"The mind is amazing; with it, we
wondrous things. In The Successful
has drawn together more than 30 exp
globe to share with you their expertise. If you read no other
book this year—read this one. Erik's panel of authors covers
almost every subject including mindset, confidence, success,
leadership, wellness and so much more. Do yourself, your life
and even your business a service—be sure to read this book
from cover to cover. There is so much potential in all of us—
tap into yours."

—DONNA STONE, Stone Business Coaching
and author of *Stepping Stones to Business Success*

"'Who is your biggest competitor?' As a business owner and
frequent podcast guest, this is a question I'm often asked.
Over the years I've come to realize it's the guy I see in the
mirror. No enemy can do me as much harm nor ally do me as
much good as my own mind. THE SUCCESSFUL MIND
shows us how to harness our powerful minds to achieve our
goals and avoid our demons. The various perspectives from
the authors provide more than a single opinion but rather a
timely and timeless guide to follow."

—TOM SCHWAB, Founder Interview
Valet and author of *Podcast Guest Profits.*

*"*The Successful Mind *gives you the roadmap you need to*
create success in your life. More than 30 experts from around
the world have come together and have created endless
possibilities for you to put into place steps to enhance and
transform your life. You are the creator of your own dreams,
and this book allows you to figure out which path to take to
create the success and happiness that you truly deserve."

—DEE McKEE, Mindful Business
Coach, Wellness Director, Soul-Ology

"What a brilliant and humble concept to bring together mindset experts into this one book. Because achieving and sustaining a successful mindset is a multi-factorial endeavour, this collection offers a wide array of wisdom. This serves as an ongoing reference so you can adopt skills at various times of your life."

—WENDY QUAN, Founder of The
Calm Monkey, Workplace Mindfulness

"Using multiple perspectives that draw from a vast array of personal belief systems, The Successful Mind is a testament to the golden thread connecting human thinking to the grander scheme of comprehensive, pinnacle success. Each of these authors, successful in their own rights, shares information that goes beyond the mind as an organ and deep into its essential role in the ever-evolving organism of humanity. Best of all for the reader, steps to this grand success can be practiced individually, as each stand-alone chapter shares—often through simple, outlined steps that involve very minor adjustments in thinking and action. Pick up your copy today and use it daily for personal, business and even spiritual success."

—KEALAH "Coach Kiki" PARKINSON, Founder
Kiki Productions, Communications Coaching, Host
of Tune In: Radio for your Mind, Body & Soul

"Reading The Successful Mind is like putting together a very important jigsaw puzzle. With multiple perspectives from mindset-experts from around the world, each chapter of this book is a unique piece of the puzzle to success. When the whole book is put together, the image is a kaleidoscope of possibility. It is up to the reader to choose which aspects of mindset to put into practice in order to take small or large steps to improve their lives."

—VIVIAN ANDERSON, author
of How High the Mountains

THE
SUCCESSFUL
MIND

THE SUCCESSFUL MIND

Tools to Living a Purposeful, Productive, and Happy Life

Authored by:

Erik Seversen, Robin Bela, Rúna Bouius, Deborah Brown-Volkman, Cynthia Corsetti, Danny P. Creed, Dario Cucci, Delisa Deavenport, Inge Dowden, Sébastien Ferré, Mary Lee Gannon, Mary Gardner, Glenis Gassmann, Samira Chandra Gupta, Peter Hill, Jory Hingson Fisher, Dr. Jacqueline Pridgen Howard, Amor de Jager, Nate Johnson, Raj Kapur, Christina Kashar, David Krueger M.D., Dr. Stem Sithembile Mahlatini, Claire Morton, Jeff Nthiwa, Marilyn O'Hearne, Alyssa Poggioli, Chi Psilocybin, Michelle Greene Rhodes, Annie Salvador, David Saville, Kari Schwear, Richard D. Seaman, Vince Stevenson

THIN LEAF PRESS | LOS ANGELES

The Successful Mind individual chapters. Copyright © 2020 by Robin Bela, Rúna Bouius, Deborah Brown-Volkman, Cynthia Corsetti, Danny P. Creed, Dario Cucci, Delisa Deavenport, Inge Dowden, Sébastien Ferré, Mary Lee Gannon, Mary Gardner, Glenis Gassmann, Samira Chandra Gupta, Peter Hill, Jory Hingson Fisher, Dr. Jacqueline Pridgen Howard, Amor de Jager, Nate Johnson, Raj Kapur, Christina Kashar, David Krueger M.D., Dr. Stem Sithembile Mahlatini, Claire Morton, Jeff Nthiwa, Marilyn O'Hearne, Alyssa Poggioli, Chi Psilocybin, Michelle Greene Rhodes, Annie Salvador, David Saville, Kari Schwear, Richard D. Seaman, Vince Stevenson.

Disclaimer—The advice, guidelines, and all suggested material in this book is given in the spirit of information with no claims to any particular guaranteed outcomes. Anyone who feels they need professional physical or mental support or counselling should reach out to a licensed doctor or therapist before following any of the advice in this book. The authors and publisher do not assume and hereby disclaim any liability to any party for any loss, damage, or disruption caused by anything written in this book.

Library of Congress Cataloging-in-Publication Data
Names: Seversen, Erik, Author, et al.
Title: The Successful Mind: Tools to Living a Purposeful, Productive, and Happy Life
LCCN 2020912343

ISBN 978-1-7323369-5-7 | ISBN 978-1-7323369-4-0 (ebook)
Nonfiction, Self-Help, Body, Mind & Spirit, Personal Growth, Success

Cover Design: 100 Covers
Interior Design: Formatted Books
Editor: Nancy Pile
Copy Editor: Rebecca Lau
Thin Leaf Press
Los Angeles

THIN LEAF

Thank you for reading this book. There are tools found within the following pages that can greatly benefit your life, but don't stop there. Make sure you get the most you can from this book and reach out directly to the 33 expert authors who want to help you enjoy life with a successful mind. Contact information for each author is found at the end of their respective chapter.

To mentors, colleagues, and students.
We are all part of the circle of learning.

CONTENTS

INTRODUCTION

By: Erik Seversen
Author of *Ordinary to Extraordinary* and *Explore*
Los Angeles, California

As I wrote the last words to the final chapter of my book *Explore*, I thought to myself, *Wow, I have a lot more to say about mindset and success.* I was compelled to begin another book right away, but the idea of spending two or more years accomplishing the task was daunting. I knew I wanted to share an important, positive message, but I was impatient about how long it would take me to write even my initial thoughts regarding mindset and success.

Immediately, I thought of some of my colleagues and social media contacts who are coaches, speakers, authors, doctors, teachers, and mentors who also use mindset as a tool to help others succeed. On a daily basis, they live and teach many of the ideas I have about success. I decided right then to get their input. In turn, the idea of organizing a co-authored book called *The Successful Mind* was created.

Within 24 hours of my idea, I began reaching out to a variety of experts who could contribute something special toward the book. I intentionally looked for individuals who are extremely successful in their fields, who come from different backgrounds and locations, and who work in diverse areas of expertise. My goal was not to have a group of authors with the same opinion about the mind and success, but rather to have multiple perspectives. The result was amazing. In less than three weeks, I gathered a world-class list of top professionals wanting to help answer the question: *What is the most important mindset a person can have to create more success in their business and their life?*

In this book, you'll encounter the answer to this question from 33 experts from a variety of backgrounds. These contributors come from all over the USA, the United Kingdom, Switzerland, France, Costa Rica, Australia, India,

South Africa, Syria, and Kenya. The areas of expertise include the sciences, humanities, spirituality, business, sociology, and healthy living. The authors of this book are professionals who work as mindset coaches, energy therapists, leadership and executive coaches, yoga instructors, doctors, nurses, pastoral counselors, speaking coaches, neuro-linguistic programming masters, addiction experts, intercultural communication coaches, high-performance coaches, psychedelic guides, and even a licensed firewalking experience coach.

Authors in this book have been personally trained by iconic individuals including Zig Ziglar, Brian Tracy, John Maxwell, Marshall Goldsmith, Tony Robbins, and many more. The book you are holding is a profound toolbox created by an amazing collection of individuals who want to help you locate, discover, and create more success in your life by making small changes in the way you think. I'm excited that you have the chance to learn from each of these world-class teachers all of whom want you to experience more success in your life.

The Successful Mind highlights three areas of success: purpose, productivity, and happiness. These are three easily identifiable "parts" of success that can be measured as they transform in your life. Each chapter highlights one of three aspects of purpose, productivity, and happiness as its main focus, but as most of the authors work with a holistic approach, almost every chapter speaks toward all three of these, even if the main idea of the chapter focuses on one.

Although this book is organized around the united theme of mindset and success, each of the chapters is totally stand-alone. The chapters in the book can be read in any order. I encourage you to look through the table of contents and begin wherever you want. Even still, I urge you to read all the chapters because, as a whole, they provide a great array of perspectives and each is valuable in providing tools for the creation of a successful mind.

Email: Erik@ErikSeversen.com
Website: www.ErikSeversen.com

CHAPTER 1

MINDSET AND THE FLOW OF MANIFESTING SUCCESS

By Robin Bela
Success Mindset and Manifestation Coach for Businesses
Edinburgh, United Kingdom

Born for Success

You could say having a success mindset is an art, an acquired skill, but in reality, it is our natural state of being. We are natural creators and are naturally sustained by our Creator, who is the source of all our needs. We lose this natural state of having everything within us when we look outside to reach our goals of success, happiness, and abundance. The energy of success and happiness comes from within us first, if we choose to see ourselves whole and complete now. This energy has been flowing through us since our birth. The reality is that we are born successful, joyful, happy, and perfect within. Perhaps that is why as children, we are natural risk-takers; we don't fear failure and intrepidly try new things with hearts bursting with joy and excitement. As children, we are already tapped into the success mindset.

Lack-and-Poverty Mindset

As we grow into adults, most of us tend to lose sight of this natural success mindset and begin to focus on seeing the lack of joy and success within us and, hence, start experiencing that as our reality. Many of us go on to live most of our lives in this flow of lack. As we continue focusing on the lack, it gets harder to rediscover the success mindset that manifests our success. The lack-and-poverty consciousness becomes a habit, so to come out of this negative mindset, we need to consistently learn to think differently.

The world is focusing on all the wrong aspects of creating success. We are born happy and peaceful, but later we begin to attach our happiness and fulfilment to the achievement of worldly goals. And we never get there, or when we do, we find more goals and continue to forever postpone being happy, peaceful, and successful.

Creating a success mindset begins by understanding what we are meant to focus on, and what we aren't. I know for years I thought I was meant to focus on only working hard. I was wrong because I was working a lot using many strategies and wasn't seeing the success I wanted in the material world or, more importantly, in achieving inner joy, fulfilment, and satisfaction. I tried all kinds of mental tools to affirm my success, but something was missing. I was not connecting to the feeling of success from within and so felt fake affirming what I did not believe in as of yet.

I was filled with fears of never "making it", and my situation felt like an unsolvable puzzle. It was a draining and tiring process. Yet I knew there had to be a way, for we are born whole, healed, and complete, and success is my and everyone's birthright.

Realigning to the Success Mindset

An exhaustive soul search led me to find my path to realign myself to the success mindset and to the flow of manifesting success. Now 15 years as a success and manifestation coach, it's my way of being each day. Also, I live and work joyously, with a deep sense of fulfilment. Outer circumstances no longer overwhelm me, and I remain conscious that the energy fuelling my success is within me always.

Do you wish to know the secret I discovered?

I call it "alchemy" or "divine support", through which I now manifest the life I desire. Once I discovered I am the creator and everything flows through me, I realized it is up to me to be the life force of creating success in my life. Initially, I was seeing glimpses of success when I would do well in my business. I started noting how I was feeling and what I was doing and thinking when I created those successes. I did not want it to be luck but tangible steps for me to follow always.

I remember once I wasn't even feeling well, but I got a big contract. I'd known before that meeting that I had tapped into the flow of manifesting, and I was feeling the essence of success from the very start of the conversation. It felt right, I felt aligned to my client's purpose as well as my own, and it was just a joyous conversation. The success was not a forced sales tactic. It was due to my alignment with the needs of my client that came from a joyful and peaceful space within, which allowed me to truly sense the happy result. If I said it was plain visualization, I would be wrong. It was more than that. It was prayer and a loving and peaceful divine alignment that led God/Source to manifest the successful outcome in a perfectly natural way.

When I talk about God, it is the Source from where we come. You can call it God, or any name based on your culture, religion, or mindset.

Once I realized that God is the source of my true happiness and peace, I did not need to achieve worldly goals but only say a prayer for them to be restored. As soon as I prayed, I felt complete contentment from within and more energized in my mind and body. My sense of happiness increased and so did the peace within me. I trusted God to bring that to me every day. My high positive energies naturally attracted all I was envisioning.

The Flow of Divine Manifestations

I now believe that the foundation for success is unconditional peace and joy within yourself. Once we learn to tap into that, we remain in the flow of divine manifestation always. We are connected to our success energies within, our joyful synchronicities, our natural state of excitement, of being in awe of life and all its possibilities. Outer manifestations also start aligning easily, effortlessly, and naturally. Problems then do not seem as problems. We see that all our troubles come with solutions. We don't feel overwhelmed with events but rather face everything joyfully and confidently. This reality can only be ours when we learn to not worry and live each day joyfully.

Getting into the flow of joy and peace through prayer is easy. It is the only medium from where we can connect to unconditional peace and joy, for no reason at all. But the hard part is learning to remain in that state long after those moments in prayer. And that is the most essential aspect to owning a success mindset.

Keep the Faith with Daily Exercise

So how do we strengthen our internal muscles and not allow ourselves to give in to worry?

It is through learning to keep the faith. We need to have faith in divine intervention and see that there is something larger than us, the Divine, God, who always has our back. When we live without faith, helplessness and fatigue overwhelm us. The longer we resist this divine connection, the longer we don't feel fulfilled, peaceful, joyful, and successful within. This is harder to achieve when we are seeing losses and failures in front of us. But it is equally imperative to look beyond the surface and tap into unconditional joy and peace by giving our worries to God, our Source. Then we need to simply trust that when we surrender our fears and relax, we start seeing the best in our life.

Learning to keep the faith is so essential, and we can practice that by releasing all our fears in a prayer to God and ask for peace and joy to return now. And next, continue to focus on being in a place of joy and peace. For that, you can affirm, "I am God's light, I am God's peace, I am God's love, I am God's joy, I am God's success, I am God's abundance".

I would suggest this exercise every morning, repeating all or any of these lines with closed eyes like a mantra. Focus on feeling the gratitude and appreciation of these words within you. It is a way to raise our frequencies for success and happiness. And anytime you feel fears creeping back, pray and release all fears, affirm these lines, and remember your true essence of being whole, healed, and a perfect child of God.

What if you pray sincerely and focus on the end positive result, and then right after, return to worrying? Is it possible for the prayer to work?

By returning to our anxious mindset we simply cancel, clear, and delete away our success mindset. Being in a success mindset isn't a one-off experience like going to a film; rather, it is a permanent state even when we're faced with unfavourable outcomes.

You cannot pray and then wonder after an hour, "Is it going to work?" or "When is it coming or happening?" Surrender means surrender. Get your hands off the situation, relax, and breathe. Surrendering to the logical mind can feel like you are not moving ahead because it likes to control the outcome, which is usually due to fear and anxiety. Slowing down is not a waste of time. You will only be more efficient and productive when you do everything from a happy, joyful, relaxed, surrendered, and non-attached place. You become open to not resisting what needs to flow to you and through you, and also not get attached to the outcome. It's a place from where positive synchronicities come naturally to you, so that you perhaps cannot even plan or figure out "how" now. Our focus is not on "how" but "what" always. Focus on "what" you love to do and like to achieve and be excited about it. Then, the steps to "how" start appearing soon.

Our focus every day must be to do our work from a joyful and a surrendered place of trusting that God, our Source, has our back! We don't need to hold our breath and live in constant mental turmoil of not achieving happiness and success. As human beings, we love to try to control outcomes, but true manifestations align and happen when we are in the happiest state of non-attachment to the results. All we must do is tap within for it. Success is first an internal process.

And, yes, keeping the faith comes by learning to be okay with uncertainties. And why would you not be okay when you trust that God has your back? So, if you are in the habit of try to figure out all the things that can go wrong and not aiming for your big vision, it's time you stop and see where you are heading, which is towards the lack-and-scarcity mentality, away from the divine connection and from your purpose of living joyfully. It is plain fearful living disconnected from God and not trusting that you are guided and supported. This can only lead you to experience a life of hardships and struggle.

Practising consistency in this process can get a bit difficult at times. My deepest hope is that you don't give up on getting and owning this peaceful, joyful, surrendered place of being. I know how important consistency is as I work with my clients to ensure they get to this place that manifests their success.

The Foundation of Manifestations

Pray for support too. This helps keep you going till you get to the peaceful, joyful, surrendered place. For me, it took a week of constant focus to get there the first time. It happened when I was struggling with a difficult circumstance, and I surrendered the problem to God in a prayer as I had mentally exhausted all other avenues. I wanted peace. So, I prayed for peace, not knowing that getting to peace was going to open all gates to manifestations for me. Peace is the foundation for manifesting all success. It leads to unconditional joy.

When I focused on praying for peace, by the end of the week, all my fears had disappeared. I began to work from an inspired place. Difficulties I was facing with some people just disappeared on their own. My social media presence began to expand with thousands of friend requests within a couple of days because of a post that suddenly went viral. Work started to increase … and it was just the beginning! I had tapped into the flow of manifesting! I was so enjoying being in this place of peace within, that I forgot about my outer goals. That's when my outer world started aligning to my success.

Success is a very natural place to be, but we complicate it. We have nothing to add or fix in ourselves but just to release all the resistance and all judgements, criticisms, fears, and doubts. Our prayers are answered when we are not in doubt and have faith.

A success mindset is very much a "feeling" process. It requires deep yearning to be peaceful and joyful, no matter the outer circumstances, and then listening within from a clear space to what you really want and need to do. Place it then in God's hands to be shown the next steps. And you will be guided because you decided and asked. You dared to take the step towards your true happiness. If you are doing what makes you happy, God supports you.

Live Your Joyful Purpose NOW

Instead of putting your feet into many things and getting tired trying to make all of them work, focus on what brings you joy, and live your purpose fully. Wouldn't it be wonderful to be bringing joy into your life and also into other people's lives simply by being in your own natural, internal joy on a daily basis? Focus on getting into the right energies and mindset, and then whatever you do from that place, you create positive results. You work from being a full cup of joy. You will discover that when outer success does manifest, usually it feels normal and you don't wonder how you got it because you are already joyfully aligned and feeling successful within.

Everything that flows through you is just an extension of your love and joy within. Everything is here in the now and within you. Our future success is here in the now. Let us live this day to our fullest, doing everything from a peaceful and joyful place, and seeing that the best is taking place for us in the coming days. *We see and feel only joyful results.* This is being in the natural success manifestation flow.

I have entrepreneurs working with me who want to achieve this divine success mindset and get into the manifestation flow because in the end, no amount of marketing and business strategies are going to work if you are not aligned within your success mindset for your purpose.

When the mind opens to possibilities to think bigger for our purpose with joy, tangible possibilities open in the outer world too. It all begins in the mind, in the unseen world, from where we carry the faith within God's support even when we are not yet able to see any tangible results.

We cannot build positive outcomes when carrying fears, limiting beliefs, fatigue, and confusion, and when feeling unsupported and overwhelmed underneath. We create this internal chaos by chasing after outer-world goals in the hope that they will complete us one day. That day never comes, and we keep running after the goals until we pause and adapt to the new mindset where we feel supported by God, and we replace the internal chaos with peace and knowledge that we are whole, healed, and perfect already. We can then start to enjoy and be happy in the now.

Aspiring each day for our inner fulfilment and alignment to our success mindset and the joyful flow of manifestation is the most important goal and needs to be the purpose of our lives. I deeply hope that this introduction to the foundation for creating success has offered you useful insights for your work and daily life.

About the Author

Robin Bela is an author, international speaker, and success mindset and manifestation coach for businesses. Robin, an MBA graduate, is also a purpose coach, spiritual mentor, transformational teacher, and energy therapist since the last 15 years. She is the author of 'Break the Pattern: Connecting To The Power Within To Create The Life You Want'. Robin helps entrepreneurs and leaders to manifest their success by creating a spiritual success mindset.

Email: mail@robinbela.co.uk
Website: www.robinbela.co.uk
Facebook: https://www.facebook.com/RobinBela.Author/
Instagram: https://www.instagram.com/robinbelacoach/
LinkedIn: https://www.linkedin.com/in/robinbela/
Twitter: https://twitter.com/RobinBela

CHAPTER 2

RESET YOUR MIND FOR UNSTOPPABLE SUCCESS

By Rúna Bouius
Founder of True Power Institute, Speaker, Executive Coach
Los Angeles, California

*A shift in perspective has the potential
to change your thinking, and if you change your
thinking, you might just change your life.*
—Rumi

Redefine Your Success

Reading this book indicates that you are interested in leading and living a vibrant and successful life. But what does it really mean to be successful? Definitions of success are as innumerable as the people on this planet because each person's idea of success is unique to them. Because we tend to be highly influenced by our families, values, and cultures, many people may not know exactly what makes up their own definition of success.

Society has focused primarily on defining success as recognition, fame, and fortune. Businesses have valued output and financial results above all else in the traditional capitalist fashion, and individuals have tried to adhere to that model.

Even though financial well-being is part of our basic cultural needs, other factors come into play when creating real wealth, flourishing lives, and sustainable success. Many studies have shown that chasing money alone isn't going to buy you happiness. We all want good health and well-being. We all crave connection and loving relationships. We all dream of inner peace and calm. We all yearn for safety and freedom. We all search for meaningful work and happiness. But few strive to determine their particular notion of success even though this is available to anyone. You can redefine your success on your own terms and live by the direction of your soul.

Amplify Your Power

When I'm asked, "What's the most important thing I can do to create success in my business and my life?" my answer is always the same. Amplify your power, your TRUE power.

If you have a big vision of a better world or want to take your personal and business success to higher levels, cultivate more power. Maybe you are going for a higher position within your organization, or you want to start a business, go into politics, or write that book. Whatever it is, know that you're going for a stretch.

A stretch always means something new and challenging. It's like wanting a faster car, you look for one with a more powerful engine. So, you need to accumulate added power to manifest your next growth spurt. I don't mean external power, like positional power, but the power you create from within by mastering your mind. The more power you have, the more change you can make in a shorter period of time towards your mission.

Befriend Change

Dreaming a new vision of success from the field of infinite possibilities is the fun part. But once that's done, and you want to realize your dream, you may come up against a barrier representing the one thing that we humans resist more than anything—the wall of ultimate resistance: resistance to change. When you are "bidding for power" by aiming for more, the manifestation of the dream requires you to leave your comfort —your beliefs, routines, habits, and the status quo. It requires you to change.

Yes, life is always in flux, and change is inevitable. The Greek philosopher Heraclitus gave us one of our most succinct and powerful concepts: "The only constant is change."

Befriending change rather than fighting it lessens your suffering.

Face Fear Head-On

Whether you're going for your next level of personal or business success, implementing a reset after dealing with COVID-19, or facing any other changes in your life, it's not always easy to get out of your comfort zone. Fear is bound to creep in and take center stage.

Fear has an important role in our lives as protection, but it can also hold us back. As we are not living in caveman times anymore, there is no need to live in constant fear. Uncontrolled fear converts to stress and anxiety and can easily block our path to success. That is the paradox of most modern fear. It isn't always grounded in reality, but only exists in our small minds.

When you are fearful, you are not in your TRUE power. The only way to move through fear is to become aware of it, acknowledge it, face it, activate your curiosity and courage, and take it on.

Understand Your Mind

The mind is part of the invisible, transcendent world of thoughts, feelings, attitudes, beliefs, and perceptions. It's where our dreaming, imagination, remembering, and judging reside, and the source of our behavior, actions, and awareness of things. The mind may not be tangible or material, but it is immensely powerful—holding the key to who we are and the secret of creation.

The brain is the physical organ most associated with the mind and consciousness, but the mind is not confined to the brain. It can be experienced throughout the body via feeling, thus, the body-mind connection.

Some liken the brain to the hardware of a super-computer in which the mind is the software thought to be a stream of consciousness divided into the conscious mind and the subconscious mind. Freud famously used the analogy of an iceberg in which the tiny part above the water represented the conscious mind at 5 percent and the 95 percent underwater represented the subconscious mind. It's quite scary to realize that our functioning is 95 percent unconscious until we realize that our conscious thought-habits can affect our subconscious actions.

Select Wisely Through Your Conscious Mind

The conscious mind is your thinking function and consists of what you are aware of in the present moment. It controls your ideas, attitudes, and behaviors, takes input from your five senses and analyzes the information, and then makes decisions based on that information. Conscious choice-making activates the process of creation and manifestation, enabling life to continuously generate new ideas, new feelings, and infinite possibilities. Then choice—as a function of your will and focus—isolates a single possibility from that pool and impresses it on the subconscious mind. Therefore, your thoughts have control over creation.

Harness the Power of Your Subconscious Mind

Your subconscious mind is a massive storage unit of information holding every single memory of your lifetime. It's emotional in nature, connected to the heart, and where the **creative mindset** originates from. It operates automatically through the autonomic nervous system and governing functions like heartbeat, body temperature, and breathing.

When you live your life unconsciously—on autopilot—this is the part that's in charge of your beliefs, attitudes, actions, and behaviors, based on your past experiences. Unable to discern between good or bad, positive or negative, life-affirming or life-negating, real or imagined, the monkey mind is in charge as the gatekeeper of your comfort zone.

The subconscious mind doesn't have the ability to choose, but rather it receives input through ideas the conscious mind has accepted as true and has chosen through the medium of feelings. The subconscious mind then gives form and expression to those ideas.

Harnessing the power of your subconscious mind through the control of your ideas and feelings is the most effective way to manifest your deepest desires. And that's power—TRUE power.

Choose Abundance Mindset vs. Scarcity Mindset

In addition to the two aspects of the mind, there are two levels of the mind in operation at any given moment—the lower mind (or small mind) and the higher mind (or universal mind). You move back and forth between these levels all the time, but the level you inhabit more frequently determines your happiness, well-being, and success.

When you find yourself in the lower mind, you experience a specific situation as life happening to you ("I'm the victim") and life happening by you. You react out of fear. This is the **scarcity mindset.**

When you are located in your higher mind, you experience life as happening through you or life happening as you. You respond from love. This is the **abundance mindset.**

Soothe Your Self-Concerned Lower Mind

When people operate from the lower mind, they believe in separation, limitations, lack, or not enough—what's called a **"scarcity mindset"** or "poverty consciousness." They find it hard to believe that there is enough time, money, space, or resources for all, so they feel the need to manipulate and forcibly extract what they want. That's an example of the scarcity mindset operating from the wounded and damaged ego. The lower mind also catches people in the fear-trap by believing that there is a real threat to their livelihood, desires, and need for recognition, control, or security.

People operating from the lower mind tend to cling voraciously to their opinions and have a strong need to be right. They get easily stressed, anxious, and overwhelmed. They avoid conflict or may pursue conflict for the sake of winning. They find faults and play the blame-game while ignoring their own responsibility. They claim to have all the solutions and never accept being wrong.

The lower mind is guided by negative emotions stored in its memory, the memory of the subconscious mind. It prompts people to react based on information from old and outdated beliefs.

The power of your will is the only way out of the lower mind, together with curiosity and courage. To calm yourself, gently talk to and soothe your lower mind like you would a child.

Reap the Benefits of Your Higher Mind

The higher mind is your soul speaking to you through your intuition as the conduit to higher powers and the creative quantum field. It transcends the boundaries of time, space, and matter, and operates beyond ego. The results of intentionally working with it can often seem quite magical.

Here are some examples of what happens when people operate from the higher mind:

- They see lessons in all situations that advance their growth.
- They see value in everything, living and leading from an **abundance mindset**.
- They believe that learning, growing, and evolving are more important than being right.
- They thrive on curiosity.
- They listen deeply.
- They constantly question their beliefs and habits.
- They use humor and play to spice up their lives.

Seven Tools to Unleash Your TRUE Power

To awaken your TRUE power to fulfill your desire for living and leading a more fulfilling and exciting life, explore these tools.

1. Discover Who You Are

One of the two most important questions that humans have asked themselves through the ages is "Who am I?" When you start to get a glimpse of who you are and expand on it reflectively, the truth of your authentic nature gets revealed.

2. Manifest Your Purpose

The other big question is "Why am I here?" which relates to your true purpose for being on the planet, often called higher purpose.

As an individual, your personal higher purpose needs to be your North Star for all decisions you make regarding how to design and live your life, and where to put your energy in terms of work and contribution.

If you are a business owner, your company also needs to know its higher purpose, beyond the bottom line. If your purpose for your business is only to make money, you are unlikely to find lasting meaning, happiness, or success.

Your purpose connects with your passions and deepest values, and your need to be of service to others. It gives you resilience and grounding in turbulent times and helps you move forward against all odds. Make sure you know both your personal and business purposes, that they are aligned, and that they are bigger than you, with a positive social impact. That is a **success mindset.**

When people learn I'm from Iceland but living in the United States, they want to know why I made the move. I tell them that after 20 years as a successful entrepreneur in Iceland, I started to experience dwindling passion for my work, restlessness, and a hunger to learn something new, to grow. I asked myself the question, "Is this all there is to life?" and the answer was a resounding "No!" I knew there was so much more—I just didn't know what that was at the time. But I was determined to find out. And now I know what that roar was, coming from the depths of my soul. It was a call to reveal and take ownership of my higher purpose—and my TRUE power.

3. Pick the Growth Mindset

Carol Dweck, a Stanford University psychologist, wrote the book *Mindset* over a decade ago. In it, she helps people from all walks of life—parents, business moguls, children—to discover what she calls **"Growth Mindset"**:

> *A Growth Mindset is characterized by an **underlying belief that abilities and intelligence can be developed**. This mindset is often further defined by contrasting it with a so-called Fixed Mindset; an underlying belief that our abilities and intelligence are predetermined and set at particular levels.*

She points out that by committing to being a lifelong learner, you can master anything you want while you are cultivating your abilities, openness, flexibility, and adaptability that will support you in surfing through uncertainty and navigating the unknown.

Here are some examples of a Growth Mindset and Fixed Mindset:

- A Fixed Mindset sees failure as a disaster while a Growth Mindset sees failure as an opportunity to grow and collect new knowledge, information, and wisdom for building future success.
- A Fixed Mindset says, "I've always done it this way," and stays in the comfort zone while a Growth Mindset loves trying out new things.
- A Fixed Mindset doesn't like to be challenged while a Growth Mindset thrives on new experiences and feedback.

You get my drift ...

Buddhism teaches you to take on the "beginner's mind" or "don't-know-mind." When you are open and eager to learn, you're always discovering something new that can expand your mind and help you to grow.

Satya Nadella, the CEO of Microsoft, has become known for his stellar leadership and brilliant business moves. He credits Carol's book, *Mindset*, for the culture he has been building in the company: "Don't be a know-it-all; be a learn-it-all."

4. Map Your Awareness

Mapping out what your mind is focusing on at any given moment is a powerful awareness tool. Start noticing and becoming aware of your current thought, emotion, behavior, and the story you are telling yourself—about yourself, about others, or about a situation. Become the observer, the witness. Are you reminiscing about the past or worrying about the future? The present moment is where you want to be. Eckhart Tolle talks about "The Power of Now."

Do you find yourself in the lower mind or the higher mind? If in the former, use your will and internal power to choose to change your mind, shift from a negative way of thinking to a positive. Go from being unaware to being self-aware.

5. Practice Letting Go

Once you start mapping your awareness regularly, you may discover old beliefs, habits, and behaviors. Question whether they are serving you anymore. Prune your inner landscape and let go of negative beliefs and emotions.

This is essential, for they have been standing between you and a fully joyful and happy life. All limiting emotions must go out with the trash—fear and anxiety, pride, shame, guilt, and the need to control. You may also find habits that need to be replaced, as well as places and people.

Let go, relax, trust the process, and replace the old with empowering new thoughts, habits, people, and circumstances.

6. Control Your Feelings

As feelings are the medium by which you perceive and choose ideas for manifestation, it's crucial that you discipline your mind only to entertain feelings that contribute to your health, abundance mindset, and happiness. If you constantly allow negative, debilitating, and judgmental thoughts to fester in your mind, you create the same in your outer world. Therefore, always follow your feelings to discern which thoughts and ideas are going to benefit your well-being and that of others.

7. Own Your Mind

I've trained with Korean energy masters for almost two decades. One of my big aha moments happened when I finally realized the statement, "My mind is not me but mine." The same goes for "My body is not me but mine." But for my body to do what I wanted it to do, I discovered I had to use my mind to command the body to hold a position longer, instead of believing in my mind that it couldn't do it.

When you are not aware that your thoughts are caught in the lower mind and taking you for a negative spin, you can't do anything about it. Once you start cultivating that mindful awareness and can locate your thoughts and feelings, you can make that empowered choice with the conscious mind, which instructs the subconscious mind what to do. Your relationship to your mind needs to change from the mind being the master to the mind being your servant.

When Mastering Your Mind Becomes Your Power Tool

When you take control of your unconscious mind and teach it to serve you, you stop functioning from unexamined limiting beliefs. Now you consciously choose life-giving and uplifting thoughts to focus on and bring into manifestation. That changes your life. Your core becomes more resilient as you now know how to overcome fears and anxiety, and meet the unknown. Your relationships flourish, and you feel empowered. You respond calmly to external stimuli, increase your effectiveness, and your purpose-driven life takes on a deeper meaning. You are life, moving through you with ease and grace. You are mastering your mind as a conscious leader. And that's power—TRUE power.

What's Next for You?

Above are seven simple and practical tools that can change your life. What next steps will you take to unleash your TRUE power and master your mind? Don't wait for it to happen by itself. Make a commitment and take action. There are no more excuses. Get the results you are looking for—that vibrant and successful life.

To your success!

About the Author

Rúna Bouius is a former CEO and entrepreneur from Iceland, and the founder of the True Power Institute. As an author, speaker, and conscious leadership guide to visionary leaders, entrepreneurs, and individuals, she is on the vanguard of the new-business-paradigm thinking, the creation of better workplaces, and the development of emerging leaders. Rúna sits on advisory boards and is a council trustee at Coventina Foundation. She's a contributing author to numerous books and publishing platforms, and a frequent speaker on online summits and podcasts. Rúna is also a co-founder of several social-impact platforms in Los Angeles, including the Conscious Capitalism LA Chapter. She will be featured in the upcoming Reality/Doc series, *The Social Movement*, season 1, on Amazon Prime in which CEOs, founders, CMOs, entrepreneurs, investors, and business owners share their genius onscreen.

Email: info@truepowerinstitute.com
Website: http://truepowerinstitute.com/

CHAPTER 3

CAREER SUCCESS STARTS IN THE MIND

By Deborah Brown-Volkman, PCC
ICF Certified Career & Executive Coach,
Marshall Goldsmith Certified
East Moriches, New York

Dreams are extremely important.
You can't do it unless you imagine it.
—George Lucas

Hypothetical Bob (not his real name) has trouble keeping a job.

People tell Bob he has tremendous potential, but he struggles to find career success. People don't understand why Bob starts a job and within six months gets fired. They want him to see what they see—a smart, funny guy, who could do well in any job.

Why does Bob keep getting fired although he has a great education and skill set? He doesn't believe in himself. He can sway the interviewer, but once he starts a job, his inner critic kicks in. Bob starts to doubt himself and holds back. He doesn't showcase his work and hands in assignments late. Employers don't let Bob go immediately. They have conversations with him to see if he can turn himself around. But to no avail, Bob stays the same, and that once-promising job, slips away from him.

Can you see yourself in Bob? A person who wants more, but whose thoughts keep you from achieving what you know you can do?

Sometimes just knowing where you're at is a great start to getting to where you want to go. How about you—where are you in your career? Do you want a new job? A new career? Or a new way of being successful in your current role?

Think about a time when you had a career goal and succeeded. How did you achieve it? What did it feel like? You probably had to overcome several obstacles. And, at some point, you may have doubted yourself. But, unlike Bob, you persisted and achieved your goal.

What's standing in the way of your goals now? Outside circumstances? Or internal thoughts about your situation?

In my 20-plus years' experience as a career and executive coach, thousands of people seek me out to ask, "What do I do?" I meet them when they are lost, frustrated, or stuck. For some, it's a one-time event that came out of the blue. For others, it's a recurring pattern that spans several years. They all tell me the same thing, "I've tried everything, and my problem won't go away."

One of the first questions I ask them is "What is your mindset regarding what is happening?"

This question typically renders them speechless.

Thinking and talking about mindset can be daunting and overwhelming. Especially when you need a problem solved quickly and all you can muster is "This is my problem." Your thoughts are all over the place, mostly in the past remembering something that already happened and cannot be changed. This is why so many of my clients tell me their stories over and over again. They are seeking closure and understanding, but at the same time, dwelling on misfortunes does not bring closure; it just keeps you stuck. I always begin my work with clients by asking them to shift their thinking. That's their way out.

Why Is Mindset So Important to Your Career and Your Life?

What you believe matters. If you can't see yourself achieving a goal, then you can't achieve it. I believe that most people don't move ahead in their careers for two reasons: 1) limiting beliefs and 2) logistics (aka, "How do I do it?").

I find that most people start with logistics, as in, "If I can figure out the steps, I'm good." Starting with logistics won't work if your thoughts are limiting your potential. If you don't clear out the negative beliefs first, you won't be able to tackle logistics. Your mind (and your fears) won't let you.

How does a negative mindset hold you back?

The answer—erratic action, fear of failure, fear of success, procrastination, repeated patterns, stagnation, and unfulfilled dreams.

On the other hand, how does a positive mindset propel you forward?

The answer—career satisfaction, consistent action, direction, power, promotions, purpose, a seat at the table, and wealth.

As you can see, your mindset makes a big difference. Does this mean that you won't have to work hard? It does not. But whatever your career goals are, the hard work will not seem as hard if you have a positive perspective.

How Do You Set Your Mind for Career Success?

When facing a career setback, people often look to the outside: who did what to us, why did they do it, and how did it happen? Such a mindset causes people to feel powerless and trapped, resulting in an inability to make a decision and see a path forward.

The outside is not the place to look. The focus should be inward. You cannot control what is occurring (or has occurred) around you, but you can control your actions, reactions, and next move. How? Follow the following three steps:

Step 1: Become aware. This is when you recognize that your inner thoughts are hurting your outer goals. For example, you are not getting a promotion at work because you don't believe you deserve it or you believe it will go to someone else. You don't do well in interviews because you are afraid to let prospective employers see the real you. You are not going after that career you have been thinking about for years because you believe you won't make money or the "fantasy job" could never happen.

Awareness is a wake-up call. In this first step, you begin to say things to yourself such as: "What have I done? How did I get here?" It hits you like a ton of bricks, and you fully recognize the repeated pattern and understand that no one is holding you back but you.

Step 2: Make a decision to change. You recognize that the weight of your negative or fearful outlook is far greater than any comfort you may derive from it. You decide that enough is enough and you want something different. For example, you resolve to speak up in meetings, be more proactive with networking, or step up your job search efforts.

In this second step, you begin to say things to yourself such as: "I don't want this anymore. I am done. Today is a brand-new day." You are not sure where you are headed, but you are more afraid to stay where you are. You are determined to take action.

Step 3: Do things differently. You spend time learning. For example, you are reading, watching videos, taking classes, etc. Anything you can get your hands on. You are in a "success mindset" school, and you can't get enough. You are growing, testing the waters, and putting new routines in place. Some days you are moving forward, and other days you feel like you are standing still or going backwards. But still, you feel better. You are on your way.

When You Can See It, Then You Can Make It Happen

Once you have a success mindset, you are ready to go after your career goals. Now it's time for logistics/implementation. It's time for a game plan. Here are the five steps, based on five questions, that I have seen my clients use for effective career planning. The aim of a career plan is clarity. If you keep your plan simple, it will be easier to follow and achieve.

What goes into your plan? To start, ask yourself the following five questions:

Question 1: What do I Want? For example, "I want a new job. I want a new career. I want better assignments at work, better relationships with co-work- ers, or a better attitude." When you say what you want out loud, does it make sense and inspire you? When you speak it to others, do they immediately get it or look confused? Determining what you want is the most important piece of your plan because it's the foundation. Do not move past this step until you are crystal clear.

Question 2: When will my "what" be achieved? For example: "Three months from now," "Six months," etc. Be specific. I notice that many of my clients are afraid to choose a date. They worry whether they can achieve it. They don't want to look bad to themselves or others if it does not work out. Choosing a date provides focus and puts you on the court. Remember, goals are achieved on the court, not on the sidelines. You may achieve your goal by this date, or you may not. This is not the point. You are going for movement because when you are playing, you have a better chance of winning the game.

Question 3: How will I get there? This is a list of the specific action steps you will take to get what you want. For example: "I will call five recruiters, have three networking/informational conversations a week, or have coffee, in-person or virtually, with one co-worker each week." Make a list of everything you can think of. Then, prioritize your list. Break your prioritized list into smaller pieces because small steps lead to big ones over time. It is also important to note that reaching goals, as a whole, is a journey and not a sprint. Goals are reached one action at a time, over time. As long as you stay consistent.

Question 4: How Will I track and monitor my progress? One of the best methods to be successful in the implementation of your career plan is to use a calendar. Why is a calendar that important? Several reasons: if you don't feel like taking a step, your calendar can help you get motivated and stay on track. If you don't remember what your next step is, your calendar will remind you what to work on. If your steps are in a calendar, you can quickly check them off your list. Plus, everything you need to do is in one place.

Open your calendar and put your steps there. Then, add in more time than you think it will take. If you believe updating your resume will take one day, put down two. If you think a conversation will take 15 minutes, put 30 minutes into your calendar. Goal achievement traditionally takes more time than we'd like and does not necessarily happen on our timetable. However, if you have a good routine and structure in place, and you don't give up, you can succeed.

Question 5: Who will be my champion and supporter? Goals are not meant to be reached alone. We are supposed to reach important goals with someone else. You may want to improve your career by yourself, but it will be harder for you if you do. Plus, it's unnecessary. There are many good people out there to help, but you have to ask. It's vital to have someone to talk to, someone who can listen to you and help keep your success mindset in place. Connection and a positive mindset go hand in hand.

Parting Thoughts

Once you have reached your goal, don't leave your mindset at the door. Keep going. Check in with your mindset on a regular basis. Goal achievement is not the end, it's the beginning. Once you have completed one goal, there is room for others. Your confidence is higher, and you are in a good position to choose something bigger and then bigger, etc. The sky's the limit. Keep your mind sharp, and anything is possible. Good luck to you.

About the Author

Deborah Brown-Volkman, PCC, is an ICF Certified Career and Executive Coach, Marshall Goldsmith Certified Global Leadership Assessment (GLA360) Professional, Resume and LinkedIn Specialist, Certified Career Intuitive Coach, and Certified Wellness Coach. Deborah is a career coaching leader, executive coaching and leadership expert (internal and external coaching), career development expert, and author of several career, job search, business, wellness, and marketing books, with 20-plus years of solid coaching experience in helping people find new jobs, new careers, new ways of dealing with challenges in the workplace, and new systems for helping people perform at their best.

Email: info@surpassyourdreams.com
Website: https://www.surpassyourdreams.com

CHAPTER 4
CAN I EVER BE ENOUGH?

By Cynthia Corsetti, CPCC, SHRM-SCP
Executive Coach—Career Transitions
Pittsburgh, Pennsylvania

I woke up early on a Monday morning. I planned to have some special meditation time, but first I wanted that steaming cup of coffee. As I waited for the aroma to fill the room from the French press, I scrolled through my messages.

There it was. A video chat from Gabe. He wanted to tell me that he'd enrolled in an MBA program. I could hear the excitement in his voice as he talked about the new opportunities that would open for him. Gabe was all in.

I took a deep breath and realized my early morning meditation would have to wait. Gabe was at it again. One more degree, one more certification. He believed he needed one more thing to finally feel successful. It was a negative mindset that had plagued him for years. No matter how much success he seemed to find, it was never enough for him.

Gabe already held an MD and a PhD. He was a respected physician and professor. Awards lined the shelves in his office. Yet, as he told me when we first began working together, he felt empty. He told me that he couldn't remember a time in his life when he felt like he was "enough."

An early memory of his older brother winning a soap box derby race resurfaced. He said he was too young to enter, so he made his own car out of cardboard. He took it with him on race day. All the older boys jumped into their cars and lined up at the starting line. Gabe tried to sit beside them in his cardboard box, and this started the crowd laughing.

The whole crowd laughed. Gabe had explained to me, "At that moment, I felt even smaller than my seven-year-old self. It was mortifying." The reality was that the crowd thought he was adorable. They laughed with joy. Gabe heard it as ridicule. At that moment and for the first time in his young life, Gabe felt like a failure. And it hurt.

Core Limiting Beliefs

This memory planted itself deep within the recesses of Gabe's subconscious. And for the next 30 years, that memory continued to play a part in his world. It wasn't on the surface. He never "thought" about it, but over the years, he felt that same feeling many times. With every emotional re-enactment, his subconscious belief grew stronger. Like the time the kids on the playground were teasing him. To Gabe, it was further proof that he wasn't good enough. And when he wasn't chosen for the starting lineup in baseball—more proof that he was a failure. The time his parents decided to divorce, and the time he didn't get into the Ivy League University. More proof.

Each situation was traumatic to Gabe. Not all at the same level, but trauma no less. Each event further solidified Gabe's limiting belief. The belief that he was, in fact, a failure. As that belief formed, it cemented the negative mindset. And while he was finding professional wins, he was far from peace.

What Gabe experienced isn't unique. Things that happen to us in life, especially in those early years, impact us. And the more traumatic those situations, the more severe the lasting impact.

An international cohort study led by Dr. William Copeland and published in *JAMA* in 2018 revealed startling facts. Cumulative childhood trauma exposure can lead to a disrupted transition to adulthood. Yes, those little things that feel traumatic to a child have long-term effects. Things like social isolation, multi-domain functioning, and not holding a job. The study also associated childhood trauma with higher rates of adult psychiatric outcomes.

Childhood trauma is more common than we realize. In fact, according to Copeland's study, 60 percent of children are exposed to trauma by age 16. And 30 percent of those children are exposed multiple times. As adults, these subjects demonstrated anxiety, depression, and nicotine and alcohol disorders. According to the study, childhood trauma predicted adult disorders and adult anxiety disorders on a consistent basis. While some trauma is more severe, like abuse and neglect, all trauma has an impact. And while we may not end up with severe psychiatric problems, we do end up with core limiting beliefs that prevent us from living to our full potential.

We've all had experiences that made us question our capacity and even our value. When an emotional circumstance convinces us that we aren't good enough (or pretty, rich, or smart enough), it becomes a belief. And like Gabe, we become more certain that this belief is true as the years pass.

Eventually, these beliefs become habits of thought. Thoughts that run through our subconscious mind hundreds of times per day. The little girl who had frizzy hair and braces as a child doesn't see the beautiful woman she is. Instead, each time she sees her reflection, she feels repulsion. Sometimes it's subtle, a feeling she quickly brushes off. Other times, it can bring her to tears.

Our limiting beliefs affect every aspect of our lives. In fact, they can rob us of our ability to have the necessary positive mindset we need for fulfillment and true success.

Here's Why It Matters

On the surface limiting beliefs can seem unimportant. You feel small or insignificant. As my dad would say, "Suck it up." Right?

Not so fast.

These core limiting beliefs shape our perception of ourselves and our lives. They become our reality and can color every aspect of life. The impact can be small. Like not asking the special someone on a date because you believe they're out of your league. Or not speaking up at a meeting because you believe no one wants to hear your opinion. Or when you keep trying to prove yourself as worthy by getting one more promotion, degree, or title.

Other impacts are larger. Like having extra-marital affairs to feel attractive. Or sacrificing your children to spend more time at the office because you know that as soon as you land the next deal, you'll finally feel successful.

The outcomes vary, but the cause doesn't. It's a limiting belief that we hold so vividly that it becomes part of our identity. And it colors every part of our world. And plunges into the depths of a negative mindset.

One of my clients got kicked out of first grade. He took lunch money from the desk of another first grader, and—*bam!*—the strict private school expelled him. He laughs about it today. He said he remembers it like it was yesterday. There were two one-dollar bills on the desk. It was a Friday. The ice cream truck would drive by his house on Saturday. Those two bills would be enough to buy the orange pushup. He didn't think of it as right or wrong. Although I'm sure he knew it was wrong. He was seven, after all.

The fallout from getting expelled was disastrous. He didn't see his friends anymore, and he had to go to a new school. And while not related to this, his parents divorced. Even though the divorce didn't happen because he got expelled, he believed it did. It was a very traumatic year.

My client's core limiting belief was, "I'm a bad person and bad things happen to me." This mindset became part of his own identity. In his professional life it manifested as a fear that he would get fired. Even when he received stellar reviews and pay increases, he worked each day in fear, terrified that this would be the day the termination would happen. The anxiety got so bad he ended up on Xanax. All because of a core limiting belief. A belief that was far back and unnoticed in his subconscious. Yet quietly present in every waking minute.

His limiting belief actually changed his behavior at work. He didn't trust co-workers or superiors. He was secretive and protective of his work. He became paranoid, and his performance declined. And based on his own behaviors, his worst fear became a reality. He got fired.

Another client became obsessed with promotions. Each time she received one, she started eyeing the next. It could appear to some that she was power hungry. But the reality was that she believed the only way she could control her life was to be in control at work. She was the youngest of six children. As a child, she learned that her opinion didn't matter. Her voice was never heard. She was often pushed aside as "the baby." She felt like she didn't exist.

As an adult, she still held those beliefs. Beliefs that her voice wasn't important. Her opinions didn't matter. And that she didn't deserve to be taken seriously. This stayed with her, and as an adult she decided, come hell or high water, to land a corner office. A position she believed would force people to listen.

This determination caused conflict. She gained a reputation of being "hard to work with." She did produce good results and got promoted. But it took her twice as long because her interpersonal skills held her back. A brilliant and intelligent professional who sometimes acted like a "mean girl" to get ahead.

Our beliefs about ourselves shape us. They become part of our identity. Sometimes they drive us to success because we are afraid to fail. Other times they stop us in our tracks because we're afraid to play big. And, no matter what success we may find, fulfillment never comes. Those core limiting beliefs rob us of purpose. Instead of living with joy, we live with anxiety and stress.

A Mis-Aligned Life

Purpose doesn't have to be grand. You don't have to be Gandhi or Mother Teresa to live a life on purpose. But you do have to live your life as the highest version of yourself. And you do have to have the right mindset. A positive, uplifting mindset. Success isn't possible without it.

Success requires a version of you that isn't held hostage by limiting beliefs. And in order for that to happen, you have to get into alignment with reality. You have to stop telling yourself the same stories. The untrue habit-of-thought stories that you've allowed to run your life.

When you're in alignment, you're living as your most authentic self. That part of you that lives deep inside buried beneath the ego. Some call it your soul. Living on purpose means aligning with the soul. This alignment aids your ability to maintain a success-focused mindset.

This is the version of you that comes out when you need it most. The version that pulls you through that PhD program when it feels impossible. Or helps you finish the marathon that you've trained for. Both versions of you are with you every single day and in every situation. The trouble is most of us allow the loudest one, which is usually the fearful one, to be in control.

I'm going to invite you to do an experiment with me here for one minute. I promise it's easy and you'll like what you see.

Close your eyes and imagine that your life is a bus. It can be a school bus or a Greyhound or even a tour bus. It doesn't matter what kind of bus. Imagine a bus.

As you climb aboard that bus, you look around at the passengers. Each passenger looks like you. Yet, each is very different.

The first passenger you notice is crying and seems inconsolable. You recognize that person; she's a younger version of you. The one who didn't get the part in the play or who didn't make the soccer team.

Further back you see other versions of you. The one who volunteers for meals-on-wheels. And the one who leads the bowling team to victory each week. You see the one that hates public speaking. And the one that needs to lose ten pounds.

One of the passengers looks confident and strong. As you look at this passenger you remember that version of you. She showed up the day you went out for the cheerleading squad but were sure you wouldn't make it. She's the one who pulled you through to land that spot on the squad. She's also the one who showed up the day you did your first surgery on a real patient. And she was also there the day you published that first paper.

Each one of these passengers, these versions of you, is real. Each one walks this journey of life with you every day. But, the most important one, the most important passenger on the bus is the driver. And more specifically, the mindset of the driver.

You get to choose which version of you is driving the bus of your life. You are in control of each one of the passengers on that bus. Some of those passengers are shouting lies. Telling you to believe the stories you've lived with for so long.

Imagine what happens to your life if you let that fearful version drive the bus. You'll see opportunities, and you'll want to stop to pursue them. But that version will tell you that you can't. You're not smart enough for that opportunity, or you don't deserve it. And the bus will drive right by.

But, if you choose the highest version of yourself—the one that you usually save for "break-glass-now" emergencies—if you choose that version to drive the bus every day, imagine what could be.

Living life on purpose means the authentic you is driving the bus. Every single day. That highest version that knows the truth and can see beyond the stories. Every day the driver of the bus can be the version of you that holds that success mindset.

It's Your Choice

The hardest part of this concept is to understand that we have a choice. It requires a new level of self-awareness. One that we can achieve by following these three simple rules.

1. Each day when you wake up, make the conscious choice to show up for the day as the highest version of yourself.

Pay attention to your current mindset. It might sound silly, but the goal is to teach your brain new thought habits. Recognize this as important. Start each day, looking at yourself in the eye, and say, "I choose to show up as the highest version of ME today."

2. Become aware of your emotions.

An emotion begins as a physical feeling within the body. Even before it reaches your brain, your body notices it. As you begin to notice where you feel your emotions, you'll be able to assign meaning to them. For example, you might feel a knot in your stomach when you are anxious, or you might feel tightness in your shoulders when you're angry.

Noticing the emotion and identifying it will give you time to consider why you're feeling it. Before you react to it. And that's valuable time. In that time, you can ask yourself, "What is it that I'm feeling, and why am I feeling it?" If you recognize that the feeling relates to a limiting belief, think of a counter story. Let's say, for example, you start to feel inadequate. You step back for a moment in that inadequacy and remind yourself exactly why it's not true. "I am not inadequate because I have already done things harder than this." Choose that thought. Let go of the fear based, limiting thought.

3. Give yourself grace.

This takes time. You're retraining your brain, teaching the subconscious that those negative stories it has held within aren't true. They've been around a long time, but that doesn't mean they're true. Often when I work with clients, we start by uncovering at least five stories they've become accustomed to telling themselves. Stories based on limiting beliefs. Stories that they know deep inside aren't true, but that they've come to believe anyway.

If you practice these three actions every day, you will get better at it. You are whole and complete and amazing. It's only your own subconscious that's telling you something different. The key is to understand that we all have limiting beliefs. And you are on the road to healing them.

Soon you'll let go of negativity and be open to fulfillment. It's how you'll find and live your purpose. Those limiting beliefs can hold you back, but they can also be a wonderful gift. A gift that lets you heal the hurts from the past and move into a new and inspiring future. A future where you not only believe, but you know … that you can create anything that you desire.

About the Author

Cynthia Corsetti's passion rests in helping men and women achieve their highest potential within the most demanding leadership roles. She is a highly sought after certified executive coach and keynote speaker who holds a master's degree in organizational leadership, has more than 2 thousand hours of direct coaching experience, and 15 years' direct experience at the highest levels of corporate leadership. Cynthia offers a solid foundation and blend of experience, dedication, and personal insight.

Cynthia assists even the most driven and successful leaders to overcome obstacles, boost productivity, increase self-awareness, raise emotional intelligence, and sharpen the skills they already possess. In addition, her signature program **Reflect, Rebuild, Rebrand** provides professionals with exactly what they need to make a smooth and successful career transition. Cynthia Corsetti is one of the preeminent coaches that draws out the champions in her clients.

Email: cynthia@cynthiacorsetti.com
Website: www.cynthiacorsetti.com

CHAPTER 5

YOUR MINDSET *IS* YOUR REALITY

By Danny P. Creed
Master Business and Executive Coach, Consultant
Phoenix, Arizona

If you think you can, or you can't ... you're right!
—Henry Ford

At my house, there are three bathrooms. Each bathroom used to have its own plunger. You're probably asking yourself, "Why did this guy have a toilet plunger in every bathroom?" Here's why. The sewer lines would get clogged all the time. I couldn't trust them. We couldn't even have anyone over for dinner because of what might happen if they went to the bathroom, which they'd inevitably do.

So, I finally had enough. I had some experts come out and run a camera down the sewer line and take a look. We also had them inspect all the toilets in the house. Sure enough, they all needed to be replaced and the line needed to be purged. The problem seems to be solved, and I've tentatively moved the plungers to the garage.

Strangely enough, this entire event had me thinking. I realized that the human mind is very much like my toilets and sewer lines—if you don't take care of it through regular maintenance and regular cleaning, your mind WILL get clogged. So many of us allow negative thinking or negative people into our lives, such that inevitably our minds get clogged with negative beliefs. Before we know it, we can't think anything but negative thoughts. We stop learning. We worry about things that don't affect us or things that we can't do anything about. We harbor unnecessary animosity. We allow petty issues to turn into gargantuan grudges. We become a person that others do not like to be around.

When all of this happens, we then start throwing blame around. We blame the news on television, we blame CNN and FOX. We blame Congress. We blame the weather. We blame our friends, our spouses, our kids. We blame everyone except ourselves.

If you've allowed this to happen and your mind is clogged up with negative gunk, it's time to clear it out and fix the problems. Otherwise, you'll live a life of angry mediocrity.

How do you clear out the sludge? How do you fix the problem? The answer is fairly simple really. You need an adjustment of your mindset. You put different things into your mind that will unclog the gunk. The quality of your life is all about the mindset you choose.

In 1928, Napoleon Hill wrote the business and personal development classic *Think and Grow Rich*. The foundation of this book rests in one sentence: *You become what you think about most of the time.* In other words, if you think negatively about yourself and the world around you, then it will be your truth. Gunk will be your life. In turn, if you think positively and progressively, then that will also be your world. Clean and clear zest will be your life. I break it down into two very distinct mindsets—SURVIVAL thinking versus POSSIBILITY thinking.

You can spot the survival mentality a mile away. When you ask someone how they are doing, the survival mentality will say, "Oh, I'm okay. I'm getting by." I once had a client who told me he had a goal that he thought about every minute of every day. He dreamed about it. He thought about this goal while he was putting on his shoes, starting the car, waiting in line, stirring his coffee, waiting for his computer to boot up—all the time. He was fixated on this one single goal.

When I asked him what this goal was, he replied, "I go to work every day, with one goal in mind—*I will break even.*"

I looked at him thinking that maybe he was kidding, but, no, he was serious. His sole aim, every day for his business, was to break even.

I often hear this form of survival thinking from people who have no greater hope than to just make it through another day. Another client told me that their goal was simply to "not run out of money." Survival thinking set their course for the future. Survival thinking killed any hope of any level of success.

I have, in turn, been blessed to work with many people who embody the concept of possibility thinking. Even in challenging times, they specifically are driven with the hope and potential that there is a positive possibility to be found.

I recently asked one of my "crazy" clients, who is a successful business owner, how his positive mindset has helped him in life and in business. He explained that he must work long and hard to maintain his POSSIBILITY mindset. He explained the difficulties that he constantly faces in order to implement his strategy of positive enthusiasm when so many others around him are predicting doomsday.

When I asked him how he did it, surprisingly, he replied, "Oh, that's easy! When the perception of our world gets bad, all of my competition seems to pull their heads in their shell, like a turtle, and hide. They just want to survive and hope for the best. At that point, I attacked the market. While my competition is surviving and worrying and watching to see what happens, I'm out there asking their customers to come to me if they need anything, and by the time my competitors reappear, I own the market. They don't know what happened. They don't understand why their longtime customers are now former customers."

A possibility mindset is a discipline. It is also an attitude. It's a stance that you take. Sam Walton, founder of the retail giant Wal-Mart, was asked in the middle of a major economic downturn how the terrible economy affected Wal-Mart. He is said to have proclaimed, "It hasn't, we chose not to participate."

Especially for a leader of people or a team, or for a business owner, your mindset is key to your existence and growth. The people that depend on you and the people that work for you will rely on you to establish the vision for the future. You must remember that someone is always watching. They're watching you to see if your view of the future is dark and negative—survival—or one that offers them hope and prospect—possibility.

The survival mentality can easily be deadly. It can be the killer of dreams and potential. It can cause you and the people watching you to be filled with fear and self-doubt. So, be careful.

Remember, in the world we live in, in many ways there is no reality. There is only the perception of reality. If you believe there is hope and potential and a world of positive expectancy, then for you and those watching you, there will be. If you, in turn, believe much of the speculative media that the end is near, that there is no hope, then there will be none for you and those that follow you.

How many hopes and dreams have been shattered by people who actually believe in their negative perceptions and negative self-talk? How many people then allow themselves to buy into the idea that they're not smart enough or good enough? They tell themselves they can never be successful because they never graduated from college or they were raised poor. If this is you, stop it. Stop it now.

Possibility thinking could also be called the NO EXCUSES mindset. It has rules and anyone can learn them.

> *Rule 1*: No more fear of dreaming about the great possibilities that might be. You must allow yourself to dream big again. You must believe anything is possible.
>
> *Rule 2*: No more excuses for what happens in your life.
>
> *Rule 3*: No more complaining. You are in charge. You are responsible. Accept it.
>
> *Rule 4:* No more blaming anyone or anything.
>
> *Rule 5*: No more criticizing. There is a universal success law called the Law of Repulsion. It says that we run out of our life those whom we criticize.

We must have the discipline to adapt and change our thinking to possibilities and potential. In order to do this, we must also change our vocabulary. The rule is to eliminate words and phrases like "problems," "I'll try," and "I hope," and replace them with "I am," "I have," "I achieved." An example would be if one of your goals was to quit smoking. The survival mentality goal would say, "I will quit smoking." The no excuses mindset would say, "I am a non-smoker."

If your fears keep you in that survival mode, understand this—you will fail. Just plan on it. However, know that failing should be part of your success strategy. Thomas J. Watson, Sr. of IBM fame, was once asked how someone could increase their rate of success. He quickly said, "If you want to be more successful, faster, you must double your rate of failure." Quite simply, his meaning was that through failure, we learn our greatest lessons.

I was mentored to believe that with the correct mindset, I would never really fail. Failure only occurred when you did not learn something from the experience. Every great success story is built upon a foundation of lessons learned from both our successes and wins, as well as our failures.

We've all heard the classic question of the glass of water. Is it half-full or half empty? A possibility mindset would say that it's neither. The glass is neither half-full nor half-empty because it can be refilled. We have the power to decide what our mindset is and how it will dictate our current life and future.

You should be honest with yourself and understand exactly what it is that you're satisfied with. Are you okay with your *now*? If you are, understand clearly that you're okay with the current circumstances. Be happy with this clarity, but once you are, then just shut up. I simply don't want to hear you moan and groan anymore about how bad your life and the world around you might be. If you don't like it, do something about it. Otherwise just be quiet.

However, if you're willing to make some changes and adjust your potential, you may need to make some hard decisions. Sometimes that might include changing the people who make up your current circle of friends. If all your group does is gripe and moan about everything and everyone, it's time for a change. You must rid yourself of the negative influences, no matter how hard it might be. You must believe that there are others like you who are looking for positive relationships and surroundings. In business, it might mean changing jobs. Have you ever attended a meeting with a positive and fierce attitude only to have someone else in the meeting, someone with a totally screwed-up view on life, someone who is angry at the world, force their negative vibe on you? Then, when you leave the meeting, you find yourself frustrated and depressed rather than positive and fierce like you were when you began the day?

Look around you and be honest about the influences that you see and feel. You're in control. You can make the choices. Personally, I haven't watched the local news for over 10 years. I haven't been able to justify why I need to know about most of the stories that lead every broadcast. How hard is it to find a good book to read? There are literally thousands of educational and motivational CD series, podcasts, and digital audiobooks that you can listen to while you're in your car driving to and from work or at home.

I often recall the words of the legendary speaker Zig Ziglar on this subject. He would say from time to time, "We all need a checkup from the neck up to avoid stinkin' thinkin.'"

Many years ago, more than I can even remember, I had a very wise mentor. One of many whom I have been blessed with. You wouldn't know him if I said his name. He was just someone who came into my life at the right place and time. His insight and wisdom still resonate with me today, maybe even stronger than ever.

I recently had some time on my hands and was going through old notebooks when I came across my notes from this encounter with him so many years ago. My friend impressed on me that his key to personal success was based on seven pillars. I had forgotten that I still had these notes from our conversations. I still remember the "Seven Pillars for a Successful Life" like the conversation happened yesterday. He would say that to have a successful life, you must surround yourself with these seven pillars:

1. *Positive self-talk.* We become what we think about most of the time. I still love Henry Ford's great statement that leads this chapter, "If you think you can, or you can't, you are right!" Your life's happiness and satisfaction derive directly from what you say and think.

2. *Positive mental food.* You must read or listen to positive things every day. With all the time we spend in the car or in front of the television, we have plenty of opportunities to feed ourselves material for growth rather than meaningless noise.

3. *Positive imaging.* We must see ourselves positively. If we see ourselves as overweight, we sometimes become okay with that image and yet are unsatisfied with it. See yourself as lean and mean, and you will be driven to work towards that image.

4. *Positive people.* You simply cannot hang around negative people and expect to be positive. We must shed our negative contacts and reach out and discover people of like mind and spirit.

5. *Positive health habits.* We must eat healthy and exercise regularly. It's just too easy to sit on the couch and eat a bag of chips. Whatever your self-image is, you can make it so (see pillar #3).

6. *Positive training and development.* You must understand that we have the capacity to learn and continue to learn our entire lifetime. Again, it's our choice. We should live by the code of CANEI, which stands for "Continuous and Never-Ending Improvement." My friend and personal development expert, Brian Tracy, told me that if you read one hour a day on a subject in your chosen field, then you would

read fifty books a year, 500 books in ten years. This would then put you in the top 10 percent of anyone in the world in your field. It's your choice.

7. *Positive attitude*. No matter how many times we've heard this phrase, there is a universal truth that successful people know and understand. The simple fact is that people are attracted to those that think, walk, and talk a message of hope. They are instinctively drawn to those who live with passion and have a bias for action. People like this get things done and aren't afraid of failure. Remember, it's not failure if you learn something from the experience.

In 2016, I was on my way to make a speech in Canada. I didn't feel great, but I didn't feel bad. Something told me to stop by the hospital for a quick check-up before heading to the airport. I was told that I had 48 hours "or so" to live. My heart was dying. I had a triple bypass heart surgery and survived.

The morning after the surgery, my surgeon asked me what I was going to do to honor my second chance. I soon realized something that would change my new life. I realized that most people spend a lifetime waiting for someone or something else to give them a second chance, when in fact, we all have the ability to give ourselves a second chance and a third chance and a fourth chance. We can change how we think and act and speak. We don't have to wait for someone or something to give us permission to change. We have the power. Yes, it's hard to stay positive in the world in which we live, but one trait that the "winners" have over everyone else has always been, and will always be, their mastery of the discipline to adapt and change, and to be positive.

Another of my valued mentors once told me, "You know, I get up every morning and I have two decisions to make. One is that I can choose to be happy, or, two, I can choose to be VERY happy." He's right, you know. Life is short and how you live it is your decision. Will you spend it surviving, or will you spend it thriving? Whatever course you choose to take, think hard, it's all on you.

About the Author

Real World, Business Coach Danny Creed is an international business coach, executive coach, leadership, and networking coach. He is a best-selling author, global keynote and workshop speaker, experienced entrepreneur, and successful business owner. Danny works with entrepreneurs, business owners, executives, and large corporations. Danny is a Brian Tracy International Certified Business Coach and has logged, to date, over 15 thousand business coaching hours. He has been involved with 15 successful start-up businesses and over 400 business turnaround challenges. Coach Dan is the six-time recipient of the FocalPoint International Brian Tracy Award of Sales Excellence and the 2019 FocalPoint Coaching International Practice of the year.

Danny Creed is the published author of these three books: A Life Best Lived: A Story of Life, Death and Second Chances, Straight Talk: Thriving in Business, and Champions Never Make Cold Calls: High-Impact, Low-Cost Lead Generation. His books are available on Amazon.com.

Email: dcreed@focalpointcoaching.com
Website: www.realworldbusinesscoach.com
LinkedIn: www.linkedin.com/in/businesscoachdan/

CHAPTER 6

REPLACE THE HARD SELL WITH AUTHENTICITY

By Dario Cucci
Keynote Speaker and Sales Mindshifter Coach
Zurich, Switzerland

My name is Dario Cucci, and I'm the "sales mindshifter." The reason I received this moniker is because during my 20-plus-year career in the self-development and service industry, I've helped hundreds of experts, personal trainers, coaches, therapists, and consultants to literally let go of their limitations around how they perceive sales. I've helped them break through and shift their negative beliefs into positive beliefs. As a result, I've helped them, ultimately, to sell more.

Let's look into how and why your mindset and beliefs on a subconscious level can have a big impact on your success at selling your services and why it is important to finally let go of preconceived ideas about "the hard sell" in order to succeed.

Is it easier to close more sales when using scarcity tactics that have been taught by many of the sales coaches out there? The answer to that is probably yes. However, when you make a sale that comes from a place of love and authenticity, because you really care and sincerely believe that your service or product will help the client, then you will find tremendously greater sales success. When you sell from a place of love and authenticity, you'll find that the client says yes, not because you've made them afraid, but because they are ready and right for you, your product, and/or your service.

One thing that I have figured out from over 10 years of selling information products and coaching programs over the phone, and generating over a million dollars in additional sales revenue for the companies I worked with during that time, is that when I sold, not from a place of putting fear into the customer around losing out on a deal, but from a place of love, sincerely wanting to assist them to achieve their goals through their purchase of the product or coaching service, it was much more gratifying.

Not only does the customer appreciate the value they get from the conversation you are having with them, but also, they will remember you and be grateful for what you have done for them. As a result of holding a deeper conversation that does not focus on a hard sell, but on serving the client, they end up buying from you.

The tricky thing here is letting go of limitations when it comes to your perceptions around selling. During my career, I had to learn to not only let go of my own internal limiting beliefs in this area but also to stop putting pressure on myself by setting unrealistic expectations. Also, I had to learn to not allow the companies I worked with to put me under undue pressure to make a certain number of sales. Reality is, when you make sales, customers end up buying from you only when they are ready, not when you expect or want them to.

To be successful at sales, you should practice getting into the Zen zone, or as I call it, step into the "communication flow," to focus on serving your customers and to practice adapting how you hold the conversation. Practice letting go of expectations while holding a conversation that allows the customer to gain value from your conversation, regardless if they buy or don't buy from you.

To let go of your limitations, first you need to be willing to reprogram your subconscious mind and install new empowering beliefs. The second thing is to practice it daily and affirm your new beliefs on a deeper level, all the while connecting with your emotions, internal dialogue, visuals, and sounds. The third thing that needs to happen is to have someone, like a coach, challenge your point of view, give you constructive feedback, and help you integrate the new beliefs while also giving you specific tasks to complete in order for you to grow as a person.

Even after having spent 20-plus years coaching and having coached and trained many business owners, still to this day, I have my own coach who helps me grow by asking me questions that challenge my point of view on the world and what I do.

There is no magic pill that gives a script or a certain strategy for you to easily plug in and suddenly make more sales. When I started to make more sales, the biggest change happened because I changed my mindset and I engaged in regular coaching, all the while I was practicing the changes in order to improve and succeed.

The first thing that will happen when you start to challenge your mindset is that you'll look at things differently. This is your critical mind doing a stress test of your new mindset. If you give into it, instead of working through it, you will end up retreating back to your old behavior. When you have a coach and mentor that keeps you accountable while helping you work through your changes, it will be much easier for you to shift your mindset and take actions to manifest your goals.

I want to share a case study story of one of my clients whom I worked with three years ago. This guy, we can call him "Tony," is from London and is very much into fitness. He has a great passion to help others get into shape. However, when we first started to work together, Tony had spent two years and lots of money on developing a website and other tools in order to get a coaching and mentoring platform off the ground, but he hadn't made one dime on it.

The first thing I worked with him on was letting go of his fixation on the platform. Instead, I asked him, "What is it that you are passionate about?"

He answered, "Helping busy professionals to get fit without spending hours at the gym."

I then asked, "How would you do that?"

He explained, "I studied health, fitness, and biohacking, and I know that when people learn how to do biohacking strategies, it helps them achieve their fitness goals much quicker."

Once we clarified what he was passionate about, I coached him to let go of trying to do the hard sell. Instead, I taught him how to deliver value through the conversation strategy, rather than a static, hard-sell website. We focused on how he could deliver his passion as a professional service with his role being the "Biohacking Coach." Within one week after he'd made that mind shift and commitment to focus on his passion, he ended up getting three new clients, which also made him a great deal of money in sales revenue.

To this date, Tony offers that service. Tony's success happened once he was willing to let go of that fixed idea and expectation to make money, and, instead, he shifted his focus to wanting to serve people by following his passion. In making this shift, it became much easier for him to sell his service and to succeed.

As soon as Tony let go of putting pressure on himself and his website and let go of trying to make something work that wasn't going to work, and he applied himself differently, he ended up becoming successful.

The same goes for you. If you are an entrepreneur, coach, personal trainer, or expert in your field, and you feel stuck in the way you do things, then it's important to finally take the steps to let go of your limitations around what you think sales is about or how you think you can grow your business.

From Negative to Positive: The Steps to Shift Your Mind

In order to let go of your limitations, the first thing is to allow yourself to become aware of the limiting beliefs you have on a subconscious level. Ask yourself: "What negative beliefs do I have when it comes to selling my services? What are the emotions that I associate with those beliefs?"

List 10 or more of those negative limiting beliefs, write them out, but don't judge them. Just become aware of them.

Once you do that, for each limiting belief, ask yourself the question: "What would be the opposite of that belief? What positive emotion would I like to feel with it?"

List 10 or more of those positive and empowering beliefs that you'd like to integrate within your subconscious mind.

Once you've done that, it's vital that you now practice those new beliefs. Take on daily actions and hold improvement conversations that will enable you to close more sales.

Let's look at one more story about how powerful mindset is, especially in making successful sales against all the odds.

About three years ago, I was invited to be a guest speaker at a multi-speaker event called MEN Empowerment Networking. I traveled from Switzerland to London for the event. The night before the event, I felt my face cramping up.

I had an intense pain on the left side of my jaw. All the sudden, it became numb, no feeling.

I realized that my speech was no longer clear, and that something was wrong with my face. I had Bell's palsy, "a condition that causes a temporary weakness or paralysis of the muscles in the face," but this was only the second time in my life that it had expressed itself. My guest speaking gig was scheduled for the next morning at 10 am, and there I was, the night before, realizing that I could not speak clearly.

However, I was determined not to give in. Instead, I figured I would see how I felt the next morning and still deliver my speech because I had committed myself to it, and I wanted to deliver value to help the entrepreneurs at the event. I was eager to shift their mindset and increase their sales.

The next day, I arrived at the venue with everything prepared and ready to go, though my face remained partially paralyzed. However, not only were the event organizers running late, instead of 40 attendees turning up as scheduled, there were only four, plus the event crew and sponsors. On top of that, there were technical issues with sound and the PowerPoint display.

Instead of just throwing in the towel and stating, "I can't work like this," I ended up telling the audience that I had Bell's palsy and that if anyone didn't understand me, to let me know. I had to adjust my speed of delivering my speech and focus on speaking more clearly, but I spoke. I did it.

Rather than doing the prepared presentation, I asked the audience, "Do you mind if I end up coaching you today, since we are such a small group?" The audience was thrilled. As a result of these adaptations, the audience feedback was great. Additionally, I ended up winning a new client, without ever hustling to make a sale.

After I finished the event that day, I went to the hospital, got medication, and booked myself for an acupuncture treatment. It took about six months to heal my face from the Bell's palsy, but that is beside the point.

What I really hope you understand is this: you never know where your clients will come from. When you are willing to be of service and deliver value that transforms people's mindset and improves their life or business, then you better believe clients will seek you out. The reason is that they get that you are the real deal and can help them. They are willing to invest in themselves to work with you.

However, you need to have the right mindset for it and be flexible enough to change your strategy on how you deliver your service, if you don't already have a strong and positive leadership mindset.

I wish you all the best with your personal life and business, and hope that what I shared has inspired you to recognize and let go of your limitations of doing the hard sell and start shifting your beliefs in order to serve more customers from a place of love.

About the Author

Dario Cucci helps business owners ramp up sales through a combination of mindset and confidence skills that eliminates fear, insecurity, and confusion around selling. Dario has helped businesses generate over $1 million in additional sales revenue for 10 years straight and increase sales revenue up to 2 thousand percent. He is the bestselling author of five books in over 10 countries. He was featured in *Bella Magazine*, Skynews Radio, ABC, NBC, and several other high-profile media outlets for his coaching.

Dario has learned from many high-level mentors including Tony Robbins, Dr. Tad James (NLP, Hypnosis and Timeline Therapy), Dr. Joanna Martin (How to Sell from Stage), T. Harv Eker (The Enlightened Warrior), Tony and Nicki Vee (MasterCoach Advanced Accreditation Certification), and Andy Harrington (Professional Speaker Academy Elite Certified Speaker and Past Ace Mentor Coach).

If you'd like to learn more about Dario, plus claim one of the free resources available on his website or book your 15 minute Sales Mindshifter Discovery call, visit www.dariocucci.net. You can also listen to interviews and content he shares on his podcast Dario's World, https://dariosworld.buzzsprount.com

CHAPTER 7

IN QUIETNESS AND IN CONFIDENCE

By Delisa Deavenport, MBA, CPC
Employee Experience Coach, Ziglar Legacy Certified
Capac, Michigan

The most successful people develop the mental tenacity to stay focused on achieving whatever they set their mind to. The mystery question—precisely how do we attain a mental state of tenacity?

Thinking back over the many years of struggles I suffered before recognizing I had reached a level of success that I could be proud of, I realize it was a long, exhausting journey. I was in my late-fifties before I found true joy, purpose, and success—my definition of a healthy mindset. I now understand that I first had to discover and cultivate those virtues in the right combination that would result in a solid foundation for sustainable personal development. Building this foundation did not instantly create a successful mindset for me, but once this foundation was formed, it paved the way for me to build a mindset for craving all life has to offer. This type of mindset led to a satisfying, balanced, joyful, and productive success.

During my young-adult years, I was a self-improvement junkie, though nothing ever seemed to stick. I could keep up the charade of change for a couple of weeks, then I would revert right back to the destructive, unhealthy coping behavior I was accustomed to. If this sounds like drama and chaos, it was. In short, it was a life of instant gratification and manipulating people to stay off my back.

One day I came across a Bible quote that changed my life. It was Isaiah 30:15, which reads, "In quietness and in confidence shall be your strength." This was my true turning point. I remember knowing that, somehow, this quote had sticking power and was going to change my life.

At that point in my life, I listened to motivational speakers with intent, as I had no distractions to knock me off my personal development endeavors. I eventually identified two virtues to cultivate that would become the foundation of my healthy growth mindset—humility and quietness. I started with humility and then moved to quietness, focusing and nursing each one separately, until one day the foundation was laid, and I realized that I was never going back to a life of destructive coping skills.

Humility

Humility is the foundation of all other virtues hence,
in the soul in which this virtue does not exist there cannot
be any other virtue except in mere appearance.
—Saint Augustine

Human beings necessarily crave attention and approval. We want to be noticed, acknowledged, and appreciated. Whether we are outgoing or shy, extroverted or introverted, ambitious or still contemplating our purpose, each and every one of us craves interaction and recognition in some form.

Why are some people better equipped to achieve those things that bring about grand acknowledgement? Some people accomplish a goal simply for show, relishing in the spotlight. They are attention junkies. Some seek accomplishments for the sole purpose of being accepted and loved. Most people associate their identity by the job or career they have and how much financial worth they have accumulated. While their accomplishments may be impressive, they often don't find much personal satisfaction.

Just before we were born, God made us in His image, beautiful, loving, and living in a cozy, warm home inside our moms with all the food we needed at exactly the time we should have it. Our emotional slate was clean and ready for us to begin building our mindset of success on it. We spent a large portion of our infancy in tears, which we assume measured some level of pain; after all, tears are usually associated with pain.

Day after day, life happened. Some moments were awesome; some, not-so-much. As a child and teenager, we did not consciously try to develop a successful mindset. We focused on novelty as our curiosity took us through interesting experiences, all the while, forming our perspectives, attitudes, and our mindset about the world and how it all worked together.

All these experiences form your level of humility. It is your level of humility that determines how much mental tenacity you have to stay focused on achieving whatever you set your mind to. Humility is one of the two virtues you need to cultivate to build a foundation for a healthy growth mindset.

Humility has two vastly different meanings that even seem to contradict each other. Herein lies the mystery why so many people refuse to accept this virtue as a foundation for a successful mindset. When you think of someone humiliating you, it is most assuredly a negative connotation. "I was humiliated when she called me a bad name in front of everyone." This definition is "the condition of feeling insignificant, having low self-esteem, being weak, inferior, subservient, low in importance or quality, and having your independence destroyed." It is astonishing how many people only recognize this one meaning for humility.

The second definition contrasts the first one. In this case, humility is the condition of "being modest or not showing pride, being courteously respectful, not needing recognition or the spotlight, not being arrogant, putting others first and being comfortable in those times they are not right." This is the type of humility that builds a successful mindset. This is the type of humility that builds integrity.

Multi-billionaire and founder of Wal-Mart and Sam's Club, Sam Walton, lived a simple life, drove an old red pickup truck, and lived in a modest house, according to Cameron Taylor in his book *Does Your Bag Have Holes?* Sam Walton is known for looking toward his employees and customers for the knowledge needed to manage his empire. Carrying only a yellow legal pad and pen, he listened intently as the frontline folks poured out their hearts over both triumphs and concerns. In a 2016 article in *Entrepreneur*, Zach Ferres highlights that Sam Walton even jumped in and helped bag customers' purchases. Describing Sam Walton as a humble man, Wal-Mart Chief Operating Officer Don Soderquist stated that he learned a valuable lesson from Mr. Walton the day he witnessed Walton bagging customer items noting "None of us are too good to do the little jobs."

The hero and savior of the United States Union, Abraham Lincoln, was not a popular president during his term. It wasn't until many years after his assassination that his true leadership capabilities were recognized and honored. According to Russell Razzaque's article "Learning Humility from Lincoln," President Lincoln recognized that leadership was about watching, listening, and recognizing what others had to say. Lincoln never let his pride keep him from appointing the best people for the job. After his election, he promptly appointed his Republican rivals, William Henry Seward, Salmon P. Chase, and Edward Bates, to his cabinet. He eventually appointed a fellow lawyer, Simon Cameron, as Secretary of War, even though Mr. Cameron had not cared for Lincoln as a lawyer and had been unkind and unruly toward him when they'd partnered together on cases. Lincoln stated that he, himself, had no right to withhold appointments based on his personal opinion of someone when that person was the absolute best for the job.

Sam Walton and Abraham Lincoln are my personal heroes. Both men possess a reverent level of humility, the honorable type of humility. The kind of humility I knew I wanted to develop within myself. I was drawn to their personalities and the similar style with which they led quite different missions. Their stories resonate with me. They each have the two virtues I realize are key to creating a foundation for a healthy growth mindset. Sam Walton and Abraham Lincoln had the characteristics of confident humility. They also knew how to draw on their deep inner instincts even when their decisions were not popular.

Quietness

Somewhere deep inside your soul, there exists a
quiet place where truth, direction and hidden strength lies.
Learn to tap into this well of knowledge and it will carry
you to places you have never even dreamed existed.

Developing the practice of drawing strength from quietness is the second virtue that created my foundation for a successful mindset, thus enabling me to live at my highest form of productivity in all areas of my life.

In the vast amount of years I spent in personal development, I craved all the self-help theories and methods explained to me. However, I struggled with how to incorporate these life-changing strategies into my life. It was a combination of occurrences that made me finally realize that there exists a place, down deep inside the soul, where your mind transcends into your heart, where emotional knowledge, direction, truth, and insight reside. I call this place my "quiet." It's a sacred place I visit often throughout the day to receive guidance. Marilyn Mitchell identifies this inner self as the "Heart." It is in this place that authentic transformation begins.

This process of tapping into your revered place of change takes time to develop, but once you have cultivated the practice, it opens up a world of possibilities. This process is not one of mysticism, hypnosis, psychic powers, mental telepathy, or supernaturalism. This is an area of the deep subconscious mind. It is the heart of your belief system about everything in your life. It is the very place people pull strength from when they are desperately fighting to live. When someone is emotionally or physically tortured, this place of comfort and quiet will make whatever they are going through bearable. It is a place where strength will help you sustain, and it is a place where strength will help you transform, depending on the reason you are tapping into it. This place of ultimate "being" is the very place monks and ascetics journey to while keeping up their severely strict, structured lifestyles of obedience.

I first was introduced to this place of "quiet" when I began using meditation to manage stress in college. I had meditated for months before actually getting all the way to this place of subconscious strength. One day, as I lay on my bed, relaxing every muscle, one at a time, all over my entire body, I slowly began to feel myself floating. After a period of time, I physically felt like I was in a dream-like state, rising above my bed. While it was happening to me, I was not frightened, but when I woke, I must say, I had a type of anxious wonderment about the experience. It was many years before I was able to tap into that level of "quiet" again because I did not realize exactly what it was at the time.

Fast-forward a few years. Aiding my journey to discover transformational strength in my "quiet" was Marianne Williamson's book *Return to Love*. In the introduction, she writes about how she fought the fight of both addiction and a chaotic lifestyle for many years. It was when she realized that she had to surrender to the fight that her life began to change significantly. I wondered exactly what it meant to surrender. I was not able to put it all together at the time, but I never forgot her words. Somewhere in my heart, I knew she was telling me something that was going to eventually create real change within me.

In 1991, a judge decided that I had a drinking problem and that I needed a year's worth of AA meetings. I disagreed, but I complied. It was at these AA meetings that I began to hear this word "surrender" again. One day, when I was reading the AA daily devotional book, the words jumped off the page, "In quietness and in confidence shall be your strength." There it was, Isaiah 30:15. What struck me so strongly about this statement was that strength came from quietness, but I simply did not know how that could be. Could it have something to do with surrender?

I thought about surrender, I thought about quietness, and I thought about confident humility. In one translation, I read the verse as "In quietness and consciousness ..." It all began to make sense. I remembered that place I went to, so many years earlier, during a meditation exercise. I realized my life was never going back to drama, addiction, and chaos. It was my time to transform.

Over the years, I understood that transformation happens when I am able to get still and relax, forgetting about the physical world around me and going inward. I mentally focus on transcending my mind into my heart where I finally reach that part of me, I call my "quiet". I talk to myself here, or I talk to Jesus. Sometimes I talk to the universe, and sometimes I talk to that part of me that hangs on to unhealthy ways.

Often, I get overwhelmed in life, and I absolutely have no idea how to untangle the thoughts in my head. I proceed into my place of "quiet." I go there for all sorts of life's challenges seeking direction. I get still and go into my "quiet," and I ask for guidance. In my stillness, with all my muscles and body relaxed, the craziness subsides, and I can clearly see the facts or direction in an objective way.

Frequently, I lack clear, convincing evidence as to why I am directed to follow a certain path of action when I am in my "quiet," but my heart feels the strong conviction of what to do anyway. When I've chosen more logical choices than what my heart has told me while looking into my "quiet," every single time, it's proven the wrong choice. I now listen to my "intuition" because, if the choice came from the sacred place of "quiet," it is the right choice. You can bet on it. And, it is available to anyone.

There are many techniques to access this place of "quiet," for example, meditation, tapping, emotional freedom, energy medicine, and the list goes on. Meditation and guided visualization work for me. I am not an expert on what happens during meditation or how it prepares and heals the body. What I do know is that you must calm down all the adrenaline and stress in the muscles to effectively tap into your "quiet." You have to let go of all thoughts, good and stressful. I often picture myself in a garden, smelling flowers and kissing bunnies, to let my worldly thoughts go.

Each time you relax, you get a little closer to that place of clear thought. It may take months to discover the actual place of true "quiet" where transformation takes place, but each time you go through a relaxation method, you feel healthier, you have a clearer mindset, and you get a little closer to that place of quiet discovery. Once you are able to tap into your "quiet," you discover your true belief system and you can contemplate why and how a change will benefit you. Think of it like your conscious talking to your subconscious and saying things like, "You are enough, and you are a strong person, confident and capable of going for that goal," or "You have a personality of snapping at people and being too direct, but you can change that and be kind, patient, and more understanding of others." That was one of my big changes. If you want to be a successful entrepreneur, it is in your "quiet" that you find the strength to overcome inevitable obstacles and stay passionate about your calling.

As an employee working in a workplace culture where it is difficult to be productive, you can find your niche, your way to contribute your worth to the company vision, while laying aside all the preconceived notions about other co-workers. All of a sudden, it is not about their personalities or limitations. It is about your ability to rise above the challenges and be a part of the solution rather than the problem. In my employee experience coaching practice, I do coaching around what needs to be done to create positive change. Then I coach exactly how to go about bringing that change in a passionate way, tapping into inner strength.

It takes time, patience, faith, and persistence to transform into the person that unequivocally has a successful mindset. It is a process, which for some, is more of a struggle than for others due to their perception of how life works. The goal is to grow into the kind of successful mindset that allows you to be productive in every area of your life. Every single one of us has the ability to acquire this wonderful gift of a successful mindset.

Your level of humility determines how much mental tenacity you have for transformation. Your ability to tap into your "quiet" will give you the fuel to develop a greater level of humility. When you are able to confidently work this combination to build your foundation of personal development, you will have created a productive life of peace, joy, and purpose. You will be wildly productive in each spoke of your life—the mental, spiritual, financial, physical, professional, personal, and familial. You will develop a successful mindset.

Find your direction in your quiet. That is my message.

About the Author

Coach Delisa Deavenport, MBA, CPC, is on a mission to work with service-oriented, small business owners to motivate, lead, and empower employees by cultivating the employee experience, which results in employees with strong engagement, high productivity, and driven innovation who deliver quality customer service in a happy, healthy environment. She is a certified Zig Ziglar speaker, a certified Ziglar Legacy instructor, a Distinguished Toastmaster, and a certified professional coach from Professional Coach Academy.

Delisa has worked in the public accounting and nonprofit world for over 30 years and has held numerous board positions with nonprofits dear to her heart. She is a member of the St. Nicholas Orthodox Christian Church in Burton, Michigan.

A Texan by heart, she recently moved to Michigan to live near family. She works out of both the Dallas and Detroit surrounding metro areas. Delisa is the proud wife of her hero, Larry Deavenport.

Email: delisa@coachdelisa.com
Website: www.coachdelisa.com

CHAPTER 8

THE HAPPY BOSS: MINDSET TOOLS FOR THE SUCCESSFUL BUSINESS OWNER

By Inge Dowden
Business Coach, Author and Keynote Speaker
Bristol, United Kingdom

Most business owners start their business for the same reasons: they want to have more money, more freedom, and more time to spend with their loved ones. And running their own business can indeed give them the freedom to make their own decisions, determine their own direction and have a lot of fun in the process. They get to decide what products to sell, where to sell them, and how to run the business. The amount of money they can earn is limitless. Of course, we all know about business owners that spend their days on the golf course or on exotic holidays.

But the reality for many small business owners is often the exact opposite of what they wanted: they work harder than they ever have before, for less money and with less time to spend with their loved ones. They find they have to be good at all sorts of things they didn't have to do before—bookkeeping, IT, people management, and even production, to name a few—and it can all be quite overwhelming. The dream has turned into a nightmare, and they don't know how to get out of it.

Let's take James for example. James is an electrician and a very good one. He loves working with clients, has a keen eye for detail, and generally solves problems quickly and skilfully. His boss, however, is a penny-pinching tyrant who rules with an iron fist and asks his employees to see if they can charge people the maximum possible for the minimum amount of work. This clashes with James's values, so he decides to leave and start his own business.

Because he is good at his job and good with people, James soon becomes very successful and takes on more electricians. The business continues to grow, and he takes on admin staff, an IT guy, marketing people, and sales staff to keep up with the demand. Although the business is now successful, James is not actually happy because suddenly his days are filled with strategy meetings, personnel issues, and paperwork. He, personally, no longer does any electrician work, and he really misses it. But he feels he can't go back because by now he has adapted his lifestyle to the amount of money he is making: his kids are in private school, the family goes on three holidays a year, and he drives a nice car. He has everything he always thought he wanted, but it feels like a prison. Not exactly a happy situation, wouldn't you agree?

So how do you get out of a situation like that? Or better still, how can you avoid getting into this kind of situation in the first place? Because ultimately, we all want to be happy. That's what we want for ourselves and also what we want for others.

Here's the good news: being happy is a state of mind that is entirely within your own control. It has nothing to do with the state of the economy, your customers, your members of staff, or the weather. I'll show you that it's possible to be happy at any given moment, regardless of what's happening around you. Once you realize the power of this, you'll be able to do anything you want.

Begin with the End in Mind

One of Stephen Covey's *7 Habits of Highly Effective People* is "Begin with the end in mind". Before you start making business plans or working out which office unit you want to rent, you need to be crystal clear about the kind of business you want to run.

Starting your business without knowing what you want it to achieve is like going on a journey without a destination or road map. Sure, once you start travelling, you'll end up somewhere, and by chance, this might be where you want to be. However, you'll more likely end up in a situation where you think to yourself, "How did I get *here*?"

Before you start thinking about what kind of *business* you want, you need to think about what kind of *life* you want. To help figure this out, you can ask yourself the following five key questions:

1. WHO is important to me?
2. WHAT is important to me?
3. What do I want to BE?
4. What do I want to DO?
5. What do I want to HAVE?

When you answer these questions, think about what *you* want. Not what you think you *should* want or what your family, friends, or colleagues tell you to want. It's important that **you have your own definition of success**. Just because someone else wants to run a multinational company, doesn't mean you have to want that. Equally, just because someone thinks it's enough to have a lifestyle business, it doesn't mean you shouldn't create your nationwide franchise company.

For example, my definition of success has always been that I want to be able to go for a walk or a bike ride on a sunny Tuesday afternoon. Freedom is my number one value, and I've created my business in such a way that I do indeed have plenty of time during the working week to do things other than work.

On the other hand, I have a client who has a daughter with special needs, and his main motivation for the business is that it should give him enough money that he knows her future is secure. And that drives everything he does.

While every business needs to focus on making a profit (otherwise you just have a hobby or a badly paid job), the money in itself is not necessarily the driver for every business owner.

And that brings me to the next point.

Know Yourself

It is essential that you know yourself. This may seem obvious, but all too often people don't realize that their personal preferences influence their behaviour, and this, in turn, determines their success. You need to know your **strengths** and **weaknesses** and what **motivates** or **demotivates** you.

A great tool to help with that is personality profiling. I'm a fan of the DISC profile, but there are many others out there. If you've never done one of them, I highly recommend you do. Not only will it help you to know yourself better, it will also help you to understand others better. And this will make it easier to communicate appropriately, lead effectively, and avoid conflict.

People like people who are like themselves. This is why there are some people that you get along with straight away: you have the same sense of humour, they understand what you want from them with only half a word, you have lots in common, and you feel comfortable with them. It's easy to get along with those people, isn't it?

However, in life and especially in the workplace, there are also people that you don't get along with so easily. They grate on you. They frustrate you. They never seem to "get you", and you don't seem to be able to get through to them. At best, they annoy you, and at worst they make you unhappy because they might be your business partner or your employees.

This is where personality profiling comes in. It will help you understand that those other people are simply **different** from you. They have a different learning style, communication style, leadership style. Their pace of life is different, and their way of thinking is different. But different isn't necessarily worse even though it may feel like that sometimes. **Different is just different**. And when you understand their view of the world, their way of thinking and their behaviour, you will find it easier to deal with it. By knowing what motivates others, you can adapt yourself to them and, thus, get the results *you* want, rather than being annoyed and frustrated and not getting anywhere.

Do you think that if you treat people the way you want to be treated, you're showing them the utmost respect? You might do. I certainly did. It's something we get taught from a very young age, and it will work beautifully with people who are just like you. But we've just seen that many people are not like you, so what happens with them? They don't respond to you at all and may even be hostile.

The key to successful relationships in all aspects of business and life is that you should **treat people the way *they* want to be treated**. That way, they will feel like you understand them, and they might even feel that you're similar to them, which will make them appreciate and trust you more. And when they trust you more, they are more likely to respond to your requests in a way that you want.

I hope that I have convinced you of the need to know yourself and others well and that you'll look into personality profiling as a tool (please feel free to contact me for a DISC profile if you want). I haven't got enough space to write in detail about the DISC profiles, but I will give you a very quick overview to give you an idea of the sort of things that set people apart:

- ☞ *D-personalities* are driven, determined, and ambitious. They have a short attention span and want you to get to the point quickly. They make strong leaders but can also be bullies.
- ☞ *I-personalities* are engaging, fun, and inspirational. They want to get people on board and are excellent communicators. They may lack focus but are great at building rapport and negotiating.
- ☞ *S-personalities* are loyal, dependable, and good with people. They are excellent listeners, well-organized, and great team players, but they don't like change.
- ☞ *C-personalities* are detail-focused and analytical. They love systems and processes, and are great at setting them up. They can be perfectionists and too cautious but will always deliver great work.

The trick is to **work according to your preference** most of the time. Sure, anyone can do anything, but if you're having to work against your preference, you're much more likely to be frustrated and unhappy.

Just look at James, the electrician: instead of doing the electrical work he loved (because it was detailed and methodical), he now has to deal with people's problems and strategy meetings. He would be much better off if he outsourced the things he doesn't like (the people stuff, in his case) and focused on the things he's naturally good at (the business processes and finances, for example).

As a business owner, it is also very important that you employ people in the position that's right for them. You want someone in accounts who has a C-preference, a salesperson who has an I-preference, and account managers who have an S-preference. You might have a D-preference, and that means that you need people with other preferences on your team, so that all your big plans actually get executed.

Focus on what you love doing the most and get other people to do the things that you don't like, but they love. That's the way to create a successful business that gives you happiness as well as money.

Mindset of the Successful, Happy Business Owner

Although everyone's idea of success is different, there are certain traits that happy and successful business owners have that link them together. By looking at the attributes of people who have the kind of life we want for ourselves, we can use them as tools to get our own success and happiness, whatever that means for us.

Below is a non-exhaustive list of characteristics/tools you could aim to get or improve. Remember that your personality will have a lot of influence, so certain things will be more natural to you than others, but because this is all about mindset, you can always learn to change.

Believe in yourself. Successful people believe in themselves, even if nobody else does. But most of the time, others believe in them too, as this characteristic often leads to success. This is not about being arrogant or deluded, but about believing that you have every right to be here and do your thing. And think about it this way: if you don't believe in yourself, how do you expect others to believe in you?

Don't be afraid to fail. This is a key ingredient for success. As Winston Churchill put it, "Success is the ability to go from one failure to another without loss of enthusiasm". And the opposite is true as well: fear of failure and, therefore, not even giving a go is a recipe for never achieving anything. You have to try things out and see every mistake as a learning opportunity. That's how you improve and ultimately become successful.

Be open to new ideas. Even though success isn't uniquely linked to doing new things, being open to new ideas plays a big part in how successful and happy you can be. Embrace the unknown and learn to deal with change. This can be easier said than done because most people dislike change, so start with small things—a new recipe, a different route to work, learning a new skill—and then work up to the bigger things—changing careers, starting a business, developing new products, etc.

Be willing to take a risk. This follows on from the previous points about not being afraid to fail and being open to new ideas. Don't be afraid to get out of your comfort zone, as that's where the magic happens. The thing with your comfort zone is that the more time you spend in it, the smaller it gets. Whereas if you're willing to try new things, even if they are a bit scary at first, that's when you'll experience growth and fulfilment.

Don't give up. Walt Disney once said, "The difference between winning and losing is quite often … not quitting". It's such a simple concept, but one that unhappy people don't get. They try something new, and if it doesn't work the first time, they simply give up. But that's not how you get good at something. You have to keep on trying and not give up. Sure, you might have to try something else and learn from what went wrong (as there is no point flogging a dead horse), but most of all, you just have to keep going. Especially when it is important to you, which is the only thing you should be working on anyway.

Keep on learning. Super successful people know that they don't know everything and will always invest a lot of time in learning new things. Whether it's reading about the latest trends in their industry, getting familiar with a new technology, or working on mindset skills, they know that it all helps to create a more rounded, more creative individual.

Value your time. Time is incredibly valuable, much more so than money, so make sure you use it wisely. Get good at time management, focus on the things that are truly important to you, and learn to say no to things that will distract you from your goals.

Don't be afraid to be different. I've talked before about the importance of setting your own goals and defining your own path to success, and this follows on from that. If you're not afraid to be different, you can be a disruptor, come up with brand-new ideas, and find new ways of doing things. Rather than follow the "but that's how we've always done it" school of thought, you can carve out a new road that leads you to **your idea of success**. But to do that, you have to worry less about what people think of you and have the courage of your convictions. It doesn't matter what other people think, you're the only one living your life, so make sure you live it the way you want to.

Learn to deal with uncertainty. This is especially true for business owners. If all you want is safety and security, then it's unlikely that you're ever going to be super successful. Because starting and running a business is full of twists and turns, and you never know what disaster is looming around the corner. If you're okay with uncertainty and you work on mitigating it as much as possible, then you'll be set for success.

Focus on what you can control. Most things that are of concern to us are actually outside our control. Things like the weather, the economy, the government, what Bob thinks of us, and what society thinks we should do. The only things that we can truly control are **our reactions** to these outside influences and the **actions** we take as a result. So, the trick is to focus on the things you CAN control and not worry about the things you CAN'T control. Once you do this successfully, your happiness will never again depend on things that happen **to** you.

Be happy to delegate. To have more time and freedom to do the things you love, you have to trust others to do a great job for you. Whether that's your outsourced providers or your staff, you have to be able to delegate properly. Tell them what's expected of them, give them all the training and the tools they need, and then let them get on with it.

Get good at systems and processes. This may sound boring, but good systems and processes are the keys to freedom and success. From production to sales, from marketing to customer delivery, everything needs to be process-driven and easily replicable.

Get support. Last but most definitely not least: get help and support when needed. I've said before that your personality preferences will influence how you feel about these characteristics/tools, and if you want to change some of them, you will probably need some help to do so. Super successful people didn't get there without help: they have mentors, business coaches, trainers, accountability groups, and people they can use as a sounding board. They realize that they are not perfect, and they will find someone to help them in the areas that they need the most.

In Summary

To be a happy and successful business owner you have to:

- ☞ Have a clear definition of what success means to you
- ☞ Know your strengths and weaknesses, motivators and demotivators
- ☞ Focus on doing what you love and outsource or delegate the rest
- ☞ Follow your own path and don't worry about what others think.

Use the mindset tools I have given you to achieve this, because **you deserve nothing less than happiness and success**!

About the Author

Inge Dowden is a business growth coach, based in Bristol, UK. After a successful career in international business, she started her coaching business in 2008 and has since helped hundreds of small business owners achieve happiness and success. She's an NLP practitioner and qualified DISC profiler, and she firmly believes that everyone deserves to be happy at work, be that as a business owner or an employee.

Inge is the author of *The Happy Worker: How to Find a Job You Love and Love the Job You Have* and is working on her second book, *The Happy Boss: How to Create a Business You Love.* In her spare time, she loves to go out Nordic walking, and in 2019, she achieved her long-held ambition to walk in the Himalayas. Originally from the Netherlands, she now lives in Bristol with her husband Nick and their two cats, Bonnie and Coco.

Email: inge@ingedowdencoaching.com
Website: www.ingedowdencoaching.com

CHAPTER 9

WITH A STRONG MIND, YOU CAN ACCOMPLISH ANYTHING

By Sébastien Ferré
International Coach HEC, Founder of Hopis
Paris, France

*A short concentration with feelings will bring you far
more than long meditation without feeling.*
—Sri Shyam Sundar Goswami (1891–1978)

With a strong mind you can accomplish anything.

We all have a source of inner strength, calm, and focus, which we can draw from directly. This is one of the secrets of a successful mind that I will share with you.

Twenty years ago, I worked in my family's business. Daily I was handling many responsibilities and a lot of pressure. At that time, I also coached my brother, a top sportsman, to assist him to achieve great success in motor sports. Each day, I had to do the work of several people, managing a team and keeping the money coming in. I was pacing around a workspace of almost a thousand square meters, responding to the incessant calls from the three phones I had on me. I was always doing several things at once. I was multitasking before the word became fashionable.

At the end of each week, I traveled to join sports competitions. I leave it to you to imagine the extreme pace of my life at that time, physically, psychically, and emotionally.

Despite my apparent success, I had a feeling, as vague as it was inexplicable, that things would change, and more and more deeply, a feeling that things had to change.

My life then took a radical turn when, at my workplace, I met an authentic spiritual master. This incredible encounter seemed to be planned. I'll confess, I do not believe in chance.

Allowing my feelings to guide me, I fully committed to a teaching that would gradually turn my life upside down. For ten years, this wise man passed on to me the teachings of his Indian guru, Sri Shyam Sundar Goswami, of whom he had been a disciple for over two decades. I am forever grateful to him.

I want to clarify here the original meaning of the word "guru." In Sanskrit, the word "guru" means "one who lifts the veil of ignorance." Goswami was an authentic master of traditional Indian yoga, rarely seen nowadays, and a world-renowned expert in mental concentration. Even today, the name Goswami embodies the vocation of knowledge and teaching. This teaching radically changed my existence.

Next, I returned to university, more specifically, to medical school, to study mindfulness with doctors, psychiatrists, and psychologists.

With a strong mind you can accomplish anything.

Having transposed all these teachings into the different areas of my life, I've had a lot of personal fulfillment and success. In my many years coaching others on this same path, I observed many individual transformations through learning calm and concentration.

We all have a source of inner strength that we can draw on directly when we're calm and focused. By learning to be calm and focused, through training and by being patient, you can find the key that will allow you to connect with this inner strength. The mind is like a muscle that needs training. In recent years, scientists, including Dr. Antoine Lutz of the Lyon Center for Research in Neuroscience and Professor Richard Davidson of the University of Wisconsin, Madison, have proven that people who assiduously practice mental discipline can achieve unusual levels of consciousness through the creation of neural connections.

Your mind needs to be trained. How? By willpower. Where there is no will, discipline cannot continue. As you train your mind to concentrate, it will get stronger and stronger. You are beginning to understand why I repeat this simple truth: with a strong mind you can accomplish anything. Mental concentration cannot take root in agitation. That's why you absolutely have to cultivate calm.

Focus on these words, follow me.

If you are looking for success or greater success, you will not find this by continuing to do the same things in the same way as you are already doing them. How could you get a different result by continuing to do exactly the same things the same way? You must be ready to make changes in the context of your life and be prepared for transformation.

It is not about reading a book or attending a conference and following what is on offer without it relating to your interiority, your own desires, your own needs. Beware of the accumulation of these passive modes of learning, during which you are just a spectator. It can be stimulating or even inspiring, but the change of context that you seek cannot be done without you! It is only through lived experience that you can truly integrate the concepts of your own transformation. It is about you, and more specifically, about your life, hence, the importance of being connected to yourself.

You have to set out to meet what drives you to seek success. And for that, turn your attention inside yourself. This is the first step to mental concentration. The real point of reference is inside you. Remember, as long as you are aware of what you are doing and what you are going through, it only takes a few small things to get engaged in order for you to find that successful mind state you seek. It's good to remember here that, in the psychological sense, we can define consciousness as the "internalized relationship that a being can establish with the world in which they live or with themselves." So we are now talking about your interiority. No one else can know you better than yourself, provided you are connected to yourself.

With a strong mind you can accomplish anything.

Focus can only emerge once you establish an active but peaceful attention to your internal perceptions. And this is only possible if you are calm. Focus is closely linked to calm. Where turmoil resides, true focus will not be achievable in the long term.

Most of the time, people are turned outward. These days, it seems everything leads us to dissipation. Most of the people I coach—including executive leaders of Fortune 500 companies—often feel consumed by external factors and yearn to reconnect with themselves. I tell them what I'm telling you now:

you are like the passenger of a car that has no driver, which can be danger-ous, if you think about it. On board, you are being driven, following a route. So, you are subject to the circumstances of the moment. Instead of being in action, you are in reaction. In this state, you have no focus. Your energy is con-stantly spent in reacting. Sometimes, the toll can even be very heavy: fatigue, headaches, insomnia, nightmares, anxieties become your fellow travelers. You know perfectly well, these are not good companions.

To succeed, you need to take your place in the driver's seat.

Comfortably installed in your seat, you must regain control of the steering wheel. Driving a car requires a lot of attention. You have to be attentive min-ute by minute. Attention, extended over time, becomes focus. At the highest level of driving—Formula 1 drivers know this better than anyone—you have to stay calm and focus with precision. At this level, the slightest deviation of the steering wheel can put your performance at risk, or worse still, your life.

The more ambitious you are in your plans for success, the more calm and focused you need to be. When you focus, know that what you think, what you feel, what you do, and even what you imagine all determine what you experi-ence. And for that, you have to be in the driving seat with your hands on the wheel. A driver must become one with their machine. When you are driving, you are one with yourself. It is this state of oneness that gives you access to your inner strength.

With a strong mind you can accomplish anything.

If you want to succeed in something, don't do anything else.

You can only succeed fully and sustainably if you are 100 percent commit-ted. These days, people do things by halves because they do two things at the same time. You're doing homework with your son and watching the news at the same time. You're talking with your spouse and reading emails at the same time. You're driving and looking at your smartphone at the same time. Believe me, if you want to find success, do one thing at a time!

Scientists are unanimous on the ill effects around multitasking. "Multitasking will slow you down and increase your chances of making mis-takes," says Professor David E. Meyer, director of the Brain, Cognition, and Action Laboratory at the University of Michigan. Using medical imagery to analyze the brain activity of people in multitasking mode has shown that the brain cannot multitask strictly simultaneously. As published in *Science* in 2010, French neurologists Étienne Koechlin and Sylvain Charron of the Cognitive Neuroscience Laboratory of the National Institute of Health and

Medical Research (INSERM) show that, multiple zones can activate at the same time, but the brain will only process one task at a time.

Remember this. If you want to succeed in something, do one thing at a time. Do one thing at a time, calmly and with focus. And do it with love.

The secret to success is to be 100 percent here. One hundred percent present in the present. You cannot succeed fully and sustainably without fully committing yourself. The heart is the reality of your person. It is the essence of your person. It is your deepest interiority. When you fully commit yourself by putting all your heart in, you put your heart into something to which you give a particular energy. Then, you will experience inner calm, joy, and eventually, success will come. Success does not take one form. The intensity of heart we can impart into an undertaking lasts far beyond our existence.

When we focus on something, we give it strength. We all have a source of inner strength that we can draw on directly when we fully direct our minds to our hearts.

With a strong mind you can accomplish anything.

Concentration is a mental process by which multifaceted consciousness is reduced to a point. Concentration gives energy to a specific point, like a spotlight aimed at a particular place until you forget the rest, while a lack of attention removes all forms of energy from things. The more you focus on your project, the more energy you will produce in its direction and the more energy you will give it. Your intention to succeed converts this energy into action. Your attention places energy, your intention transforms it, and your heart is the engine. If you stay focused (one thing at a time!), you can put all that energy into motion bringing your project to life, moment by moment. You don't grow a flower by pulling on it, you water it and you wait patiently. To be successful, you must stay calm and focused, remaining simply present, moment by moment.

The more calm and focused you become day by day, the more incredible energy you carry. You go from a dissipated consciousness to a focused internal energy. You become like a magnet. You can then bring about and naturally attract success.

If you've stayed with me so far, focused on these words and nothing else, I know you can feel what I'm talking about. You feel it, and you visualize its full potential. By continuing in this way in your life, you will be more and more present, in the present. You will then be able to fully express your potential, and you will become more and more yourself.

By carrying out your plans, your whole being gets fulfilled.
With a strong mind you can accomplish anything!

About the Author

Sébastien Ferré is an HEC Paris International Coach and graduate of the Lille Faculty of Medicine with a specialization in stress and anxiety management. After completing a mission for the United Nations, he worked as a psychological coach in the world of high-performance sports. Over ten years, he received the teachings of Shri Shyam Sundar Goswami in the philosophy of traditional Indian yoga.

Sébastien has worked for several years as an executive coach to leaders and teams of multinational Fortune 500 companies. An expert in mental concentration, he works with individuals and groups on their personal, professional, and spiritual development pathways, either remotely or face to face. He regularly organizes courses to initiate mental concentration and practice according to the teachings of Shri Shyam Sundar Sundar Goswami.

Email: sebastien.ferre@hopis.fr
Website: http://hopis.fr

CHAPTER 10

SUCCESS IS FREEDOM, NOT MORE HOURS

By Mary Lee Gannon ACC, CAE
Executive and Career Coach
Pittsburgh, Pennsylvania

You've done all the right things. You went to college. You studied hard. You even have a postgraduate degree. You have a nice family. You are dedicated to everything you do. But you just aren't where you thought you'd be right now.

Someone else got the promotion. Someone else has direct reports who compete to be on their team. Someone else seems happier. Someone else's kids call them all the time. Someone else's spouse is crazy about them. Someone else has a spouse.

I've not only walked a mile in your shoes, I've broken a few heels and changed shoes dozens of times, thinking that if I tried just one more thing, I'd be happier and more successful. I'm talking business books, self-help books, conferences, groups, courses, time management tools, changing friends, changing relationships, counseling, networking, retreats, informational interviews, to-do lists. The harder I tried, the more stuck I became.

What's Your Grit Story?

Leaders hire, promote, and position colleagues to advance based on their ability to do one thing more than any other—adapt. If you can demonstrate how you have been resilient and tenacious, you are likely to achieve. That's why I urge—know your grit story. You certainly don't want to share all the intimate details of it with prospective hiring managers but defining what makes you unique in the area of persistence builds your confidence for when you are asked to talk about yourself. A grit story demonstrates how you addressed a challenge, your strategic thinking ability, and your execution skills.

At the age of 35, I was a stay-at-home mother of four children under seven-years-old, living what looked on the outside to be the country club life, but behind closed doors was in an unpalatable marriage. Every day I used to weigh the merit of my children growing up with mom and dad together in dysfunction against the meaning of life with us separate. My biggest fear was that my girls would grow up and find themselves in a similar circumstance or my son would replicate the same. And I would be responsible. After all, it was okay for mom.

When I noticed that a piece of my soul was dying and was completely void of hope, I finally filed for divorce as a leap of faith. However, I was not at all prepared for the avalanche that befell me. Within six months, my husband filed his businesses into bankruptcy on loans I had cosigned. He re-opened the business under a new name yet in the meantime, he canceled the children's health insurance, shortly after which the children and I were homeless, on welfare, food stamps, medical assistance, and without a car. The children had to change schools midyear and were on the free lunch program.

I never saw this despair coming. Yet, the children managed it with grace. They made new friends with an open mind. They handled not having a dad at events with innocence. They treated poverty with humility. It was remarkable.

I remember the day I took my two-year-old son with me to the gas company to plead for utility assistance and realized how grateful I was for these programs. I made a commitment right there, looking into my son's sweet eyes as he played with an action figure in the chair beside me, that living on public assistance was not a way of life for us. It would be a bridge to freedom, not a boat circling the shore dependent on the weather to stay afloat.

Being a child in a divorced family is difficult enough. Then to be a casualty of the war of divorce is way more than anyone can imagine until you live it. Today, my children are warm, caring, thoughtful, successful, well-adjusted young adults. Maria, Brianna, Andrea, and Max survived this period in their lives and thrive today because they learned the most important skill of life early—how to cope and adapt. It amazes me how many people in the work-force do not have this skill or know how to develop it.

What I will share with you is what I've learned by experience. These are not hypothetical theories but strategies that I've implemented, observed in my children, and seen the benefit of over years with my executive coaching clients. If you are to thrive, you must learn specific skills to cope with disappointment, realize hope for a vision you believe in, keep your childlike innocence, have front-sight focus to stay on track and thrive, and earn and influence the way happy people do. You can absolutely have your dream career and dream life. But first, some things must be released, learned, and accepted.

Recognize the Treadmill to Nowhere

While I was DO-ing everything I could think of to improve my sense of accomplishment and happiness, I was getting farther and farther away from noticing the toll it took on my peace, my leadership, my relationships, and my family. I played to my strengths, had a dedicated work ethic, and always measured my successes that communicated my value. I became the CEO of a $26 million organization in a very short time. But I was working long hours, was detached from my children, and never really felt that I deserved to be happy. I was exhausted from continually having to prove myself on the treadmill to nowhere.

I was living for the perception of others—my children, my boss, my board, the community, my parents, my friends, my colleagues. I wasn't living for myself. I had lost "me" in the process of shame. I thought my success would earn me favor. I used it to cover up my depleted sense of self-worth. Deep down I was embarrassed that my marriage had failed, that my life had ended up in anguish, that my children had to live in poverty, and that I hadn't been good enough to make it all work.

Confidence is being competent and effective. I was, indeed, career confident. I secured jobs I was never qualified for on paper because I knew what to measure and had a reputation for exceeding any goal set before me. It wasn't long before recruiters were calling me. I turned down prospective positions twice where counteroffers were made to secure me in place.

By all accounts I was triumphant over tragedy. I bought a home half a mile from the one we'd lost in the most affluent suburb of our town. We went on vacations. The children were in sports and activities. They went to camps. We got a dog. We got another dog. We got two cats. I had finally arrived at the destination of what seemed like success. But it didn't feel that way because I didn't feel worthy to be happy.

Why should I be comfortable with happiness because surely another challenge would rise up and swipe it away? Of course, I didn't deserve happiness, or all this would never have happened. Survival at all costs was my mantra. The corporations valued my results. But results came at a price. I saw my staff as soldiers and my family as my primary responsibility. I had difficulty seeing people as people—as individuals with fears, intimacy, needs, wants, and souls. I had difficulty seeing myself and my children that way too. Everybody was a path to survival.

I remember one afternoon at the local swimming pool when my 8-year-old daughter, Brianna, came up to my chair and said, "Come on, Mom," as she pulled my hand. "Get in and have some fun with us." I couldn't move. I didn't know how to have fun. And worse, I didn't think I had earned fun, so I didn't know how to accept it when it was inviting me in.

That's when I began to understand the power that life messages hold on us.

Stretch Your Safety Barometer

We are born into this world having come from the safe, protective, and soothing environment of our mother's womb. We are thrust without choice into a cold and unfamiliar world where every moment holds a new experience. To survive we learn very early to trust our parents or primary caregivers. With our parents we belong—we are safe. Our parents teach us how to stay away from harm. We mirror their responses. And we begin to make sense of the world.

What we don't learn in childhood is that our experiences are one facet of life. Our interpretation of those experiences is another.

Our early ancestors understood the role of safety for survival. They knew that in order to withstand the elements and feed themselves, men needed to hunt in a pack with women tending to children and home. Your existence hinged on belonging to a tribe. Your distinct role contributed to the survival of the tribe. If you were exiled from the tribe because you did not live by the tribe values, you were subject to carnivores, weather, the aggression of competing tribes, lack of safe shelter, and starvation. If you had to live alone, likely you would die. Just as at birth, a sense of belonging led to safety.

We are programmed to fit in with others because historically that is where we are safe. As humans we are not calibrated to do it alone. And as we coexist with people we trust, sometimes we adopt philosophies from them that may not feel true to our core, leaving us with a sense of unrest. Conversely, as we coexist or work with people we don't trust, we can interpret their wrath as an assault on us personally, leaving us feeling as if we don't belong—an unsafe and unsettling feeling for sure. Either way, throughout our lives we have interpreted experiences through the filter of our safety barometer because self-preservation is our innate instinct. Am I safe or not? Those with a high safety threshold are risk-takers. Those with a low safety ceiling are more risk averse.

Whether you want to skydive is not what's important, though physical challenge is a sound way to build confidence and resilience. What is important is that you recognize how your safety barometer shows up in your career and relationships. When you feel threatened, defeated, dismissed, undervalued, personally attacked, or any number of negative emotions, and can't self-regulate false assumptions in order to release them, you will likely do something you regret. The result of this can lead to doubt, worry, self-criticism, lashing out, anger, immaturity, judgment, self-judgment, inaction, or overcompensation. These thoughts and behaviors kill careers and relationships. They rob you of peace and executive presence. And the worst part is, once you've been stereotyped for these (not executive material, hothead, not a leader, not strong, too emotional), it is very difficult to undo the stereotype without a noticed behavior change.

Lasso the Need to Be Right

The need to be right is at the root of every argument, conflict, and war that ever existed. It's a product of the ego needing validation. People who are difficult are also needy. If you work or live with someone who is difficult, they're likely to be more amenable when they know you have their back or at least respect them.

During my divorce and for years after, I needed validation that I was a good person, good wife, and good mother because I had adopted insurmountable shame about my situation. Though my ego needed external validation, I never asked for it because subconsciously I didn't feel I deserved it. This resulted in a continual longing for legal justice that never came, for validation from my children who were then teenagers and hated their mom on a good day, and for romantic love that was fleeting for a single mother with four children. I wanted to belong somewhere. So, I spent many hours at work because I was good at that. Corporate America is a welcome recipient of your time and energy.

As an executive coach, I counsel my clients dealing with colleagues who have big egos to find something about the difficult person they can authentically respect. It might be their dedication to the organization, their work ethic, their education. I suggest that my clients win trust by communicating their respect. The needy ego will appreciate the validation. This makes it easier to work together and to get what you want. But you must swallow pride and manage your own ego in the process. Keep your eyes on the ultimate goal. Not your need to have your own ego validated by them.

I learned the art of patience by letting my children have their opinions of me without defending myself or needing them to validate me. They couldn't possibly know what it was like to be in my shoes. Nobody could. We grew closer as a result of no expectations.

I was learning to trade the treadmill to nowhere for the freedom of self-acceptance. I had to shed the need to be deemed "right" by external forces in my divorce, parenting, and life. Outside parties can judge you. Your children can judge you. Your colleagues and the community can judge you. It is you that must be true to your character and draw a boundary between what you will and will not allow.

Permit them to be right about their judgment. It is incredibly liberating. You need not waste time, energy, or resources defending yourself only to feel defeated and exhausted when you can't change their minds. You cannot convince fools of their foolishness. You can leave them to it.

In this space you must feel as if you are safe and belong in the comfort of your own humanity and humility. Your job is not to win them over to convince your needy ego that you are right. Your job is to be safe in your own conviction that you need not be number one at anything but being yourself. Here you win respect.

I remember another day at the local swimming pool where the parent of a classmate of one of my children asked me, "If your marriage was so bad, why did you have four children?"

Recognize judgment for what it is—an offshoot of unhappiness. People who judge others judge themselves far worse. Happy people do not hurt one another.

I paused and thought about her question. In that space I had to lasso my ego because at first, I wanted to reach out and drown her. Once I could set that thought aside with humor, I replied logically without emotion from a servant leader perspective, "Probably for the same reason you have two children. Nobody goes into a marriage thinking it will end. My children are the best part of my life. I would never resent my children. Would you?"

This thing called life is a complicated engagement. Add into the mix your career and relationships, and you have a real menagerie of emotions, behaviors, and results. The happiest and most progressive people are the ones who can shake off self-doubt, know they belong anywhere they go, and accept joy as a part of their soul, not a condition.

About the Author

Mary Lee Gannon, ACC, CAE has a unique perspective as an award-winning certified executive coach, author, and 19-year corporate CEO who helps leaders have more effective careers, happier lives, and better relationships while it still matters. She is the founder of MaryLeeGannon.com, a consulting firm that helps leaders position their mindful impact—the same impact that took her from welfare to CEO of organizations worth up to $26 million.

Mary Lee is an International Coach Federation Associate Certified Coach (ACC), An American Society of Association Executives Certified Association Executive (CAE), a Duquesne University Certified Professional Coach Graduate (CPC), a scholarship recipient of the Search Inside Yourself Leadership Institute at Georgetown University's Institute for Transformational Leadership originated at Google, an alumnus of the UCLA Mindful Awareness Practices Program and the Harvard Medical School and McLean Hospital Coaching in Medicine & Leadership Conference. She is the author of two books: *Reinvent You—From Welfare to CEO* and *Starting Over.*

Mary Lee's personal turnaround came as a stay-at-home mother with four children under seven-years-old who endured a divorce that took her and her children from the country club life to public assistance from where she re-invented her life to support her family. Get her free career plan at www.MaryLeeGannon.com

Email: marylee@maryleegannon.com
Website: www.MaryLeeGannon.com

CHAPTER 11

AN INTROVERT'S GUIDE TO BEING AN INSPIRING LEADER

By Mary Gardner
Communications Consultant, Speech Coach
Winter Park, Florida

There is a huge untapped market of potential leaders to head our companies, our businesses, and in every sector of leadership. This group of people works among us, they're working beside us, sometimes they are our bosses and the people we manage. Introverts—they're intelligent, they're introspective, they're wise and experienced, and as a group, they make up about half of the population.

In an interesting reveal, the Myers-Briggs organization showed introverts made up 50.7 percent and extroverts 49.3 percent of the United States general population. But a myth has pervaded the business world for far too long: *introverts aren't cut out to be leaders.* Studies show that 65 percent of senior execs see introversion as a "barrier to leadership," and only 6 percent think introverts have what it takes to oversee a successful team. Sadly, according to a recent study in *Harvard Business Review*, only 2 percent of people in senior leadership roles identify as an "introvert."

It's time to shift this mindset. At the same time that people start giving introverts a chance, there are some strategic things that the introvert can do to increase influence, gain confidence, and step into their future stronger to eliminate being passed over for important leadership roles.

In my work coaching introverts from all over the world, I have found introverts thoughtful, incredibly intelligent, mostly kind, and willing to have others feed into their lives. They seem accepting of others' points of views even when they don't see eye to eye. They may or may not agree, or even respect a person, but often they don't feel the need to let everyone know their every single thought. They're much more private and tend to hold their conversation in unless engaged in a serious discussion. Not much for small talk, the introvert values more meaningful connections that are not a waste of time.

Introverts gain their energy by going inward and spending time alone instead of with people. Extroverts, on the other hand, gain their energy by being with other people and thrive on activity.

The individual who has a balance of both is called an ambivert. An ambivert is someone who falls in the middle of the introvert/extrovert continuum. Ambiverts have a blend of traits from both introverts and extroverts, as well as their own unique strengths.

As an ambivert, I am self-expressed and enjoy talking and meeting new people. Yet, I can listen with precision, can detect nuances in a person's tone of voice, and have an eye for detail when it comes to the tiny shifts a person may be able to make to up their game. I also understand the deep need of the introvert to be alone and quiet.

My clients usually find me at a point where they've been passed over for promotions, dismissed from important meetings, not engaged in speaking invitations, and left out of events or important and significant opportunities. They know they are often more intelligent, get the job done in a quicker and smarter way, but because they simply are not as vocal, they feel and know that they're being overlooked.

By the time we speak, they have realized that unless they up their game, develop new communication skills, and exert themselves, they will be sidelined for good. In my work, I couple the introvert's desire to become a top leader with my knowledge of the competencies of what makes an "inspiring leader." Inspiring leaders are those who received the highest scores on the competency of "inspires and motivates to high performance" in studies.

These tangible and intangible qualities are perfect for the introvert, as studies show that only 12 percent of inspiring leaders are extroverted, and the majority of inspiring leadership skills are simply a shift in communication.

Here are a few stories from clients who have adopted new skills to enhance their careers:

Lisa, a CEO, is introverted, a former accountant, and very intelligent. She came to me because she had an upcoming event where she had to present on stage in front of the local business community. Her usual way of being was very quiet, kind, always a good listener, and one who seeks first to understand rather than to be understood. She often waited to be spoken to, never interrupted others, and never commanded attention in any way. She was always very supportive of others and truly an uplifting person. She was working with a business mentor who suggested she work with a presentation coach to become more visually dynamic and develop a commanding presence on stage.

Lisa desired to be a more dynamic leader and presenter as well. In our work together, Lisa began to understand the power of vocal command, positive energy, body posture, and strong messaging. We began by creating powerful words that would engage the audience. She wrote them down and rehearsed. We worked on her vocal volume. She needed to project louder, so we practiced on stage until her voice carried to the back of the room. Then I showed her how to open her arms on stage to embrace the whole audience like in a hug. I had her practice using hand gestures to emphasize a point she wanted to make. We practiced over and over together to get her to feel comfortable and authentic.

On the day of the big reveal, she was on stage with other leaders in her field. Even though it was a panel discussion, she embraced her new style and new inspirational messages that brought pizzazz and entertainment to her audience. She even made them laugh.

These things were all new for her audience to see. They had never experienced or seen Lisa as being a powerful communicator before. There was an undercurrent of a positive buzz that was happening in the audience during her time on stage and after because she was so dynamic. It was the first-time people saw this CEO emerge powerfully.

Afterwards Lisa shared with me that many told her they were absolutely shocked and delighted to see her performance. She was extremely pleased with their response and was eternally grateful for the opportunity to work on her executive presence. This session taught Lisa to break out of her shell, and a result of this work, she was awarded the CEO of the Year Award by her local business community. A huge accomplishment for a quiet introvert.

John is a finance professional in telecom, also an introvert who is kind, doesn't want to intrude on others, and likes to think before he speaks. John came to me because he found himself without the promotions he wanted and was challenged by his managers to step up his communication skills.

By hearing about his mindset of never wanting to hurt anyone's feelings, I asked him the following questions: "Do you believe that your employees need a strong leader? Do you believe you have skills you can help them learn? Can you start by engaging with them more and finding what they are doing RIGHT, and NOT only addressing them when you need to correct them?"

He started integrating new techniques slowly. After meetings, John started complimenting his employees. He started working more synergistically with them on projects. As a result of gaining some insight into how they worked, he felt more comfortable "sharing" his wisdom. (The word "sharing" is non-threatening, and usually people are open to hearing from someone who is willing to "share.")

As John gained confidence from his interactions one-on-one, seeing and calling and complimenting staff for what they were doing right, and understanding how beneficial these interactions were to both himself and his co-workers and employees, he saw the value of this process and began to feel more and more comfortable. He then felt open to speaking up more and took on the leading role in meetings.

Additionally, we worked together on varying his tone of voice, interjecting energy, and understanding the value of pacing his delivery, which enhanced his performance as a speaker and as a leader. It was just a few weeks before his managers started hearing his name mentioned often in a positive light.

As a result, John made appointments to have one-on-one meetings with his bosses. He engaged with them MORE and not LESS. He started to create personal relationships through networking with many across the organizations, which allowed more influencers to get to know him.

John's communication style continued to improve, and by the time he and his manager had his year-end review, John's name was at the top of the list for a promotion. He was given more projects and was asked into key meetings. John's experience of coaching exploded his confidence, leadership, and his career.

Tessa was a high-level technical expert. She was in her late-30s, solid in her career, and extremely comfortable as a problem solver. She came to me because, as a leader, her entire group of 10 that she'd managed was reduced by her superiors down to just two people. She was perplexed about why she wasn't given more people to manage and that, instead, her leadership role continued to shrink. As a proficient problem solver, she knew she had to crack the code, so she hired me to improve her communication skills.

Upon hearing Tessa's core belief, it was obvious to me that she always had the answers. Her style was to solve the problem herself and then hand the work off to her team. Her personality was very blunt, direct, not extremely friendly, but, as a genius in her area of expertise, she usually did find correct answers. Tessa also knew that her team believed she had a good heart, in spite of her tough delivery, and she trusted they could complete the tasks she assigned.

I started by asking Tessa, "What do you think your associates experience when dealing with you? What sorts of feelings are coming forth from them when dealing with you? Are there other ways to solve the problem than the method you currently use? Would it be possible for the team to brainstorm new ways to solve the issues?"

She needed to learn that though she had many of the answers, the team would not be able to embrace them until she developed an effective team-building delivery process. She needed to learn some basic coaching skills.

Slowly I modeled to her what she needed to learn. Once Tessa realized I was her greatest advocate and cheerleader, she started asking me questions on how she could improve her leadership and "likeability" skills. By working together with her associates, Tessa learned to help them grow personally and professionally. We worked on making her delivery of her messages more friendly, on learning persuasive skills, and on her strategy to get things done by creating advocates in her company.

It was an ongoing process with many aha moments, but Tessa's willingness to be coached had a tremendous positive impact on her career, her team, and her company.

After coaching many introverts to bust through to leadership, I've come up with these basic guidelines to raise an introvert's influence:

Know Thyself. As an introvert, you know that you are thought-provoking, you prefer one-on-one conversations to large groups, you often get drained from large social interactions, and you prefer time to yourself. You prefer writing over talking, can feel overstimulated from too much noise or activity, and often need time to process conversations. It's important to know how you, personally, react to people, to your environment, and to situations, and that you set up strategies to deal with them. Getting a baseline by asking for feedback from your co-workers, superiors, clients, or friends can help you understand your areas of need. From that, you can set up strategies and systems.

If there is a particular person who is overly talkative and sucks up a lot of your time (energy vampire!), then create a strategy to deal with this person. Perhaps when they call or you run into them, act enthusiastic to see them but take a glance at your watch and say, "Great to see you! I'm running to a meeting in a minute but hope all is well?" Notice, that is a yes or no question, and you're not inviting a huge conversation. But you're coming across as genuine, caring, and friendly, and still not giving up your valuable time and energy to this person.

If you begin feeling overwhelmed by being surrounded by people, take a pause. Taking mid-day breaks to stretch or to go on mental vacations is a good way to slow the over-stimulation. Going for a walk or putting on some music can also re-energize you.

Take the time to know what systems work for you, so you have a strategy in place!

Fill Up Your Cup! In the morning, by starting the day nurturing yourself and getting ready for the day, you help yourself be more emotionally ready to deal with whatever comes your way. In the current norm of stressful environments, this preparation is key. The morning routine is very important as it sets up your day with the intention of it being productive and positive. According to researchers from Harvard Business School and Stanford University, workplace stress can be as damaging to our health as secondhand smoke, so managing it by starting the day with exercise and meditation, journaling, praying, or whatever makes you feel strong and ready to go for the day should be a top priority.

Get to Know People One-on-One. Inspiring leaders are those who spend more time with individuals they lead. Studies show that inspiring leaders are better at creating emotional connections by asking about the other person. They are better at establishing a clear vision. They are ardent champions of change. They are perceived as effective role models within the organization, and they encourage creativity from their teams. These intangible skills can increase someone's influence, merely by their investment in one-on-one conversations with people.

Create Advocates Through Networking. My clients who have networked with their peers and management have increased their influence quickly. The concept is that in order to move up the chain, you need advocates. Individuals who don't want to "bother" their bosses might notice others moving ahead at a swifter pace and have sometimes assessed incorrectly that those others are "brown-nosing." In reality, including your managers and bosses in problem solving, running ideas by them, and keeping them in the loop creates a stable relationship and promotes synergy. In addition, networking with people inside the organization as well as customers on a personal level has profitable benefits. People like people who like people. This can be a year-long strategy and be done on a one-on-one basis. Perfect for an introvert!

Adopt Coaching Skills. Coaching is a skill that focuses on moving others ahead. Inspiring leaders are constantly trying to motivate and inspire others to do better. How you do this is not by telling people how to do something, but by asking questions of how the person will do it. The benefits of coaching are many: eighty percent of people who receive coaching report increased self-confidence, and over 70 percent benefit from improved work performance, relationships, and more effective communication skills. Eighty-six percent of companies report that they recouped their investment on coaching and more (ICF, 2009).

Coaching is basically learning how to ask the right questions. The result is the person being coached discovers and owns their next right step in the process. The coach listens intently as the mentee makes new discoveries. This process develops trust between the coach and mentee. This collaborative process creates more synergy and builds the relationship. When leaders have focused conversations with their team members in order to learn their skills, passions, and strengths, this aids the leader in knowing what to ask.

Leading Meetings with Pizzazz. Upping the game by implementing small changes can dramatically alter the way a person in a business, firm, or industry is viewed. Some techniques to dramatically enhance the audience's experience of a meeting include:

1. Create an icebreaker to get people talking.
2. Use people's names as much as possible, which gives people a shot of "positivity."

3. Start and end meetings with a pertinent story that makes a point.

Clients who have made these tiny changes have received accolades immediately from those they are leading.

Ramp Up Your Public Speaking. We have all seen and experienced platform speakers that elevated the audience from their typical way of being to experiencing enthusiasm for taking on a new challenge. Many introverts are amazing speakers. As a matter of fact, many well-known actors are introverts, as it is a well-known fact that introverts are introspective and think before they speak. Having quiet time to prepare a presentation, knowing what words to say, and then practicing how to say it can make an immediate difference in your influence by altering the audience's perception of you and your message.

The key components of great speeches are simple:

1. Write the presentation down.
2. Start with a personal story or something humorous.
3. Back important points with a metaphor, quote, or story to create impact.
4. Practice.
5. Have fun with it!

Introverts are an untapped resource for incredible leadership. When introverts adopt inspiring leadership qualities, they can become a major force within their companies and industries. Introverts who practice excellence, not perfection, are chipping away at the myth that introverts can't be strong leaders. More and more people are realizing that introverts can lead in dynamic and positive ways. A few mental shifts and adding some tools can greatly benefit not only the introverts who are becoming powerful leaders, but also the companies and industries they lead, as well as our world in general.

About the Author

Mary Gardner is a nationally recognized speaker and public speaking and executive communication coach, and consultant. She hosts online courses and in-person workshops and seminars. Mary rose to prominence in the industry as a top celebrity agent at Keppler Speakers in Washington, DC. She then founded The Coaches Certification Institute in Princeton, New Jersey, the first business and life coaching and training school on the East Coast. She is an avid communicator with a passion for helping others find their charismatic voice. Mary has worked to raise the profile of many executives, celebrities, professional athletes, and influencers, and transition them to new, lucrative careers in the motivational speaking circuit. In her role as the president of the Inspirational Speakers Academy, she has created a workshop series that fast-tracks former professional football players into an exciting new career as professional motivational speakers.

Mary draws on her experience as a television and radio host, where she appeared on *Nightline*, *The Today Show*, CNN, ABC's *20/20*, CBS, Fox, and MSNBC. She has addressed corporate and college audiences across the country, and her client list includes Goldman Sachs, Mercedes Benz, Computer Associates, and numerous Wall Street financial institutions. She also has experience as a professional spokesperson.

In a coaching capacity, Mary has worked with astronaut Mark Kelly, professional athletes Billie Jean King, Martina Navratilova, Peggy Fleming, NBA Hall of Famer Bernard King, NFL Greats Mike Haynes and Randy Grimes, as well as TV anchors, CEOs, and executives who are respected experts in their fields.

Mary's main objective is to help people improve their skills in business development and communications, storytelling, interviewing, and public speaking.

Email: Mary.Gardner11@gmail.com
Website: www.marygardner.com

CHAPTER 12

YOUR BUSINESS SUCCESS IS DELIBERATE, NOT ACCIDENTAL!

By Glenis Gassmann, B.com CA
Business Coaches' Coach and Strategist
Melbourne, Australia

Have you ever wondered how some people can sail through setting up a business and then continue to grow and scale that business without ending up with as much as a scar? Then they end up either selling or putting in a manager to run that business while they follow another passion of theirs and duplicate that process? While others go from business to business, all the while carrying debt and wounds from one business to another?

I wasn't born one of those humans that I described above that knew what it took to have a successful business the first time around. However, I consider myself lucky to have emerged from my first business somewhat battered and bruised, but also stronger for the experience and not covered in scars.

However, there was enough pain from those bruises for me to discover where I could make changes for next time. I went about and changed my mindset, which in turn changed my behaviour, quickly followed up by actions for my second business, the one I'm in now. My changed mindset is one that allows me to be in the world of success daily.

Of course, there are always two sides to anything. In business, those two sides are the business owner's mindset and the daily actions taken inside a business based upon strategies to make it profitable. Although I am equipped to discuss both sides, today we are focusing on the business owner's success mindset.

There are three steps to set yourself up with and master your business success mindset—intention, daily practices, and monitoring progress. They don't sound new or original, do they? However, what I have found that is when you perfect these three steps on a consistent basis, you will see your business success soar.

Throughout this chapter I encourage you to be like a student, open to new learning and aiming to think big. For if you had nothing to learn about having a business success mindset, you wouldn't be reading this in the first place.

1—Intention

Some people call your intention your "why". I like to think of intention like this: there is something not working, or not working as well as you would like it to work in the world. As such, you have an immense passion to ensure that through your business offerings, whether it be a product or service, you would make a difference to that issue, so much so that you are touched, moved, and inspired to keep making that difference.

This issue that isn't working or where there's some kind of gap, which you are looking to alleviate through your business, should be something that you are really passionate about. If you didn't get your business going, then you would have a sick feeling in your gut about this issue not working for others and knowing you could fix it or make a dent in it.

This is something that is much bigger than you and your survival. It would be so inspiring that it would pull you out of your warm bed on a cold winter morning so that you could start the day knowing that you were making a difference to someone or something in this area of your passions.

Your intention of what you are going to make better in the world is your context, and it is why you started your business in the first place. You may need to have a look at what that was. Is it still your passion? Does it still inspire you to jump out of your warm bed on a cold and frosty morning? If not, then you might need to review, tweak, or even create a new intention that stirs something inside you. This would be based on something that you see you can fix with your business and something that people need.

Without this high-level intention based on something outside you, when the going gets tough in business, as it will, this will be the one thing that will keep you going. It will be the one thing that you know in your heart of hearts you can't get rid of. It will be the one thing that you simply will not give up on.

To create your intention, you will not be thinking of results that could occur from the success of your business, like making $180,000 net for the year, buying the car and boat of your dreams, or just making enough to pay the bills. Your intention should have nothing to do with what you can get and everything to do with what you can give, provide, and help with. Think about your intention in terms of what your customers will be receiving from you and your business. Then turn that into a statement that moves and inspires you into action every day.

For example, my first business was an accounting practice. In the first few years, when I was in survival mode, I never had an intention other than survival, which is what I find in most business owners in their first business. Being new to the world of business, every day there are new challenges to either jump over, duck, or step aside from. My success, in terms of return on investment in time and money, was not apparent at that time. On reflection, what I learnt from those first few years of challenges has been priceless, and it is all still with me today as I coach other coaches in businesses.

About halfway through my 15 years as a principal in an accounting practice, I created my intention that led the way for success with my mindset as well as a return on investment in time and money. That powerful intention was—to exceed our clients' expectations.

This intention gave me my purpose for those cold winter mornings. It had me eager to deliver not only what was expected of me as an accountant but to exceed my clients' expectations, from the little things like knowing how they took their tea or coffee when they came into the office, to taking the time to understand what was going on in their world other than in the world of business in our conversations. Let's just say those two small changes, ones that didn't cost anything, started a snowball of mindset shifts within me, the team, and our business results.

They were not the only two changes we made in the business. The other change was a radical one that separated me from most of the practitioners at the time. This was to stop the process of time sheets, charging clients in six-minute units for any work we performed. Not only was this method old-fashioned, unproductive, and, in some cases, made up by the many people preparing the time sheets, it didn't fit under the new intention "to exceed our clients' expectations".

Consider that if the senior partner of the firm had a junior doing the work with a charge-out rate that didn't match the skills required to accomplish the job, the client either was over- or under-charged for the work. It occurred to me that if you had a degree in accounting and had so many years of experience, you charged out at X, and if you had double those years of experience, you charged out at Y. Thus, the rate charged was not at all connected to the complexity of the job and the actual knowledge of the individual performing it that you'd think would make up the value of the work being done for the client.

Seeing as integrity was, and is, one of my highest values, I made a radical change for the better and in line with my new "intention". This was the beginning of the shift in mindset of the business, team, and me. No longer were we measured by an hourly charge-out rate that someone had said was "normal" within that industry. We were measured on performance of an individual job, based on the complexity and knowledge required to achieve the positive result. In turn, we started giving fixed prices, and from the engagement and communications we had with our clients, we knew exactly the complexity of the work as well as who was suitable to achieve the result for the client as well as exceed their expectations. This had the client know our expert status and worth as their accountant.

The other added benefit it had was our team members knew their own value and worth, and not as measured by an hourly rate and how much time they had to complete the job that may or may not have been commensurate with their level of skills and knowledge. In this way, a total mindset shift occurred across the business, so that we were able to fully take on exceeding our clients' expectations each day and achieve business success.

If you are still wondering if your Intention is big enough to pull you into action even when you are up against the wall with nowhere to go, do some thinking on it once you finish this chapter. My rule of thumb is that if you do not get a "pang" in your stomach when you voice it out to a prospective customer, then it's not big enough.

My current intention is—to reduce business failure rates worldwide. That still has me touched, moved, and inspired each time I voice it. I know I am well on my way with 14 coaches working with me on the same intention across the world, who each have over 10 clients on a regular basis and who are teaching a process that triples leads and doubles profits in the given businesses.

Let's get to the second step in mastering your business success mindset.

2—Daily Practices

Like everything, until you do it daily, you will not begin to master the little things that will have your business perform on a high level. It's the small things practised every day across a few areas of your business that will make the exponential difference.

When it comes to mindset, we must keep our eye, or mind, in this case, on our intention. Our intention sets the context of the daily routines, whether it be with your mindset or business actions. Next, you perform them daily.

The other thing to be aware of is the 80/20. Please don't get disillusioned if you didn't do something for a couple of days and give up altogether, i.e., the 20 percent of the 80/20. It's what you do most of the time, i.e., the 80 percent, that gives you a particular level of performance. Just like in losing weight, if you eat a chocolate bar each day on top of what you normally do and don't exercise, you will gain weight over time. If you do that one day a month, it won't make a lot of difference.

The overriding context of your business mindset should be fun and enjoyable. This is your passion; it is not hard work. This is what you were made to accomplish, so be kind to yourself in the process.

The daily practices to master your business success mindset are:

1. Inside your context, write out a three-year GOAL(s) you want to accomplish. This would be a paragraph at the most. Be clear, concise, and specific. You may want to use SMART goal setting here.
2. Then within that three-year GOAL, write out a 12-month goal, along with four quarterly milestones that you should achieve to reach your 12-month goal. Once again, be succinct, not a lot of detail here.

The world is changing and evolving on a faster basis now than ever before, so I find that having a 12-month planned goal, as well as a three-year MAJOR GOAL, for your business is sufficient to pull you forward on a daily basis without constraint, and it allows you the ability to shift and pivot if needed.

3. Once you have this set up, take the first milestone for the first quarter and break that up into three clear goals (one per month) that you would need to achieve to accomplish the quarterly goal.

4. Now you take your first month and write your list of outcomes (not tasks) that must be done and determine who is going to work on each particular outcome (i.e., what team member if you have a team).

This step-by-step process is very important to set up after you have your intention. It allows you to focus on the outcomes, and the tasks will flow inside that outcome, milestone, goal, and intention.

Taking action is the backbone of mastering a business success mindset, even when you don't feel like doing so. It will also allow for you to NOT be swayed and get caught up with the "new shiny object" syndrome. What I mean by that is that people who go from one shiny new object to another, spending profits on unnecessary expenses that are not in line with the end milestone, goal, and intention are not focused on the main aim of the game, i.e., their intention. Or, it could mean that their intention is not big enough or inspiring enough to have them take focused action.

Example Goal Mapping

Here is an example of how I have mapped out my goals, milestones, and outcomes.

Intention: to reduce business failure rate worldwide

Three-Year Goal: an international business with 100 coaches worldwide having made an impact on over 10 thousand business owners by showing them how to grow and scale their businesses with strategy and mindset

Twelve-Month Goal: Thirty coaches, each with successful businesses who are coaching and training 25-plus clients on a yearly basis

Quarterly Milestones

1. 15 Coaches
2. 30 Coaches
3. Automatic marketing for clients for coaches
4. Replace myself as general manager

Quarter One—Outcomes

Milestone: fifteen coaches

What	Who
Master Sales Process	Myself
100 warm leads in the pipeline	Subcontractor
Set up retention system	Admin

Before discussing step 3 in establishing a business success mindset, there is also another set of daily practices that assists with your business success mindset, and they are personal practices.

It has been in my experience that a successful business has a business owner that is healthy, not only in mind but also in body. Here are some basic practices that you might consider incorporating into your daily routine:

- Eat healthy foods.
- Exercise daily.
- Drink plenty of water.
- Get sufficient sleep.
- Ensure you have a daily relaxation routine.
- Be grateful (at least) once a day.
- At the end of the day and before you go to sleep, reflect on at least one thing that you have achieved that will progress your intention and acknowledge yourself for that.

3—Monitoring Your Progress

This is the step that is the most critical to mastering a business success mindset. Yet it is the most often overlooked and the reason why businesses don't achieve the momentum they need to move forward with velocity.

How do you know how far you have come if you do not know your progress? There is a saying, "If you can't measure it, you can't improve it". This is by far the most important factor in any business, and business owners should set this up in the beginning.

To set yourself up for success, the first step is measuring your progress. Note: I am not saying measuring what you haven't achieved, that comes from a negative mindset point of view. Rather, I am suggesting that you come from a positive point of view and measure your progress, putting in place different actions that will improve the status of your business for outcomes that were not achieved without any assessment or judgement on the person who was designated that task.

The most significant point in shifting my business mindset was when I shifted my thinking from "something was wrong or right" to "something either worked or didn't work". I took out the personalisation of right or wrong with any person inside or outside my business, including myself.

For example, I changed our daily progress meetings from sitting in a room around a table to standing at the coffee machine. At the standing meetings, I ask a series of questions to each member of my team. They include: *Are you on track to achieve your weekly goals? If not, what is the challenge? Do we need to schedule additional time outside this meeting to go over that? And, if you are on track, what else do you need from me for the day/week?*

That's it. Each member knows that at the end of the week, they will have an agreed-upon performance measure to achieve.

We discuss the performance measure at the end-of-the-month account-ability meeting, where we go through the five following questions:

1. What did you want to achieve?
2. What did you achieve?
3. What did you want to achieve, but didn't?
4. What are you going to do differently for next month to achieve your goals?
5. What are you going to achieve next month?

These are high-level questions that will encourage each member of your team or yourself, if you don't have a team, move forward towards your quarterly milestone. I encourage you to get a coach to ensure you have a positive experience with this meeting. Answering these questions with integrity and authenticity will help you progress quickly towards your milestone and goals.

The most critical part of this process is not to make anything or anyone wrong. Deal with the real facts of what is happening, and always find something you can acknowledge the other person or yourself for.

This is progress, and when this is done consistently over a period of time, you will achieve your milestones, which, in turn, lead you to achieve your goals. Repeating it each day will build muscle around this for you, and your business success mindset will shine through. You will be able to achieve anything and everything you desire for your business. What else might surprise you is all the additional benefits that arrive from taking these actions.

Mastering a business success mindset can simply be said to involve the following: have an intention and a clear set of goals, milestones, and outcomes that are monitored and checked on a consistent and regular basis. Your progress with this will manifest into a business success mindset, and this process can be applied to all areas of your life, not just business.

Enjoy the process and success.

About the Author

Glenis Gassmann is a former accountant turned mega-successful business strategist and marketer. She provides business coaches with an automated turn-key business system solution to grow and expand their business.

Specialising in sales and marketing for small business owners, Glenis has over 30 years in business and has developed a keen understanding of the complex issues facing small business owners in today's volatile economy. She coaches and effectively teaches business owners how to apply strategies quickly and successfully in the right order that allows them to grow and scale their business. Small changes across key areas in a business will bring exponential results.

Her team has spent more than 10 years and $2 million developing the world's first e-learning marketing system (MBA for business owners) being used by more than 5 thousand small business clients in 50 countries around the world to grow their business to multi-million-dollar status and beyond.

Learn more about Glenis Gassmann on her website or email her directly.

Email: glenis@morecustomersmoreprofits.com
Website: https://millionairecoachingbusiness.com/

CHAPTER 13

TRANSFORM WITH POWER AND POISE

By Samira Chandra Gupta
Executive Presence Coach, Firewalking Instructor, NLP
Gurgaon, Haryana, India

The chills of a shiver go deep into the spinal cord despite the heat of the fire bed in front of me. My monkey mind is unable to focus and is constantly telling me to step aside and walk away from the red, yellow, and orange coals. I could feel the rhythmic contraction and expansion of my heart. The intention of conquering my fears became less important and the fear of getting burnt became paramount. I was anxious and fearful, but it was a commitment I had to make to myself, it was a question of "now or never!"

"Walk to win", said the firewalking instructor, "It requires courage, confidence, and focus. If you choose to conquer your fear now and are willing to bathe in the glow of embers, you will not only embark on a gorgeous life-changing journey but also come out as a 'never-before' version of yourself—brave, beaming, and blissful," he encouraged.

It was time. I had to finally take control of my escape mindset, the "I cannot" mindset, the "what-if?" mindset, the "it's not possible" mindset, the "what if I fail?" mindset. All kinds of fears and limiting beliefs filled my mind and body. Everything was happening so suddenly that I felt disconnected with who I was and what I wanted.

But I had to take charge and bring back the connection between my body and mind. I had to give the right command to my mind to take over matter (the body), to create a powerful moment in my life. This was the moment of facing all my fears and limitations. I had to cross this bed of fire for a new life. If there was anyone who was going to help me, it was me.

Suddenly I felt a shift in my thoughts. There was a ray of hope, a new desire to accept the challenge, a new courage to break through the barrier. This was nothing but the power of my own mind, which was now thinking of possibilities, opportunities, and the joy of accomplishing an important landmark, which could change my life forever.

The glowing embers were suddenly inviting, and the eight-foot-long fire bed of 600-degree Celsius heat did not appear scary and impossible. The encouragement of my firewalking instructor and the motivation from the cheering crowd added to my courage and confidence.

The determination to transform my mindset and my beliefs to feel the power within was so strong that I took the first step, and then the second—and then there was no looking back! As I stood at the other end of the fire bed, I observed what I had just accomplished. I was elated yet very calm, excited yet in control. I wanted to scream yet took a deep breath and was grateful for the moment. I realized that a lot was left behind on that fire bed that hadn't been working for me in life, and a lot was gained that I needed to have a successful life.

Fearful or Fearless?

What exactly is fear?

When we are born, we do not possess the capability of logic or inhibitions. As children, we are fearless, ready to fall, run and crash, play with dogs, and jump into unknown water. All of this without any fear of getting hurt, because at that time, we are not introduced to fear. It is only through our growing years that fear starts setting into our subconscious mind due to our environment, education system, cultural superstitions, media, and our upbringing at home. These fears become limiting factors when we want to achieve something big. Every time we face a new challenge, some fear is triggered and comes out as a barrier, a roadblock, not allowing us to go full throttle and get what we want. We must address these fears through reprogramming of the subconscious mind.

Firewalking Can Help Break Fear Patterns at the Subconscious Level

"The only reason you believe at first that something like this is not possible is because you had this belief instilled in your mind as a child", said Agugliaro. "Somewhere along the way, you were told not to touch fire because it was hot and would burn, so you stayed away, and this became a strong belief".

In the same way, many of our fears become limiting beliefs in our lives and hold us back from going forward or keep us from achieving bigger successes in life. Our limiting beliefs are deep-rooted at the subconscious level and require a deeper intervention to alter them into empowering beliefs.

The purpose of walking on fire is more than just a break-through firewalk. It is to walk from the paradigm of "what I know" to the paradigm of "what I am yet to discover". However, our programming stops us from discovering the new. Our conditioning is such that we are unwilling to accept the unknown. In such situations, our brain starts to send warning signals of the pain and discomfort we may go through.

In life, when faced with challenging situations, the subconscious mind programmed by the fear mechanism, obstructs our path to growth. Reluctance and resistance become the immediate reaction to challenging situations. People seldom become successful by reacting to challenges instead of responding to them. To overcome a challenging situation, we must set the right intent, the intent of growth, because everything begins from a thought! A firewalk can become the catalyst for our shift from a fixed mindset, one that functions on the fear mechanism, to a growth mindset, which is confident to face challenges head-on. Firewalking is a metaphor for courage, confidence, and belief. When we alter our paradigm, we change the results to any challenge we face.

Firewalk, A Tool for Transformation

The first walk is governed by the fear mechanism built in us and the hesitation coming from what we know. Hence, it is usually done in haste, focusing more on the feet, i.e., matter.

The second walk is governed mostly by ego, where the brain is aware that it is possible because it has been done once already, so this time it is done for power i.e., mind.

A high ego firewalk leads to suspension of thought. With the suspension of thought, the intent is lost. This is why you should set your intent before walking on fire.

The third walk is often the profound one, where you establish a connection with your soul to understand the importance of a bigger purpose, which happens when you set a clear intention. Setting the right intention can help you connect with the universe to channel the energy that can heal, rejuvenate, revive, and restore your higher self. Knowing why you are doing this gives you clarity and helps you remain calm, and the focus shifts from the body.

Firewalking Can Help Professionals at Work

Firewalking is much more than just a simple adventure. It is a tool that takes leaders and teams to new levels of performance, teaching them to leave behind blockages and walk courageously to overcome their limitations and barriers, leading to higher productivity, self-confidence, and self-motivation.

In order to walk on fire successfully, people must practice positive intention, laser sharp focus, and courage. The rewards at the end of the fire bed are these strong messages engraved in the mind: "I can do anything now", "I am unstoppable", "I am limitless", and "I am a winner".

The shift from limiting to empowering beliefs must be done at the subconscious level. This can happen either through months or years of cognitive self-development work, or it could happen with just one powerful experience. Since firewalking works brilliantly, it is also used as an effective tool in the neuro-linguistic programming (NLP) workshops to rewire and reprogram the mindsets of participants for purpose, power, and productivity.

History and Science of Firewalking

Firewalking is an age-old tool used by tribes for hundreds of years. In 1200 BC, the first recorded firewalk happened in India during the Iron Age. In the modern era, Tolly Burkan is considered the founder of firewalking. He was the first person to make it available to the public by offering firewalking classes that anybody could attend.

As per Burkan, proper blood circulation prevents the feet of a firewalker from burning—as long as the walker is relaxed, allows strong blood flow, and keeps walking. According to him, the ability to firewalk is more than just physics, it's your state of mind.

Loring M. Danforth, a Bates College anthropology professor, says that scientific explanations do not debunk, diminish, or invalidate the value of the firewalking ritual. He further says that firewalking can have the power to affirm a person's life. It can change lives.

What Happens After a Firewalk

Let me share what a firewalk is capable of doing. Firewalking helps us break our limiting beliefs and barriers that hold us back from accessing our success and unlimited potential. Firewalking can help us transform destructive habits and negative thinking patterns into increased creativity and clearer thoughts. Often, we get trapped in negative habits—smoking, narcissism, ungrateful-ness, etc.—and are unable to get rid of them. Despite a desire to get rid of these patterns, we spiral back because of a lack of will, confidence, and faith in ourselves. Firewalking helps us find new self-confidence and self-esteem. It is a demonstration of strength and courage that is hidden inside us. When we unravel this newfound strength, we are able to make a strong commitment to the self to break the negative patterns and create a successful mindset.

Firewalking helps us face our fears and deal with them. We get better at decision-making and not letting situations drift out of control. Faith in our own capabilities can create a huge difference in our decision-making power. Once we develop faith, the assumptions of "what if?" will change to "I will make it happen". This is nothing but a shift from a fixed mindset to a growth mindset.

It helps us bring out our inner genius to conquer challenging tasks and move forward in life. We are able to set better goals. Earlier, our goal setting was determined by what was possible and impossible, which was determined by our experiences and others' experiences known to us. Hence, our true potential is often undiscovered. People who dare to set unbelievably lofty goals are people who achieve great heights. An accomplished firewalk can break our inhibitions and empower us to soar to great heights.

It alters the way we look at life. We start finding joy and happiness in our day-to-day lives. We often plan things ahead of time, and when they do not turn out the way we planned, we get disheartened and recede to the victim mode. Walking on fire enables us to get rid of the planned and be welcoming to what's there to come. Unless we leave behind the old, we will not be able to move forward. Firewalking helps us deal with the resistance in our subconscious mind and opens it to new possibilities. It helps us get rid of the prejudiced perceptions, irrationality, primitive thinking, and superstition.

Those who have walked on fire,
leave sparks of light everywhere they go.
—Unknown

When a person is standing still for a minute or so in embers of 600 degrees Celsius, something extraordinary happens. There is awareness, consciousness, and focus in the moment, which creates a strong will and determination to achieve the impossible. Many people who practice firewalking account for an undying feeling of inspiration and focus in life. When asked what they think about while they are on fire, people often say, "I am connecting with my loved ones and sending them love", "I feel the fire inside me, and I am ready for life's challenges", etc. Firewalking stimulates people in a way that they experience the power of higher self, elation, ecstasy, happiness, and fulfilment. Firewalking demonstrates what the mind synced with the body can accomplish—a successful mindset!

Although firewalking is my speciality, any act that can alter your state of consciousness significantly, modify your definition of self, and bring about a transition in your way of thinking and being, can be empowering, enriching, and transformational.

Be a Spark Lighter

Having a successful mindset can help you enhance your productivity and purpose, but the doors to opportunities will open if you can be spotted through your strong personal brand, which is about knowing who you are, accepting who you are, and presenting the best version of yourself to the world.

Looking and feeling successful are equally important to achieve greater heights. You may have the potential to achieve great success but without creating the right perceptions, the opportunities may not come your way. These perceptions are based on how you dress, groom, accessorize, move, walk, talk, and behave. Your impressions become others' perceptions.

*You never get a second chance to
create the first impression.*
—Unknown

A strong personal brand is a promise of your credibility, integrity, quality, and responsibility. So, when people do business with you, they have faith that the job will be done with excellence. A good personal brand will attract opportunities and power, and a successful mindset can convert those opportunities into business. An unkempt personal brand can sabotage your success. Being mindful of your appearance, behaviour, communication, and confidence can contribute to success in your personal, professional, and social areas of life. Build your reputation and the revenue shall follow—this is the power of infusing personal branding with a growth mindset.

Combine all the elements of inner and outer transformation to come out as a person who is ready to rock 'n roll to charm, impress, and take on the world.

"Don't settle for mediocrity, strive for excellence!"
—Mac James

My own mindset has transformed over the years through various tools of personal development, and firewalking was a big piece. This transformation has helped me find my purpose, and now my mission is to empower every soul who comes in contact with me, with power, purpose, grace, and finesse. If you have the opportunity to experience a firewalk, I highly encourage you to do it, but in whatever you do—be fearless! Be powerful! Be impeccable! And you will be successful!

About the Author

Samira Gupta is the founder, chief image consultant, and an executive coach at Auraa Image Management and Consulting. Her firm is based in New Delhi, India. She is an expert of leadership training and coaching for middle- and senior-level corporate management, bringing about a holistic transformation by breaking limiting beliefs of the subconscious mind. She has personally coached over 800 individuals and has trained over 150 thousand corporate professionals in the sectors like IT/ITES, luxury real estate, consulting, banking, FMCG, luxury retail, premier hospitals, hospitality, aviation, education, and government. She helps people find their purpose, clarity, vision, and mission, enabling them to reach their dreams and goals.

Samira has studied hundreds of hours from the top mentors in areas like image consulting, life coaching, relationship coaching, executive coaching (MGSSCC), body language, GLA 360, NLP, hypnotherapy, rapid transformation therapy, fine dining and wine etiquette, and firewalking instructor training. She loves touching people's lives and has found her purpose in transforming and empowering others.

Email: samira@auraaimage.com
Website: www.samiragupta.com | www.auraaimage.com

CHAPTER 14

REFLECTION AS A TOOL TO SHAPE A POSITIVE MINDSET

By Peter Hill
Development and Leadership Coach
Kingston upon Thames, United Kingdom

*What lies behind us and what lies before us are tiny
matters compared to what lies within us.*
—Ralph Waldo Emerson

As a coach, I accompany my clients on a journey of self-discovery. They learn how to learn from their experiences and develop insights into their own role in how their experiences unfold. These insights help them gain a deeper self-awareness, opening up new possibilities that they can act on to address any challenges they may face.

Through this process, my clients discover more about themselves, their unconsciously held beliefs and cultural biases, and the impact of these on how they see the world. In choosing to read this book, you too have made a positive decision to take action and to learn more about yourself. You are ready to take psychological responsibility for your own thoughts, emotions, words, and deeds.

Taking responsibility for how we feel and how we respond to our feelings helps us move from being the victim of our own drama to being able to observe the drama for what it is. Namely, something we helped create and can, therefore, change. This shift in mindset moves us towards greater self-acceptance and away from self-judgement and the judgement of others.

This positive move towards greater self-knowledge and self-acceptance is a necessary step in embracing lifelong learning. To set the scene, we will look at how we understand ourselves and how our unconscious influences our feelings, thoughts, and behaviours. Then, I will share techniques you can use to build a more mindful way of being as you progress on this journey.

Underpinning this chapter is a growing body of research on the brain and the roles our unconscious and conscious processing play in our decision-making. This sets the context and explains why change is difficult. My interpretation is broadly aligned with a wide range of contributors to this field. That said, I encourage you to explore the literature yourself and draw your own conclusions.

Why Change Can Be Difficult

Our brain is created full of potential, which our experiences then shape. The brain links experience with emotion to make meaning and create memories, which are encoded in the brain. The brain responds to stimuli from all our senses through these "programmes" (neural pathways), which operate predominantly at an unconscious level, controlling how we behave, think, and feel.

These programmes operate on a set of, often forgotten, assumptions shaped by early experiences. As our lives change and we mature, these long-held assumptions may no longer hold true, if they ever did. Consequently, we can become prone to poor perception and invention. If we realise that our perception of reality is not reality itself, we become open to the possibility of misunderstanding.

Acknowledging this possibility enables us to learn from experience and create new knowledge about ourselves and the world around us. New knowledge allows for new assumptions and new habits. Over time, these habits become embedded, forming a part of our brain's unconscious programming. Old habits die off and old programmes fade.

However, we are creatures of habit, and our brain looks for predictability and likes certainty. The process of developing new habits introduces a degree of uncertainty and a loss of predictability. Hence, practising new behaviours can be uncomfortable, they are new and can be clunky at first and may even feel unsafe in certain circumstances.

We might also perceive trying something new as inauthentic. However, there is a distinct difference between being inauthentic and feeling uncomfortable. The moment you first got on a bike, you were uncomfortable, not inauthentic; you were learning something new. Now, you barely think about what you're doing to control your bike.

Let's be clear, behavioural change, changing habits, isn't about personality change or changing values, and it isn't about being inauthentic. However, to make these types of changes takes practice, repetition, feedback, and adjustment. It takes a curious mind and a willingness to put aside self-judgement and judgement of others. It requires commitment and a positive mindset.

The Work

People come to coaching, or turn to a book like this, seeking support in the face of a challenge. These can be stressful situations, such as a difficult but important relationship, loss of a partner or a job. They can be the consequence of emerging opportunities, like a new role, or existential angst—a feeling of conflict or disconnection in their life.

These are times when habits that might have served us well may no longer be doing so, or moments when we simply don't have the habitual response to deal with them, perhaps because they are new situations. We may even come with an incomplete awareness of what is going on but knowing that something is out of kilter.

In order to create new habits and to escape old ones, we need to become more mindful of what is happening within us when we respond to new experiences or repeated negative ones. We need to take psychological responsibility for our own behaviours, feelings, and thoughts, and we need to focus on what we can do and not what we think others should or shouldn't do.

Most of us feel our opinions are objective, built on experience and an unbiased assessment of a situation. However, in reality we are all subject to confirmation bias. Our brains pattern-match what is happening now to memories of past events to find our most likely explanation. As it does, it focuses on what upholds our beliefs and ignores conflicting information.

Consequently, different people can draw different meanings from an event due to the way related memories were structured. For example, one person may feel bullied by someone shouting at them, another excited by the passion on show, and a third questions their own perspective on seeing such strongly held views. It is the same event for all three; the only variable is their subjective realities.

To change how we feel about something, we need to alter how we perceive it. Mindful reflection can help us test our reading of events and look for alternate meanings. New meaning brings a new emotional response, new habits, and a change in our reality. Thus, we avoid repeating old mistakes. There are many models that can help this process, and I will outline three that are easy to apply.

Recognising the Difference Between Intent and Impact

You and a colleague are dealing with a stressful situation. As you open the discussion, you have an *intent* in mind. What you say has an *impact* on your colleague, which comes with a consequence, in the form of a response from them, backed by their *intent*. The *impact* of this on you has a consequence, and the cycle continues to a conclusion.

If you only see your intent and not your impact, you are living in a self-centred world. Remember, meaning always resides in the listener, not the speaker. You have to check their understanding, as the listener is drawing on their own experiences to interpret what you do and say. There are three possible outcomes between intent and impact:

1. A match—both of your beliefs are reinforced, and your strategies are justified. This may be all that is required although you both may choose to test your conclusions with others.
2. A mismatch—you both become more entrenched in your positions, falling into a negative cycle. Positions polarize, and both fall into the trap of thinking: "I'm right, you are wrong".
3. A mismatch—you note the rising tension and recognise there might be a misunderstanding. You become curious and ask open questions to understand what is concerning your colleague.

Outcomes 2 and 3 occur when there are differing perspectives. Failing to recognise these situations can lead to outcome 2. However, when we feel our stress levels rise, we have an opportunity to step in and change the flow. We can become curious about this tension and ask clarifying questions to understand our impact. Perhaps we were unknowingly insensitive or made an invalid assumption.

When someone feels listened to, they are less likely to feel defensive and more likely to be open-minded and to reciprocate, giving you the opportunity to clarify your position. One or both of you might see merit in the other's perspective, causing a reassessment. This opens the way for the co-creation of new ideas.

There is a lot of good literature out there to support the development of your approach to having such discussions, for example, Nancy Kline's *Time to Think: Listening to Ignite the Mind* and Judith Glaser's *Conversational Intelligence: How Great Leaders Build Trust and Get Extraordinary Results*.

Giving and Receiving Personal Feedback

Johari's Window is a useful way to support the exploration of differences between people. It divides self-knowledge into four areas:

- ☞ *Open Self*—what I and others know about myself
- ☞ *Hidden Self*—what I keep to myself
- ☞ *Blind Self*—what I am unaware of, but others know about me
- ☞ *Unknown Self*—what is hidden from everyone

This can help for building a better understanding of others and for developing self-awareness, improving communication, and developing interpersonal relationships and team dynamics. The model relates to biography, behaviours, feelings, attitudes, motivations, skills, preferences, styles, and experience.

Expanding our open area—Open Self—helps build trust and rapport. The greater the trust, the more open people are to giving and receiving feedback. Feedback shrinks our blind area—Blind Self—to reveal our impact on others and help us adapt our style and build empathy. Our Unknown Self shrinks through self-discovery by applying learning from, for example, this book, self-development courses, coaching, etc.

Sharing isn't about total exposure; how much you share is something that you have to judge, and it will vary depending on context. For example, you will probably share deeply emotional life experiences with partners, family, and close friends, but you may have different boundaries at work. Organisational culture will also influence your decision on what to share at work.

What you can do is use this framework to help yourself be more proactive in how you build relationships, taking time to share things to help build trust and to show an interest in others to build rapport through demonstrating empathy. This isn't about manipulation; it's about recognising we are a social animal and want to belong and feel valued.

Giving and receiving feedback is critical to building the Open Self, understanding, empathy and trust. However, feedback is often associated with poorly managed performance management systems, making this a sensitive exercise. I use the following model:

- *Situational*—the feedback must relate to a specific event or events.
- *Relational*—the feedback must only be about the experience of the person giving it.
- *Factual*—don't assume anything, only report the facts as they unfolded.
- *Non-judgemental*—do not speculate on the motives of the person you are giving feedback to.
- *Reciprocal*—acknowledge your part in the situation and how it unfolded.
- *Shared Responsibility*—ask what you can do differently to help in the future.

For example: "Mary, you've arrived late four times now without explanation, leaving us waiting and then rushing the agenda (factual). I feel you don't see this as a priority (relational). I value your contribution and feel it is critical to our success, what is causing this and what can I do to help (relational)?"

This technique reflects a curious and open mind, an absence of judgement, the taking of personal responsibility for yourself and the offering of support whilst being clear about impact, which, as we know, isn't always aligned to intent!

A great source of insight into building relationships can be found in Daniel Goleman's *Emotional intelligence: Why It Can Matter More Than IQ*. If you want a deeper insight into where emotions come from, try Lisa Feldman Barrett's *How Emotions Are Made: The Secret Life of the Brain*.

SOAP

This model is particularly powerful for learning from difficult experiences that leave you with negative emotions. SOAP is an acronym constructed as follows:

- *Subjective Account*—my first-hand experience of something. What happened to me, what I felt, and what my emotions were. Physically what was happening to me, where did I feel it? What were my thoughts and internal dialogue during and after? What metaphors come to mind as I remember?
- *Objective Description*—what actually happened, what would an observer have actually seen and heard? What was said, how was it said, at what volume, how were we behaving?
- *Analysis of Incident*—was I aware of my internal dialogue at the time, what was the impact of my style of communication, are there patterns or themes emerging in my behaviour, emotions, and thoughts? Does my subjective experience match the objective description?
- *Personal Learning*—was my inner dialogue aligned with what was unfolding? What were my unspoken assumptions, are they still valid? What could I do differently next time?

Approach this with a sense of curiosity and without any self-judgement. Be thorough and stick to the brief. This isn't about marking your performance, or that of others. As you analyse your subjective and objective description, some things to look out for include:

- *Negative Self-Talk*—negative self-talk, about self, others, or events can become habitual and will leak into our impact on those around us, bleed into our everyday language, and impact how we communicate, all whilst being unaware of it. Challenge its logic and look for contrary evidence.
- *Black and White Thinking*—"I failed, therefore, I'm a failure, I will always fail". Nobody gets something right the first time every time or completes everything perfectly every time. Failing at something does not mean you are a failure; it means there is something to learn.
- *Attributing Thoughts to Others*—"He's a bully", "She is trying to undermine me". It is unlikely we know as a matter of fact that this is true. Either way, by focusing on it, you are limiting your choice of

response. Put speculation aside, and focus on what actually happened, what you did, and what you could do differently.

☞ *Personalising and Catastrophising the Impact of What's Happened to You*—"I didn't understand what was said, therefore, I must be stupid", "I'm always getting picked on for extra work, they must dislike me". This distorted thinking is over-generalising and turning negative experience into absolutes. You are in danger of painting yourself into a corner.

☞ *Self-Centred Thinking*—Getting caught up in the personal impact of an uncomfortable experience makes it easy to lose sight of the experience others are having. Put yourself in their shoes to see a different perspective, notice if you are diminishing the validity of someone's position by making assumptions about their motives.

Summarise the essence of your experience in a coherent sentence, for example: "I was thinking that I would sound rude *(belief)* if I interrupted her flow *(situation)*, and I felt myself getting hot and my throat dried up *(physical sensation),* and I became more and more stressed *(emotion)* and just couldn't bring myself to contribute *(behaviour)*".

Including these five elements can help in your analysis. For example, "Did others contribute, were they rude? If I wasn't rude, what might I have said? How did others intervene? Have I ever intervened in a similar way before? What was different that held me back this time? Why does that difference matter so much to me?"

Each step in the process is important. When you identify personal learning, think through how you might act upon it. Without action, there is no change; however, taking action requires courage. Find ways of testing the ideas you generate in a safe environment, for example:

☞ Find someone you trust to share your SOAP with, someone who can ask open questions to help you test your thinking.

☞ Look for situations where you feel safe to try something new, for example, with a friend or a close colleague.

☞ Is there someone who can give feedback when you try something new?

☞ Do you have a mentor who can support and encourage you when you want to try something new?

If you want to explore other forms of transformational learning, try Bill Torbert and Associates' *Action Inquiry: The Secret of Timely and Transformative Leadership*. I would also recommend Marshall Goldsmith's *Triggers: Sparking Positive Change and Making It Last.*

Concluding Comments

"I, and I alone, am responsible for my thoughts, feelings, and behaviours. Nobody can make me think, feel, or respond to events. It is down to how I interpret them". Many things that happen to us are outside our control. However, our thoughts and beliefs are within our control, and we can choose our own response.

When we feel challenged by an experience, critical reflection can help us step back to understand what is happening and to choose our response. Our ability to process data, visualise alternate realities, and create new options means we can shape our own future more that we might at first imagine.

The more we use self-reflection, the more we will recognise patterns of behaviour that no longer serve us well. Practising ideas that come from our personal learning starts the process of behavioural change. Eventually, we will start to recognise these patterns as they emerge and find ourselves reflexively changing our response in the moment, embedding those new behaviours.

This is not to say that our challenges aren't real or that emotional responses should be denied. However, if we are not mindful of our responses, their impact can be debilitating. When we recognise this, we do not need others to change or situations to change for us to feel better.

If you want to read something a little off the beaten track in terms of understanding how minds work and why change is difficult, I can recommend John Haidt's *The Righteous Mind: Why Good People Are Divided by Politics and Religion*. It gives a great insight into why we become illogical, biased, and foolish when we disagree with each other.

About the Author

Peter Hill is an International Coach Federation accredited coach and has a master's degree in coaching and mentoring practice from Oxford Brookes Business School. He has extensive experience in both the public and private sectors, in leadership and consulting roles, particularly in the context of driving significant organisational change.

Peter is passionate about supporting teams and individuals to facilitate real changes in their lives. His purpose is to help them challenge their status quo to uncover new perspectives and reveal new choices for what they do, why they do it, and how they do it.

Peter's focus is on providing the environment for people to give full expression to their situation, to feel able to reflect on and learn from their experiences, and, in so doing, expand their individual and collective self-awareness, enabling them to better address the individual and collective challenges they face.

Email: peter.hill@changeplussolutions.co.uk

CHAPTER 15

A POSITIVE MINDSET OVERCOMES ADVERSITY

By Jory Hingson Fisher
Faith-Based Business Coach;
Certified B.A.N.K.® Coach and Trainer
Baltimore, Maryland

She called me Pollyanna. After examining the results of a psych test I'd taken, my marriage counselor called me Pollyanna. *As if that were a problem!* According to the New Oxford American Dictionary, a Pollyanna is "an excessively cheerful or optimistic person." I didn't protest. I found it odd she seemed concerned. As if optimism were something I needed to fix.

My "Pollyanna mindset" has served me well over the years, getting me through many challenges and disappointments.

Imagine the infinity symbol or a figure eight. The flowing, continuous line crosses over itself again and again. That's how our experiences and mindset affect our present and our future, which, in turn, affect our experiences and our mindset. In my current profession, I help savvy women of faith build successful businesses and lead joyful, meaningful lives. I've yet to meet *anyone* with a successful business and a joyful, meaningful life who hasn't overcome adversity and who hasn't intentionally cultivated a positive mindset. The line crosses over itself again and again. Like the figure eight.

The challenges I share in this chapter are ones that have shaped me into the person I am today. I pray my challenges encourage and embolden you to press on and pursue your purpose with determination, gusto, and joy.

Parents

My father—an officer and a gentleman, a Pearl Harbor survivor, and a devout man of faith—inspired me to look on the bright side of life regardless of circumstances. He was my cheerleader, my role model, my pillar of strength. This highly accomplished naval officer would do anything for his country and family. And through it all, he maintained a spirit of optimism and a mindset of success.

My mother, God rest her soul, was supremely talented as an artist and athlete; however, she was never able to muster a mindset of confidence and success. Her negativity led her to isolate herself. Her isolation led her to drink. The contrast between my optimistic, cheerful father and my pessimistic, depressed mother couldn't have been starker. I remember *choosing* as a teenager to be more like my dad.

Life is difficult. Oh, the things I could tell you over a glass of wine. We all have stories, don't we? I'll share a few examples of how our experiences and mindset affect our present and our future. It's all about choice, my friend. What mindset do you choose?

Husbands

I spent my junior year of college in Madrid, Spain, and fell head-over-heels in love with a Spaniard. Two years later, we moved to the States and got married. I was certain my passionate, handsome husband was perfect for me, and we'd live happily ever after. He wasn't, and we didn't. Cultural differences played a big part in the breakdown of our marriage, as did immaturity and communication challenges. I filed for divorce five years later and went to law school. Manuel and I became good friends again eventually; however, our marital relationship was a harsh, soul-crushing experience for someone raised by a loving, soft-spoken Southern gentleman. It almost defeated me. But it didn't.

My faith, friends, family, mindset, and strong sense of calling helped me press on. I knew I was here on earth for a reason. I was determined to find, follow, and fulfill my purpose, no matter what!

In law school I met the man who would become my second husband. Phil has a big heart, which is what attracted me to him. He's been a wonderful father to our three girls, but it was a rough marriage in many ways. After twelve years of conflict, I moved out and filed for divorce. Again. I'll never forget telling my very concerned mother, "Don't worry, Mom. I always land on my feet." She knew I would, and I did.

So, there I was, a single mother with primary custody of a five-year-old daughter and two-year-old twins, living in a tiny cottage and working part-time. I held on to a few phrases that kept me going:

- ☞ *I am called to make a difference in this world.*
- ☞ *My daughters and I will be fine.*
- ☞ *My continued faith and positive mindset are vital to our success.*

Fast-forward a couple of years. I met Dave Fisher, my knight in shining armor who bears a striking resemblance to Sir Patrick Stewart. We've been happily married for over two decades, and our seven grown children are all leading purposeful, productive lives. I credit faith and a positive mindset for helping me turn years of marital stress into a life of peace and joy. Call me Pollyanna if you'd like. I land on my feet every time.

Health

At age 55, I found out I had two holes in my heart. The local cardiologist took one look at my chart and exclaimed, "You should be dead." Okay, statistically speaking he was right. But I knew God had me here on earth for a reason, and apparently that reason had not yet been fulfilled. I wasn't scared. I was curious and very much at peace. Heading into surgery at the University of Virginia Medical Center, the cardiologist who repaired my heart said, "God obviously has a plan for your life." Amen and amen.

I stepped down from my position as a law professor and associate dean of Liberty University School of Law to practice law part-time and start up a coaching business from home. That was 13 years ago. My repaired heart is doing well, thanks be to God.

I no longer practice law because my husband and I moved to Maryland in 2012, and I didn't want to take the bar exam again. I chose to ramp up my coaching business instead.

All was going well. All *is* going well. It's just that now I have another diagnosis. I had symptoms for years without realizing I have multiple sclerosis. (MS is different for everyone. I think the only symptom we *all* have is extreme fatigue.) I get infusions twice a year to help keep the nerve damage from progressing. I manage well, and I choose to remain grateful and optimistic.

So now I work from home, accompanied by my faithful dog, Cowboy, and sweet little guinea pig, Jitterbug. Dave is with me in the evenings and on weekends, but commutes to downtown Baltimore during the week. Because of my age and compromised immune system, I'm advised to "stay home and stay safe" while the pandemic rages. You think mindset is important to me now? More than ever, my friend. More than ever.

Career Challenges

Did you notice that I didn't say "failures"? I hate that word. So many memes out there like "failing forward," "fail your way to success." Definitions of "failure" include the word "lack" as in "lack of success." I don't like the word "lack" either. It's not what happens that matters. It's how we respond that counts. And that can turn devastation into joy! If you're wondering what types of challenges I faced, below are a few examples.

Challenge Example #1: I failed (oh that word!) the bar exam. I had no idea I'd have extreme anxiety just before and during the two-day exam. I freaked out but still thought I'd done well enough to pass. Having graduated from a top ten law school, I was humiliated and ashamed when I saw that my name wasn't listed among those who had been successful. I questioned why God had prompted me to take the bar when I wasn't even planning to practice law.

I. Was. Devastated. I vividly remember my dad saying I needed to "get back up on the horse again." That was the only time I ever raised my voice at my father. This "failure" went to my purpose, calling, intelligence, *raison d'etre*, and my "failed" marriage. It confirmed names Manuel had called me. It confirmed self-doubt. What if I took the exam again and FAILED another time?

I knew I had a choice. If I *didn't* take the bar exam again, I would never know if I could pass it. More importantly, I would never have the opportunity to practice law, should I decide to do so.

I chose to get back up on the horse. I studied constantly for six months to boost my confidence, AND I got a prescription for Xanax. The night before each day of the exam, I took a pill to be able to sleep. Each morning of the exam I took a half a pill to avoid freaking out while answering the questions. Two months later we got the results. I had passed one of the most challenging bar exams in the country. *Hallelujah!*

Did I end up practicing law? Oh yes! For nearly 30 years. Isn't that amazing!

Challenge Example #2: We've all experienced wanting something really bad and not getting it, whether that be a Christmas present or an engagement ring or a pony or a job. My biggest career-related disappointment was putting my hat in the ring for judge and not being selected. Again, those dark, am-I-worthy emotions flooded my soul; but mostly, I was flat out disappointed! I wanted to serve our community as a juvenile and domestic relations district court judge with all my heart and soul, and I believed I was well-equipped to do so.

Did I cry when I read the announcement in the newspaper? Most definitely. Did I think it was a political, pre-arranged decision? Yes. But, in time, I chose to put that negativity behind me and move on. I knew I couldn't maintain a "poor me" mindset and fulfill my calling. I'd end up a bitter attorney with a chip on her shoulder and transform into a grumpy wife and mom.

A year or so later, I became a founding faculty member of Liberty University School of Law. Not being selected as a judge turned out to be a great thing after all. Isn't that amazing!

Challenge Example #3: I didn't know how to "get" coaching clients. As a lawyer, I never had to think about marketing and sales. I served as an assistant county attorney, senior legal aid attorney, court-appointed attorney, and assistant public defender. No shortage of clients with *those* jobs. We had to turn people away.

But then I started coaching from home with no clue how to attract prospects. I'm here to tell you it was a struggle for years. Do you know how challenging it is to keep a positive mindset when you're thousands of dollars in debt? My numerous coaching certifications, websites, continuing education classes, and mentoring programs filled my time and nourished my love for learning but did NOT help me earn a significant income. I felt like I had failed (oh that word) as an entrepreneur.

I knew something had to change., I was determined to figure it out, and I did.

After serving several years as a life purpose coach, I became a business coach who helped entrepreneurs attract prospects and convert them into raving clients and customers. The work was rewarding emotionally *and* financially; however, in my fourth year, I finally went to a neurologist to see what was wrong with me. Good thing I did. After months of testing, the diagnosis was confirmed: multiple sclerosis.

I had to shut down my in-person mastermind program.

I had MS and no active or passive income. That could have done me in, but it didn't. I became a certified coach and trainer with a global sales and communications company (Codebreaker Technologies) and now have the ability to serve people all over the world online. From home. Earning active *and* passive income. Isn't that amazing!

Recipe for Success

Nine years ago, I wrote a blog post titled "Recipe for Success." It is about what drives us. The questions, "What motivates us?" and "What inspires us to 'do something' with our lives?" have intrigued me for years, for decades really. I suggested we need not only a successful mind, but also a successful heart. It's not just our "mind-thoughts" that drive us, motivate us, inspire us. It's our "heart thoughts" as well.

> *As a man thinketh in his heart, so is he.*
> —Proverbs 23:7

I told you about my parents. Perhaps for deep psychological reasons, my mother's heart was broken, which affected her thoughts, which affected her actions, which affected her husband, her son, and me. My brother's and my negative feelings toward our mother then hurt her heart (and mind) even more. Mom's drinking was tough on our whole family. As I told you earlier, I made a conscious decision to be more like my dad. *I chose life.*

I was a cheerleader all four years of high school (voted Most School Spirited), active in my youth group (Young Life), and voted on to the Christmas Court my senior year. After graduating with honors, I was selected Miss Tysons Corner by a panel of judges. I mention these accolades to demonstrate my resilience and determination. With all the sadness at home, I intentionally chose a mindset of JOY. Call that Pollyanna? I call it smart! I call it breaking out of a patterned negative mindset.

To achieve anything worthwhile in life, we *have* to acquire a positive attitude. Positive thoughts lead to positive actions, which allow us to make a positive difference in the world. To maintain a positive mind(set), our *heart* needs to be positive as well. We have a saying in my church: "Open hearts. Open minds." The two go hand-in-hand.

Live Life on Purpose!

How can you feel insignificant when you know God has called you for a purpose? How can you be afraid when you know God is holding you in His hand? I truly believe that God created each of us for a purpose and that He helps us discover what our divine purpose is.

For several years, I coached clients through a program that helps people get clear on their calling. The joy and peace they experienced after attaining that clarity was beautiful to behold. We all experience hard times in this life. When you know your purpose, you're able to weather the storms and come out stronger and better on the other side.

No matter where you are in life's journey, my prayer is that you too will find, follow, and fulfill your divine purpose. I pray you will love your Creator, love yourself, love your neighbor, and choose life!

Trust in the Lord with all thine heart;
and lean not unto thine own understanding. In all thy ways
acknowledge Him, and He will direct thy path.
—Proverbs 3:5–6

About the Author

Jory Hingson Fisher has enjoyed a diverse career in government, law, and entrepreneurship. She was an attorney in Virginia for 28 years, specializing in criminal law and domestic relations, and was a founding faculty member and associate dean of Liberty University School of Law. Jory is passionate about helping savvy women of faith build strong, successful businesses and lead joyful, meaningful lives. She enjoys being a sales and communications coach and trainer and is certified in B.A.N.K.® personality science.

Jory graduated Phi Beta Kappa, *summa cum laude* from Southern Methodist University, received her master's degree in Spanish from Middlebury College, and earned her law degree from the University of Virginia. Her honors and awards include ACHI Magazine Woman of Achievement Award; Alignable Small Business Person of the Year; and the DAR Award for Women in American History. Jory is featured in America's Leading Ladies and America's STAR Entrepreneurs.

Email: jory@joryfisher.com
Website: www.joryfisher.com
LinkedIn: https://www.linkedin.com/in/joryfisher/

CHAPTER 16
THERE IS GREATNESS IN YOU

By Dr. Jacqueline Pridgen Howard
Speaker, Trainer, Christian Life Coach
Clinton, North Carolina

To be mindful is to be intentional.
—John Maxwell

Mindfulness and mental clarity in any situation are always beneficial. It is essential to be able to acknowledge and accept your feelings and thoughts. These truths impact your decision-making abilities, relationships, and life in general. It is reasonable to say that mindfulness heightens self-awareness, which helps you better understand your emotions.

Regardless of your position or field of expertise, mindfulness benefits everyone. When a situation sends you spiraling, or you get caught up in confusion, it is to your advantage to learn the value and power of "pause." These are the times when it is essential to step back, stop, pause, and pray. Your self-awareness around your becoming overwhelmed and the need to reset can reduce personal stress, help you re-center, and improve your overall concentration and decision-making. It can also spark leadership creativity, not to mention the added health benefits of lowering blood pressure and associated symptoms of anxiety.

Today's world, so full of distractions, can be very hectic. So much so, we may accept these distractions as our norm. A chaotic life is not the life God has planned for us. This book provides strategies to help you reclaim your inner peace, build confidence, and grow. Start trusting your instincts and begin setting boundaries that will enable you to minimize intrusive distractions that invade your peace. Mark 4:19 reminds us that to be caught up in the worries of this life can cause us to miss reaching our goals. Proverbs 4:25 encourages us to look straight ahead and focus on the future. Since daily decisions shape our future, can you see the benefits of intentional thinking?

God-focused, Christ-centered meditation focuses your thoughts on God and builds your spiritual relationship. In Philippians 2:1–5, Paul tells us to be mindful and live with an awareness of the mind of Christ. We begin to know God's mind through the study of the Scriptures and a Christian believer's prayer/meditation, which is ongoing (1 Thessalonians 5:17). Meditation also appears in the Bible in the context of studying the Word of God (Psalm 48:9; Psalm 63:6). Christians ought not to get distracted by tomorrow's worries (Matthew 6:25–34) and should take every thought captive (2 Corinthians 10:5). The emphasis is placed on controlling our thoughts. Paul also points out that we are to "be transformed" by renewing our minds (Romans 12:2) by thinking positive thoughts (Philippians 4:9).

Let's take a moment to reflect. Are you self-aware? How easily are you distracted? Sometime, knowing a few strategies can help you recognize patterns within yourself:

1. *Look at yourself objectively.* What makes you happy and what bothers you? Look for patterns in your thinking and behaviors. Identify your triggers.
2. *Keep a journal.* Journaling helps clarify your thoughts. It enables ideas and feelings to process in a safe environment.
3. *Write down goals.* Writing goals move them from an abstract to concrete. By listing the strategic steps needed to reach goals, you can gauge movement towards their attainment, identify barriers and resources, and establish timelines for completion.

Whenever you improve in one area, other areas are enhanced. For example, self-awareness also benefits your relationships. How? When you know who you are and what you want, you can better communicate. And, when people understand your needs, they are better equipped to fulfill them.

My work experience in public school finance, teaching, administration, ministry, coaching, and speaking has shown me that leadership is an integral part of everything we do. It encompasses every area of our life because everyone is, at some level, a leader. Allow me to use this definition for a leader: one possessing the power of influence. That being said, we know that everyone has the potential to influence at least one person.

Consequently, we all have a sphere of influence. Just as we all have differing levels of influence, we all have varying degrees of greatness within. It is up to you to know your gift, connect with it, nurture it, and develop it. It is not about measuring what we have against another's ability but, instead, embracing and cultivating our own.

In essence, self-awareness, authenticity, and the development of integrity add value to who you are and enhances your gift. As you grow, you gain respect and increase your circle of influence. Know your strengths and improve them through personal development activities. Then, share your journey with others and assist them along their way. Become a transformative leader—one who empowers others and helps to build stronger communities.

Be intentional with your thoughts as it relates to goal attainment. Understand that negative thoughts are powerful and will sabotage your success. Additionally, be aware that thoughts influence brain function as well. Negative thoughts have been associated with impairing logical thinking and even slowing down our muscular activity. Researcher Nadine Jung's article in *Frontiers in Psychology* says her experiment "showed a clear effect of emotions on reasoning performance. Participants in a negative mood performed worse than participants in a positive mood." This study shows that how you think can affect what you will accomplish. Proverbs 12:25 reads, "Anxiety weighs down the heart of a man, but a good word cheers it up." We all know that you cannot operate at full capacity when you are anxious and depressed. The emphasis on having positive thoughts is mentioned in Philippians 4:8, "And now, dear brothers and sisters, one final thing. Fix your thoughts on what is true, and honorable, and right, and pure, and lovely, and admirable. Think about things that are excellent and worthy of praise." Here again, we are encouraged to think positively, which creates hope and enables us to apply ourselves to the task at hand with eagerness or expectation to do well.

Remember, your state of mind dramatically influences your outcomes. Therefore, be cognizant of your thoughts. And, before you start traveling down a road of negativity, purposely and intentionally choose:

1. a growth mindset and choose to dwell in possibilities
2. an openness to becoming a lifelong learner at all levels

3. a positive attitude and choosing faith over fear

Your mindset plays a vital role in all that you do. It is the determining factor in how well you cope with complicated matters. People respond to situations from either a fixed or a growth mindset. Those with a fixed mindset can experience more anxiety and stress than those with a growth mindset when working through challenges. People with a growth mindset accept that they will not be proficient all the time but are confident that they can learn what is needed. They work towards gaining knowledge and locating the resources to accomplish the task. They believe in their potential, and that training, resources, and time allocation will guarantee task achievement.

We all have faced a challenge that forced us out of our comfort zone. Perhaps, it was a new job or a change in duties. Even now, you may be working areas where you lack proficiency, but with the right mindset, you can embrace the change. Be confident and look at it as just one more opportunity to grow. Whereas, those with a fixed mindset often feel inadequate when faced with change. This fear of failure is an unhealthy attitude causing them to be reluctant to accept new responsibilities that demand new learning. In turn, this hinders or prevents them from reaching their potential. People with a fixed mindset often cover up what they don't know and feel threatened by others who readily take on new assignments or grasp new concepts quickly. Thus, the mountains of angst and stress are added to their lives, forcing them to hide what they are afraid of.

What about constant complainers who have a long list of complaints every day? They feel hopeless to affect positive change in their lives. This demonstration of external locus of control decreases the motivation to get it together with work for change. This feeling of helplessness prohibits their forward movement towards the attainment of their goals and desires. Why? Because they have relinquished their power to others.

If you find that your external locus of control is stronger than your internal locus of control, try this tip. Remind yourself that you have the power of choice. The knowledge of this fact will increase your internal locus of control. Yes, it is empowering to know that you can make decisions for yourself. You choose, it is your choice whether you relinquish that to others. Look at what is within your control. And finally, one of the most powerful things we can do is to remove negative self-talk. Remember, our words create the direction for our lives.

Humans are creative beings, and creativity begins with thoughts, which are perceptions of our reality. Are your thoughts generating abstract words or concrete words? Are you connecting emotionally to the words you speak? Can you envision the action that they will create? Always consider the power of your words and how they impact what you can and cannot do. They possess the ability to influence how you feel. And how you feel affects what you do. Are you using words that motivate and inspire you? Or, do your words sadden you and make you doubt your ability? That is why it is especially important to become self-aware. Knowing this will help you choose words more carefully and maintain vigilant guard over your usage.

Self-awareness is a significant factor in how you progress towards your life's goals. First, just let me say that regardless of where you fall on the spectrum, there is always hope. Even if you doubt yourself and have a fixed mindset, you can change if you are willing to put in the work. Are you willing to put forth the necessary effort to make a positive change that will add value to your life?

According to Carol Dweck, Stanford professor, a fixed mindset is when people see their qualities as fixed traits that cannot change. They feel we are born with a certain degree of ability and intelligence that is static. Past experiences may cause someone to have a fixed mindset.

Tips for Cultivating a Growth Mindset

1. Guard your tongue. Proverbs 18:21 ESV.

Death and life are in the power of the tongue, and those who love it will eat its fruits. Proverbs 17:27 states, "Whoever restrains his words has knowledge, and he who has a cool spirit is a man of understanding." What a vivid reminder to be mindful of our conversations, even our inner conversations. Maybe you forget your keys, and without any thought, you say to yourself, "I'm so crazy. Why did I do that?" Or perhaps, you talk yourself out of applying for your dream job by saying, "I don't even need to apply for that job, I won't get it."

Understand that your thought shapes your reality and develops your mindset. What have you said or thought about yourself today? Have you made any negative statements, or did you utter empowering words to uplift and encourage yourself to move forward? I like to think of the Little Engine That Could, who used the mantra, "I think I can, I think I can …" until he did. Your thoughts can generate energy and power to overcome.

2. Dwell in possibilities and remain hopeful.

Never Give up! Reframe and focus on what is good. A pessimist is always looking at what they don't have and what is not working in their favor. When that happens, they miss the beauty and value of what they have. Don't let that be you. May I challenge you to start looking at the glass as half full instead of saying, "Shucks, it is almost gone." Get in the habit of being grateful. A grateful heart lets you live out of an attitude of abundance instead of fear and lack.

3. When setting goals to be realistic, think about what it will take for you to succeed.

There is sacrifice associated with attaining any goal. What are you willing to sacrifice to gain? There is sacrifice associated with attaining any goal. Are you ready to give up time and resources to attain your goal? The goal you seek must have a higher value than the sacrifices you make. If not, you may feel it is not worth your effort to attain it. Once you have determined that you are willing to make the required sacrifices, start developing your strategic plan by using SMART goals. List the specific steps to be implemented to reach a goal. Here's a quick review of SMART goal setting:

- ☞ **S**pecific. *Are your goals simple and specific?*
- ☞ **M**easurable/Meaningful. *How will you know when goals are reached?*
- ☞ **A**chievable. *Are your goals realistic and doable within the scope of your resources?*
- ☞ **R**elevant. *Are your goals reasonable?*
- ☞ **T**ime-bound. *How are you going to be accountable for completing each stage of the process? Create a timetable for completion.*

4. Commit to lifelong learning.

When you learn, your horizon broadens, and you can choose to adopt and incorporate what you have learned. Incorporating things that resonate with your core values will help you become your best self.

5. Surround yourself with positive, motivated people.

Learn from those doing what you aspire to do. Spend time observing their habits and listen to their conversations. Years ago, a quote attributed to Jim Rohn said that you are the average of the five people that you spend the most time with. However, David Burkus, speaker and business school professor, says that it goes far beyond that. He says, "You're not the average of the five people you surround yourself with. It's way bigger than that. You're the average of all the people who surround you."

6. Be self-aware.

Learn which habits you have that are counterproductive to your forward movement. Identify and begin eliminating them. Learning is an important element of your personal growth because our world is continually changing. In the past, processes would change over time. But today, because of technological developments and social demands, we experience rapid innovative changes, which cause processes to change quickly. This can occur in a matter of months, or some instances, it may seem as if overnight. To remain relevant, learning is not an option. It is a necessity of the 21st century.

Everyone can learn, but not everyone possesses the willingness to learn. No matter what your capacity to learn is, choosing to learn is essential to your personal growth. And, as you learn, you can add value to those around you. The opportunities to learn are endless. We have a formal education that can be found in brick-and-mortar institutions, and now more than ever, we have seemingly limitless online opportunities. You can earn degrees without ever spending a day on a campus of higher education. There are many free informal learning opportunities. For example, via the Internet, you can learn from YouTube videos, podcasts, online articles, chat rooms, and forums, to name a few.

The next benefit is that learning improves your self-confidence. How is that? It makes sense, the more you know about something, you are confident that you have the competence and ability to do it. Now this aspect is one that makes me excited. We know that the aging process naturally causes the brain to have some tissue loss. The great news is that new learning helps compensate for that loss. I am all in. Let's stimulate those neurons and create some new neural pathways. Our life expectancy has increased, and we want to remain as sharp as possible for as long as possible.

Finally, learning helps combat boredom and bring excitement and pleasure into your life. Choose to become a lifelong learner! Commit to learning something new this week, month, or year. You decide.

Our faith in our ability to achieve any goal motivates us to accomplish it. Otherwise, we may give up prematurely. When we lack faith, we begin to feel our effort is futile and may stop trying. That is why someone who has lost faith in their relationship may decide to terminate it. Or, they may resign themselves to living in an unhappy or unhealthy environment. However, if they believe that their situation can be improved, they will look for ways to repair it, which may include some type of counseling.

Self-awareness covers every area of your life. So, be gracious with yourself as you explore, and love yourself, which grants you the grace to unselfishly love others. Some strategies for this include:

1. Embrace yourself. Know that we are all perfectly imperfect people. No one is without flaws.
2. View challenges as new learning opportunities. Don't panic. Determine what resources and skills are needed. How can you acquire what is required? Who can support you in the process? What are your barriers and options?
3. Replace negative self-talk, such as "I can't," "I am so stupid," or "This is too hard."

Lastly, you lessen your effectiveness without even realizing it when you always seek approval of others. For example, you may want to share an idea with the group at work, but instead, you remain silent in fear that they may not receive your plan favorably. Then, someone speaks up with an idea similar to yours but not as good. Nonetheless, their idea was well-received. Who do you blame for that missed opportunity? Be brave and stop negatively impacting your career effectiveness by seeking others' approval. Take steps to eradicate limiting beliefs of a fixed mindset. Grow and thrive. Let the world know that you have a purpose, and there is greatness in you. It is all in the way you think.

About the Author

Dr. Jacqueline Howard is an Elder, Certified Coach, John Maxwell-trained, Distinguished Toastmaster, and former school administrator, who uses her formal education, personal experiences, and wisdom to add value to others. With over 33 years in education, she is a committed lifelong learner. Dr. Howard passionately helps others live authentically as they seek to fulfill their purpose. As the founder of Moving On With Coaching, she hosts retreats, creating a safe place for women to explore their faith, learn strategies, have fun, get inspired, and be rejuvenated. Dr. Howard's transparent, down-to-earth style makes her immediately relatable.

Dr. Howard has published several books—*Angels, Introduction to Angels, Moving on With Coaching Daily Journal, Leading God's Way*—and co-authored the *Happy Mind Matrix*. Dr. Howard always brings God's perspective on any topic. Trust her to help you expand your mind, increase your spirit, and live in alignment with God's Word.

Email: Movingonwithcoaching@gmail.com
Website: www.movingonwithcoaching.com
Website: www.jacquelinehowardleadinggodsway.com

CHAPTER 17

GUARDING YOUR HEART ABOVE ALL ELSE

By Amor de Jager
Certified Life Coach & Pastoral Counsellor
Pretoria, South Africa

Your state of mind determines how successful you will be. Your mind needs to be healthy, and you need to look after it daily to make sure it is healthy. It is no one else's responsibility to look after your mind or to set your mindset. It's yours alone. Because mental health plays an intrinsic role in your level of success, it is critical to address your mental health and not ignore it or assume it's fine.

When you are mentally fit and healthy, you have a clear view of what you want, what you would tolerate (and not tolerate), and what you will let into your life. When you don't have a clear view on your state of mind, and you take everything people say and do personally, you end up with a lot of things that worry, upset, and bother you. These things can really get in the way of your success and how you work to success.

Mindset is one of the most important aspects to look at when you want to achieve success in your life. We are going to look at this by digging deeper in the meaning of "guarding your heart".

When it comes to success, you probably wouldn't think of "guarding your heart" as one of the top ten tools on helping you achieve it, would you? A few years back, I wouldn't even think about it being in the top hundred, but today it is the most important thing that I've learned. Not only is it important when you want to be successful in life, but in every other aspect of your life as well.

In Proverbs 4:23, Solomon says, "Above all else, guard your heart, for everything you do flows from it". Let's start by looking at what Solomon's statement means. Solomon's starting phrase, "Above all else", clearly shows that this is top priority. He didn't say something like "When you have time", "When you feel like it", or "When nothing else works", etc. Solomon clearly states that this is very important—this must be your top priority. Everything else can then follow, but this is the most important. First things first, we must guard our hearts, *above all else.*

Before discussing the meaning of "guarding our hearts", let's turn to the last part of the verse that states, "for everything you do flows from it". Take a minute to ponder this. When you take some time to really let it sink in, you can feel how powerful this is. Solomon states that EVERYTHING we do flows from our heart. Not some things, not just family things, spiritual things, or feelings—but every little and big thing, and everything in between as well. This means that what we do in our business and work also flows from our heart. Have you ever thought about that?

For everything to fit together, we must also look at the "guarding your heart" part. What does it really mean to "guard your heart" above all else? It means to look after your heart as your first priority. And a lot of people don't understand the concept of our "heart". Our heart is not merely the muscle that keeps blood pumping in our veins. Our heart is our thoughts, our feelings, our emotions, conscience, and beliefs. In other words, our hearts are our state of mind, our mindset, our internal perspective. And all these things flow over into actions and words.

Our feelings and emotions flow over in actions. For example, when we get angry or feel sad, our actions will show it in our body language and what we say. What we believe also shows in our actions, we live it every day, sometimes without even really thinking about it. There is not one person who believes something, and their actions and words don't show it. Think about it. You don't need to try to do it, you automatically do it. That is why it is so important to guard your heart because what you think, feel, and believe is almost like a habit. You don't think about it, you just do it because you have been doing it for so long and that's what you're used to. You form patterns, and the longer you keep up with a particular pattern, the harder it is to break the pattern or change it. That is why your heart, in other words, your thoughts, feelings, emotions, conscience, and beliefs must be guarded every day. This determines the things you do and the words you speak, and these have consequences, determining where you are going. The New Living Translations translates the same verse, Proverbs 4:23, as, "Guard your heart above all else, for it determines the course of your life".

The last part of the verse states that "it determines the course of your life". And this means the course of your marriage, your business, your family, your health, every part of your life.

When we take a step back and look at this from afar, it looks like a very small and simple thing: guard your heart. Three words that have much more to them than what you first think about them.

This tool, guarding your heart, is a priority for a successful mind. You need to start somewhere to change your mindset and clear your mind of the things that don't belong there. Let's look into that.

Clean Your House

We had a look at our heart and the importance of guarding it. Now I want to use a metaphor to explain what can happen when you don't look after your heart properly.

As I said, we need to look after what we think about constantly, the habits we are forming, the people we are allowing to influence us, etc. All these things come down to our state of mind. When we constantly think (and worry) about what someone said, we are giving them power over us. We are allowing them to actually control what we think. When we start thinking about things that we can't change and continue to worry and get upset, we are allowing those people to get us off-track from that which is actually important to us. In turn, we can't focus on the way we want to go and the success we want to achieve because there are things (and people) blocking our way.

The example I use is one of a house. Everyone knows that there is always a lot of work to be done in a house. There are always dishes, laundry, dust, and dirty floors. You can do all the work today, but there is a promise that there will be more tomorrow—no matter how hard you try for it not to be there. So, what happens when you just leave everything? It stays there, and it gets worse every day. It doesn't disappear (even if you want it to). You must do the work every day to keep your house clean and tidy. No one else is going to do it for you.

When you leave the dishes and laundry for a few weeks, there will most definitely be a huge pile of both in your kitchen and bedroom. When you ignore the dust and dirty floors, in a weeks' time, the dust will be a few inches thick, and the floors will look a few shades darker. I promise that neither you, nor your spouse, will be very happy about it. And this makes room for arguments, unproductivity, a bad state of mind, etc. Just like cleaning a house, you need to take care of your mind daily in order for it to be clean, healthy, and fit.

Cleaning is not a once-a-week thing or when we feel like it. There are days where we can leave the dishes and laundry for another day, but it will pile up if we don't do them. We really need to make it a priority to think about what we think about daily because if we don't, we can easily fall into the habit of postponing things and leaving it for another day. The danger here is that we don't deal with what we need to when it needs to be dealt with; we start to procrastinate.

When we have a negative thought, stop it right there. We should not take it into our day, our meetings, the conversation we have with our spouse or children. Deal with it there. We need to make choices daily that will change the way we see things, how we perceive things, and how we act. We need to guard our hearts in order to have a "clean house," for this will determine the course of our lives.

You need to clean your "house" daily. Be careful what you constantly think about, the feelings you reinforce, and the people you allow to influence you. Start with this habit and see how it changes the course of your life.

Think About What You Think About

I encourage you to take some time alone and think about the thoughts, feelings, beliefs and habits you daily reinforce in your life. Is that what you want in your life? Is this what you want in ten years from now? Remember, all of these determine the course of your life, where you are going to be in ten, twenty, and thirty years. Are these feelings, thoughts, and beliefs good for your mental health, emotional state, and spiritual growth? Are these things that you believe about your business and success helping you to grow your business? Are the thoughts you have every day about your work positive ones that show up in your actions in a positive way—or not? Are the feelings and emotions you have towards yourself healthy for your well-being? Are you slowly building yourself up or breaking yourself down, little by little?

Take time and write down these feelings, beliefs, emotions, and thoughts. Think about where you first started to feel/think/believe these things and why you keep reinforcing them. Maybe you want them part of your life, but maybe you don't. What are you going to do about that then? What other thought patterns and beliefs are you going to start reinforcing to change the negative and destructive patterns that you now have in your heart? What is your plan of action to stop negative, destructive thoughts, feelings, beliefs, and people from getting too much of your attention? How are you going to deal with thoughts and feelings the moment they enter your mind/heart? Don't leave them for another day.

Once you get into the habit of cleaning your mind daily, positive thoughts will become your normal thoughts, and happiness will continue to surround you as you guard your heart above all else.

About the Author

Amor de Jager is the founder and owner of Nikao Life Coaching and Pastoral Counselling. She obtained her Baccalaureus Artium in Christian Counselling and Education in 2016. In 2018, she obtained her Bachelor of Art (Hons.) in Theological Studies and Biblical Counselling, and her postgraduate certificate in education. In 2019, she completed her life coaching diploma.

Amor loves God, people, and nature. She believes that life is about choices and that you are the only one responsible for where your life path will go, and end. She strives for an abundant life and wants everyone to have part in the abundance that God gives to His children.

Email: amor@nikao.co.za
Website: http://nikaocounselling.co.za

CHAPTER 18

THE QUALITY OF YOUR LIFE DEPENDS ON YOUR PERCEPTION OF LIFE

By Nate Johnson
Leadership and Mindset Coach
Los Angeles, California

*What you see and what you hear depends
a great deal on where you are standing. It also
depends on what sort of person you are.*
—C.S. Lewis

The Law of the Instrument

Also known as "The Man with a Hammer Syndrome," the Law of the Instrument is a cognitive bias we all have, whereby we over-rely on a tool that we're familiar with. From Buddha to the Bible, sage lessons have been provided about this bias throughout history, but it's Abraham Maslow and Abraham Kaplan who are given most of the credit for conceptualizing the idea in the modern era.

Maslow defined it this way: "I suppose it is tempting, if the only tool you have is a hammer, to treat everything as if it were a nail." What this means is that everything we see (only nails) is based on the boundaries of our perception (having only a hammer), and the boundaries of our perception are only limited by what we accept as the boundaries of our perception.

As an example, how babies and infants see the world constantly changes. At a few months old, their world is limited to where they can crawl. When they stand, they can literally see higher to things they didn't know were there. When they learn to use language, they can absorb new information and form new thoughts. Their perception, and, therefore, their mindset toward what they can do, continues to expand with each new skill they acquire and each new challenge they overcome. Their limits are not reality, just their reality.

Adults, on the other hand, experience a plateau, or worse, a contraction to our reality. Our skill acquisition slows down; therefore, the way we perceive the world begins to cement. Our feet are set, and we become stuck in place with the tools we've acquired. Our limits are now defined.

Or are they?

If your limits are self-imposed, this must imply that they are not real. There must be something you're not seeing. But if you want to move beyond the boundaries that surround the world you've created, you must first be willing to believe that there is something on the other side.

Having Limits Is Different from Knowing Limits

Every man takes the limits of his own field of
vision for the limits of the world.
—Arthur Schopenhauer

Most people believe their reality is reality. They believe that if they can't perceive something as true, then it must not be true. What they perceive as true must be the only truth. They only have a hammer and they think a hammer is all there is; therefore, they treat everything as a nail.

See, we're all playing with a limited set of tools—of knowledge. But the way you start to see the truth—the way you open yourself to possibilities and to realize perceived limits may not be actual limits—is to be open to the possibility that other tools exist and then to start to look for and acquire them.

How to See Beyond the Limits of Your Perception

Have you seen the film *The Matrix*? In it, Keanu Reeves stars as Neo, a computer hacker to whom it is revealed (spoiler alert!) that what we call reality is just a computer-generated simulation—it's all in the mind.

Even though it's not real, Neo learns that because your mind perceives it as thus, if you die in the simulation (the Matrix), you die in the real world.

However, Neo has a gift. He has the capability to see the Matrix for what it is—merely lines of computer code. And when he's in the Matrix, he, himself, is also made of lines of code, not flesh. And he understands that code can be manipulated, controlled, rewritten, redefined.

You do not need the capabilities of a superhero in a simulation to start looking at your world for what it is—an infinite playground of possibilities to be experimented with—and begin to build a different future. All you need to do is think of these three guidelines in order to see beyond the limits of your perception:

1. You must first be self-aware and notice the limits of your perception.
2. Then you must question if they are actual limits ("Is this true?").
3. Then make yourself open to the possibility that they are not.

You may, in fact, have already been exposed to truths through books you've read, advice you've been given, etc. But you just weren't ready or hadn't had the life experience you needed in order to notice them. It's like when you read a book and then re-read it 10 years later and find it means something completely different to you when you're older. You might finally get things you missed the first time because you have a new perspective. The book (reality) hasn't changed. You changed.

As Robertson Davies put it in his novel *Tempest-Tost*, "The eye sees only what the mind is prepared to comprehend." Your mind is a receiver, and it will only pick up what it's programmed to pick up. So, program it to pick up more. Below are some examples of seeing beyond perception:

- *Educational Perceptions*
  Until the past 10 years or so, getting a college education was seen as the only way to succeed in life. But, with insane tuition costs, decreasing barriers to start businesses with low overhead, and the rise of startup culture, people

are realizing that a college education is not the gatekeeper it once was perceived to be.

- *Physical Perceptions*

Our senses of sight, sound, smell, touch, and taste are pretty measly compared to other creatures in the animal kingdom. This shows, it would be foolish to think that whatever we can't do cannot be done at all. That's why when we exhaust our physical limits, we invent instruments to augment how we perceive the world, and those instruments completely change our reality and make new things possible.

- *Mental Perceptions*

Even our mind and imaginations have limitations. For example, because we live in a 3D world, we can't actually imagine anything with more than three dimensions. But even though the human mind is incapable of comprehending four dimensions and beyond, we know they are a possibility because we've developed—some would say "discovered"—math. From this knowledge, literally whole new worlds are revealed.

- *Analogy Perceptions*

People like to do what's easy, and reasoning by analogy is easy because we're basing what's possible upon what we commonly see, know, or have experienced ourselves. Elon Musk illustrates this when he hears the conventional wisdom that battery packs are expensive because they've always been expensive; therefore, they always will be expensive. This is reasoning by analogy—comparing a conceived reality to something you've experienced. Musk, however, would invite us, instead, to think from a physics point of view and reason by First Principles, which breaks things down into their simplest components. He hears experts say battery packs cost $600 per kilowatt-hour, so it will never get better than that. But when he breaks a battery down into its material constituents, then finds the spot market value of those components, he finds that it, in fact, costs $80 per kilowatt-hour. That's $520 per kilowatt-hour saved. Therefore, a whole new clean energy market was created—just by changing perception.

- *Positional Perceptions*

This might be the most difficult of the perceptions to challenge because it deals directly with the ego. Imagine for a moment, that you are standing in front of a blue square sheet of paper suspended in a room. All you see is this one-dimensional square, so you believe this is reality and everyone else sees it the same as you.

You observe someone standing to your right, looking at the side of the sheet, and you assume they just see a thin piece of paper. You become curious and want to see from their view, so you start moving to your right. As you do, however, you notice that the square isn't one dimensional at all—it's actually a cube. Not only is it 3D, but this other side isn't blue, it's yellow with red polka dots. All of the sudden, your reality has changed, just by moving your position slightly.

The look of amazement on your face prompts the other person to ask why you were looking at the thin side of the polka dot paper, and you tell them it's actually a cube and the side you were looking at is blue.

Unlike you, however, the other person refuses to believe you and chooses to stay put. Their reality is set. What they perceive is only what they can observe. The limits of their world are self-imposed. But you know there must be more to discover, so you let them be and adventurously move on.

Everyone sees the same things (physical things, thoughts, concepts, life) from different points of view, and your perception is not an absolute reality—it's your reality. And you can change your reality each time you change your angle.

Your Mindset Is Within Your Control

Reality is what you perceive as real and only a minute fraction of the things you'll encounter are actually nails. So, if you want to change your reality and, thereby, change your mindset, then expand your tools.

In order to do that, you must just think. Think for yourself. If you perceive something as hard, think why you think it's hard. Is it because that's what people always say? Have you tried before and failed? Because you failed, does that mean it's objectively hard or was your method simply wrong? Have other people defied convention and achieved what you want to achieve with relative ease? How did they do it?

If you perceive yourself as a certain type of person, think if that's actually true or if you're just applying a label to yourself for a feeling you sometimes have.

For example, "I'm an anxious person." Is that true? So, you've had a panic attack, maybe. Does that mean you always have panic attacks? Are there times when you're completely calm, relaxed and confident? Then your labeling yourself as anxious is false. Sometimes you have anxiety. But if you don't have it all the time, then anxious isn't a viable label defining you.

When you learn that everything you think is simply a condition of your perception and that while external events are not in your control but how you perceive them is, then you realize you have the power to turn everything into a net positive.

As Marcus Aurelius said, "The impediment to action advances action. What stands in the way becomes the way." When even your obstacles become fuel for you to progress, then you no longer have any fear of what might happen. Everything can be turned into a positive. Everything is at your feet, ready to be used.

About the Author

Nate Johnson is a coach, writer, and speaker who's always down for an adventure. In a former life, he cut his teeth as a suicide prevention counselor and business development manager at *Inc. Magazine*. He is founder of a digital marketing company, whitewater rafting guide in New Zealand, and cattle rancher in the Australian Outback. Having survived a boating accident in the Philippines, Nate started several businesses and confronted his stage fright by taking improv classes. He is no stranger to the emotional highs and lows of pushing yourself to experience your fullest potential. Nate has a lovingly no-BS approach to helping his clients wake up to what's really possible in their lives and then making that a reality.

Email: nate@natejohnson.coach
Website: www.natejohnson.coach

CHAPTER 19
MINDSET SHAPES YOUR WEALTH LIFE

By Raj Kapur
Financial Expert, Wealth Mindset and John Maxwell Coach
Alexandria, Virginia

Your mindset shapes your wealth life.

Most people are not even aware of their wealth mindset. Their wealth mindset is many times set at a very low level, yet they keep on wondering why others are rich and wealthy, and why they are working hard but still struggling. This is generally due to the conditioning that they grow up with and the experiences which form their beliefs. Later, as adults, such people find themselves going through life without any conscious awareness of their mindset. Many people believe, as I used to, that it is only hard work that is the key to success.

I recall finding myself in a job and thinking my worth was more than what I was making, but not much more. At that time in my life, earning a salary of $100K was an alien idea that my mind could not even comprehend. I felt if I ever reached that level, I would have all the success I needed. To get more money, I worked harder and worked extra jobs, but they paid low wages.

Once I learned that my mindset was shaping my wealth life and that my subconscious mind was running my limiting beliefs on autopilot, I realized how I'd misunderstood wealth and my ability to attain it. The learning came about after I took an NLP (Neuro-Linguistic Programming) workshop. The interest became so strong that I learned NLP in depth and then went on to become a certified hypnotherapist to understand how the mind works.

Nowadays, there are hundreds of books and videos on these topics, but at that time, in the early 1990s, this information wasn't widely available. After being introduced to this awareness, I started my own businesses on the side, all the while working another job. Twenty-five years later, my business has generated over a million dollars, while I was also working the other job. Every step of the way, I've gained valuable knowledge, whether the step ended up successful or not.

Learning that my own beliefs were running me on autopilot was the first and foremost awareness that I needed. Once I became aware of that, then I knew I could make the changes needed to succeed in the way I wanted.

Are you aware of your beliefs that are running you on autopilot?

Many of my friends, colleagues, and clients have had this same problem in their own lives when it comes to money and wealth. Their sense of their worth comes from what they get paid in the company they work for or the business they are running. When they need or want to earn more, they work longer and harder to bring in a bit more. Everything is focused on working and getting that salary or those wages. It never occurs to them that there are other ways to generate wealth.

The conditioning sometimes is so strong that anything else seems like an impossibility. It is impossible to generate more wealth until you believe that you are worth more. You will generally get in life what you think you are worth, and your mindset determines that, whether you are aware or not.

Once you get this awareness, then you need to come out of the trance of the conditioning that has been running your life. Understanding that your beliefs are affecting your wealth mindset is of utmost importance.

To first understand this concept, consider the following. We know that objects in our environment are made of matter, a state in which they appear visible. We also observe that other conditions in our world are invisible. For example, you sow a seed, and soon enough, a small plant comes out of the earth, which later can form into a complete tree. Our bodies change in size as we grow, but we do not see the energy that makes them increase and grow.

We think, but we do not see our thoughts.

Consider music. If you take a radio and tune it to the right frequency, you can hear music. So, the music is always there, but until you are not tuned in to the right frequency, you cannot hear it. However, it is there.

The point—we live in a world which is visible, but also in an invisible world of forces and energies that will produce visible things. Understand, everything in this world has two existences: one begins in thought (invisible) and the other on the visible front.

The building you are in, the city you live in, the car you drive all began with a thought in someone's mind. Sometimes we can act on our thoughts quickly, but sometimes we have to wait until the conditions are favorable to have accomplished a thought. To bring the thought from the invisible—the idea of a car, for example—to the visible—a car itself, for example. No matter how we do something, first, we think of it. It starts with the thought; next, it manifests in the exterior world.

How does this apply to your achievement of great wealth? Your great wealth too must start with thoughts; next, it manifests in the exterior world. Your achievement of wealth won't happen from luck, from hard work, from anything outside yourself. It happens first by you thinking it. After that, the exterior manifestation occurs.

You need to program yourself with the right mindset (thoughts) for the attainment of wealth. Once you have the right beliefs established in your conscious and subconscious thoughts, you position yourself to manifest that wealth in the exterior world. You will then perform the right actions and will be on your way to successful wealth generation. Again, it all comes back to your thoughts leading the way to your attainment of wealth. The invisible first and then the visible.

Let us first take a deeper look into how your mindset and beliefs are developed. Think of the sort of role models you have had in your life. Have any financial role models taught you about money and wealth? What were you taught about money by your parents, teachers, society, friends? What experiences have you had with wealth, money, jobs, business, borrowing, lending? What is it that you are being taught about money now? The reason to find the answers to these questions is so you can determine any limiting beliefs around wealth attainment you have. You need clarity on what is limiting you.

Here are some common limiting beliefs that run people's financial lives by establishing a weak foundation for their wealth mindset:

- Money is the root of all evil.
- Money does not grow on trees.
- Money is difficult to make.

- ⌁ To attain wealth requires taking advantage of people.
- ⌁ I am not smart enough.
- ⌁ It is not spiritual or unethical to make money.
- ⌁ Love and relationships are more important than money.
- ⌁ Money causes rifts among families and groups.
- ⌁ Money can come and go, but education stays.
- ⌁ Investing is for professionals.
- ⌁ Little folk like me can't make any money.
- ⌁ I should not risk my money. Don't take risks.
- ⌁ I may become dishonest in the pursuit to make money.
- ⌁ It takes money to make money.
- ⌁ Money is limited.
- ⌁ More money means more problems.
- ⌁ I cannot make money loving what I do.
- ⌁ I just can't make money.
- ⌁ I'm not willing to pay the price to make money.

Are any of these limiting beliefs running you and setting up a weak foundation for your wealth mindset?

Reprogramming to Establish a Robust Wealth Mindset

Before we proceed, there is one question that I need to ask you—do you really, really want to be wealthy?

Before, like most people, you say yes, give it careful thought. A yes will require you to instill a new mindset, new habits, discipline, learning, and commitment. Believe me, it is all worth it, but it does require work. You see, without sacrifice, there is nothing gained.

Once you have identified your self-limiting beliefs and "wealth-wounds," next comes the part where you evaluate and start to work on making the changes towards a new you.

Remember, what we focus on consistently materializes, and if we are always having thoughts of lacking, then that is what gets materialized in our lives. What you need is to be free to make your own choices.

When you create goals, you tell your subconscious mind via your conscious mind that you desire more, that you are not satisfied with the current situation. Create goals that can take you out of your comfort zone and stretch you.

Ask yourself, "What is the abundance of wealth, and what does it mean to me?" To me, abundance is having all the wealth to enjoy my life, feel free, and not feel trapped working for someone. It means to have wealth to help others, have experiences that enhance the quality of my life, help family and friends, and give for the causes I believe in. So, what does the abundance of wealth mean to you? The reason it is important to specify this is that what you focus on expands. When you focus on the abundance, your mind gives you the reasons to be abundant. Everyone has different reasons to have wealth and money, so go in-depth and find those reasons which will catapult you in the direction of attracting wealth and money, and your subconscious will be primed to receive it.

Three Reprogramming Practices

A vision board, visualization, and affirmations are three practices to help you shift from unproductive mental habits to a powerful wealth mindset. These three practices are ones you can engage with actively, consciously, and regularly to establish new beliefs and thoughts in your subconscious and conscious. In order for these three practices to be effective in the manifestation of wealth in your life, you must first program your mind to assume that you already possess the wealth you desire. So again, it starts with the invisible via the thoughts in your mind, to transfer to the visible, which is the material world. For this, you act, talk, think, feel, and behave as if you are already wealthy. The subconscious mind cannot distinguish between an actual experience or an experience that is visualized using all the senses.

A vision board is a visualization tool that refers to a board of any sort used to build a collage of words and pictures that represent your lofty goals. It is a powerful tool to manifest your life's desires. It can work in all realms of your life, including wealth. You can create one on paper or even digitally, whatever works best for you. On your vision board put things that you want—your lofty goals—and quotes and pictures that motivate you to take action. Action is the key here. Keep the vision board in your sight, so it frequently reminds you of your lofty goals. Remember, you are already telling yourself when you construct the vision board that you already have all this wealth, so when you see the vision board in your daily life, you look at it to remind yourself that you already have all the wealth-related items it depicts.

In visualization practice, you will envision the wealth you desire as if you already have it and are experiencing it. Through the five senses, visualize objects, relationships, feelings, experiences, that all relate to you and your wealth-filled, abundant life. For example, when you envision yourself as a wealthy person, visualizing yourself driving a nice car is not enough. You need to use all your senses to make the experience real to your subconscious mind. Imagine the car by seeing it, feeling the seats, smelling their fine leather, hearing the car's throttle, feeling and hearing the wind, feeling the steering wheel, and such. The point is to make it as real as possible by using all your senses. By putting in detailed effort in your visualizing, you program your mindset from the perspective that you already have the wealth you desire.

By regularly visualizing yourself in highly articulated wealth scenarios, you supply your subconscious mind with images and descriptions of the wealth as if you already have it. In turn, you create new neural structures and thinking patterns in the brain. Accordingly, you start reacting to real-life situations in different ways. You start taking new actions, which lead to new results. This leads you to change your beliefs such that you'll see wealth possibilities for yourself that earlier seemed impossible. And you start seizing these opportunities so that, in time, your reality comes to manifest the wealth scenarios you've been visualizing.

Affirmations are also powerful at establishing a wealth mindset, and thus, a life of wealth. I recommend that twice a day you affirm what you want to be, first when you get up in the morning and second, before you retire to sleep. Doing this feeds your subconscious mind with what you want to become. Here's an affirmation I used for a long time: "Every day, in every respect, I get better and better."

When your beliefs start to change, your actions change, you change, your mindset changes, and you start on the road to becoming wealthy. Circumstances and people begin to show up in your life who catapult you towards success.

Please be sure this dream of wealth is your dream, your vision, not someone else's. You have to own it with your whole being in order for it to manifest from your vision board, visualization, and affirmation practices.

As stated before, many people struggle with money because they have not conditioned their mind towards the attainment of it. Many just wish for more money. Others simply work really hard and believe that hard work alone will one day pay off and lead to great wealth, but this hard work continues without the achievement of the pay-off.

Many people do not set a goal of exactly how much money they want in life. When you ask, most people will answer, they want "more." What is "more"? Upon further probing, it seems very clear that everyone wants more, but most do not have an idea of what and how much more. Specific details in your vision are important.

Most people are also not ready to do what it takes to get that specific greater amount of money. These people will always be wishing for more and envying the rich, but that's it. The point—you have to be crystal clear in what you want, and then you have to make it a burning desire. It cannot just be a vague, weak want or envy. "Riches do not respond to wishes. Riches only respond to definite plans, backed by definite desires, through constant persistence," stated Napoleon Hill in *Think and Grow Rich*.

Quick Review of the Wealth Mindset

The secret to building wealth is very simple: after having satisfied yourself that your desire is worthy, you fix that desire. To fix the desire, use your imagination to develop a well-defined picture and see it as if it is, in fact, true. You now envision yourself in that picture, doing exactly what you would be doing, thinking, saying, and feeling as a wealthy person. Hold this mental picture, use a vision board for help, and concentrate on making this image complete. See, feel, and hear yourself in the picture, use all your emotions to make it as real as possible. You need to make it so real that you can actually feel it. There is room for great creativity here. This is the reason we have an imagination.

To initiate change, start acting and behaving as if you have already obtained the financial success that you wish for. This will inspire you and help you move forward every single day. Once you have done this, you will need to have faith that the rest of the work will be taken care of by the "Universal Power."

First and foremost, know what you want. Be crystal clear and then move on it without any delay. As you implant the picture of your wealthy life in your unconscious mind, the external reality will follow.

About the Author

Raj Kapur is the founder and CEO of Options Ahead, Inc. He received his master's in business administration from Dowling College in Long Island, New York, and is an award-winning C-suite leader and certified executive and leadership coach. Raj has built, developed, and led large, globally competitive teams, providing them transformational coaching to maximize productivity, improve staff morale, and inculcate powerful leadership skills. He has experience in for-profit and non-profit sectors.

With over 25 years' experience and leadership wisdom backed by a toolkit of the world's best leadership resources and cutting-edge techniques and ideas, Raj has leveraged proven leadership methods to develop super leaders that transformed not only themselves and their teams, but also their entire organizations at various levels. Raj has led extensive workshops, seminars, coaching sessions, mastermind sessions, keynote engagements, and group and one-on-one coaching sessions. He has coached thousands of individuals during his career and created powerful instructional programs and courses.

Email: raj@rajkapur.com
Website: www.RajKapur.com

CHAPTER 20

BEING THE BAMBOO: OUR MODEL FOR THE SUCCESS MINDSET

By Christina Kashar
Corporate Executive Coaching Expert
Damascus, Syria

Success in your business and personal life is both science and art.

Different people measure success in a range of ways. But what's certain is that successful people have one thing in common: they've trained their minds to be goal achievers. At the core of reaching goals is your mindset.

Mindset is the primary catalyst driving your feelings of self-worth, competence, and confidence. In order to achieve success in almost every arena, it's vital to have the right mindset and strategy. It has a tremendous effect on your performance.

A person's mindset can be defined as "the set of beliefs a person has about themselves." There are two basic mindsets that control how most people see themselves—the fixed mindset and the growth mindset.

- *Fixed mindset*: those who believe that their intelligence and qualities are unchangeable attributes
- *Growth mindset*: those who believe that basic qualities, skills, and intelligence are things they can cultivate through effort and perseverance

The key to a growth mindset is the belief that you can develop your intelligence. Those with a growth mindset believe in progress, not perfection, and see challenge as an opportunity for learning and stretching themselves.

As an executive coaching expert who has coached more than 12 years in many business arenas, I regularly witness my audience's infatuation with success, especially when we share techniques, tools, and strategies for success. We often talk about the wowing success factor of grit. Grit helps us push away the desire to give up, especially when things get rough. Fortunately, we can learn grit and continually develop it over time.

Based on my direct experience, I'd like to share effective strategies and mental tools to help you, our valued readers, to grow your business, live a better life, and fuel your best self in order to elevate and develop your own positive mindsets.

Let's dig deeper and find out: what will it take to reach authentic success?

Growth Mindset: Grow Personally

Personal growth truly is the cornerstone of achieving success. The small actions you take on a daily basis can make success a series of small wins coupled with the big-picture changes you make long term. Growing yourself will set you on the path to true success, and you'll guarantee a better tomorrow.

You should always be looking for ways to improve yourself, leaving no stone unturned via your growth mindset. Here are some proven strategies for growing yourself:

- *Establish a vision of your success.*
  See yourself doing what others say you do best—and be productive applying your vision as talents and skills.

- *Develop powerful strategies.*
  With strategy, success has direction and goals. Set a strategic plan, support it with suitable tactics, scheduled activities, and outcomes that will help to assure its success. It'll be bullet-proof.

- *Focus on your strengths.*
  Build on your most powerful strengths and grow your weakest ones.

⇗ *Eliminate excuses.*
Stop excuses from reaching your dynamic mind.

⇗ *Challenge your mind.*
Try bold strategies that are completely outside your comfort zone. This guarantees mindset growth.

⇗ *Adopt flexible thinking patterns.*
This allows resilience to blossom. Flexible people don't see problems, they see opportunities for growth, challenges to embrace, and obstacles to overcome. Their confidence is driven by their ability to let go of the negativity that holds so many otherwise sensible people back.

⇗ *Set smarter goals.*
Identify what you want to truly change or achieve, and set goals that will get you there, especially a 12-month goal, whether it's getting a promotion, an academic achievement, writing a book, etc. Having a plan in place will help you succeed.

⇗ *Read two or three books each month.*
And discuss the books with others. Keep in mind that "readers are leaders, and leaders are readers."

⇗ *Enroll in online or live courses and trainings.*
This will stretch your mind's dimensions with new learning.

⇗ *Be very careful how you spend the first and last two hours of each day.*
Most people wake up reactively, adhering to the world's needs, not their own. In a world of unlimited communication, people don't disconnect from society to analyze their lives. Spend the first two hours of your day aligning your short-term efforts with your long-term goals. Take time to meditate and read, then spend an hour doing an intensive workout like circuit training. The last two hours of your day dictate your energy for the next day. Chill out, thank yourself for being the best version of yourself that day, and plan your next day.

Note to Self: Learn to work harder on yourself than at your job. Stay hungry for your personal development.

Focus on Reaching Your Happiest Self

What's the point of achieving any form of success if you aren't filled with joy and able to share it with others?

It takes effort and discipline to be continually happy. However, with the right mindset and behaviors, you can guarantee your happiness. Here's how:

- *Invest in authentic relationships.*
  One of the most important things you can do is make sure you have strong, healthy, and reliable personal relationships. Grow the ones you already have or focus on making new ones. Authentic relationships require an investment of time, energy, and effort, so select the right people to spend time with and enthusiastically invest in those relationships. They'll help you to reach your full potential. Be with people who inspire and rejuvenate you.

- *Practice healthy self-talk.*
  Regularly talk to yourself via encouraging affirmations. This is a mental vitamin pill to success. Avoid doubt and destructive criticism.

- *Calibrate your daily mood.*
  Regularly boost your daily mood through self-care, taking a 30-minute walk, and listening to new music.

- *Engage less with technology.*
  Give your mind space to think, analyze, and relax without the distraction of a laptop or smartphone. Try giving up technology for one hour before bed each night. Say no to unhealthy habits and addictions by tech-detoxing from time to time.

- *Don't get in your own way.*
  Three things that bring great people down are ego, fear, and greed. If you look back at the downfall of any leader throughout history,

you'll find they exhibited at least one of these traits, if not all of them. Sometimes your worst enemy is yourself. Successful people's mindsets know that fear is a choice. They become addicted to the euphoric feeling they get from conquering their own fears and become fearless.

⚜ *Make your time count.*
Instead of complaining about how things "could have" or "should have" been, a happy mindset reflects on everything it has to be grateful for. Then it finds the best solution available for a given issue, tackles the problem, and moves on. What if negativity comes from someone else? Successful people avoid it by setting limits and distancing themselves from it.

⚜ *Have fun and take care of others.*
Gratefully enjoy the things money can't buy and give back to your community and those in need. Regularly say thank you to the people who really deserve it. It makes the good days sweeter and the tough days easier.

> *Note to Self:* genuine happiness fuels and boosts the mindset to reach its optimum performance toward success.

Find Your Purpose

The world's happiest people own a strong sense of purpose. Whether it comes from their work, their role as a parent, or even their hobby, they are happier because they have a purpose in life. It acts as their driving force and gives them momentum to keep going.

If you don't feel like you already have a strong sense of purpose, that's okay. It's not that hard to find one. Eager to find your purpose or grow it? Here are my guidelines:

⚜ *Do what you love.*
When you let passion drive your acts by doing what you love instead of doing what others think you should do, then you align yourself with purpose, and success will knock on your doors.

☞ *Changing things up is healthy.*
If you feel like nothing in your life gives you the purpose you're looking for, take time to ask yourself what would. Switching careers? Volunteering for a noble cause? Taking care of a pet? Engaging in a new spiritual practice? Changing up how you spend your weekends or whom you most often engage with?

☞ *Get back to the basics.*
Many of our priorities get misguided when life gets too busy or hectic. Reorder your priorities by asking yourself what matters. What makes you feel the most fulfilled and alive?

☞ *Prioritize your commitments.*
It's hard to have a purpose when you have tons of things going on. Try to streamline your activities and commitments so that the most important things are front and center.

☞ *Seize the present moment.*
Live in the present by engaging it in all its dimensions.

> *Note to Self:* truly embrace your purpose and bond
> with it. Refine, polish, and radiate it.

Be Serious About Your Mental and Physical Well-Being

Health is about more than just our physical state of being. It's about what's on the inside too. Mental health is just as important as physical health. Think beyond that health is solely about eating fruits and veggies, sleeping seven to nine hours a night, working out several days a week, and taking steps to keep the body in tip-top shape. Aim to take care of both your physical and mental health because both must be robust in order to achieve the success you long for.

Take care of your brain. Exercise your brain, feed it, nurture it, as you do the body in order to prep it and keep it ready for being the container for your success mindset. Being mentally sharp is one of the most important components of being as successful as possible. Regularly challenge yourself by learning about new topics through reading or online videos. Success begins as a state of mind!

> *Note to Self:* Make your overall health, physical and mental, a priority, and take even better care of yourself.

Bamboo Tree—A Story

I would like to share the "Bamboo Tree" story, which is built into my mindset. It teaches us success lessons on perseverance, growth, and development—all of which we must engage with in order for the strategies and effective habits I've suggested in this chapter to come into effect for us and our success mindset. Here's the story:

> *Like any plant, growth of the Chinese bamboo tree requires nurturing—water, fertile soil, sunshine. In its first year, we see no visible signs of activity. In the second year, again, no growth above the soil. The third, the fourth, still nothing. Our patience is tested, and we begin to wonder if our efforts of caring and watering will ever be rewarded.*
>
> *Finally, in the fifth year, we experience growth. The Chinese bamboo tree grows 80 feet in just six weeks.*

The real question here is: does the Chinese bamboo tree really grow 80 feet in six weeks? Was the Chinese bamboo tree lying dormant for four years only to grow exponentially in the fifth? Or, was the little tree growing underground, developing a root system strong enough to support its potential for outward growth in the fifth year and beyond? The answer is, of course, the latter. Had the tree not developed a strong, unseen foundation, it could not have sustained itself as it grew so quickly. The same principle is true for people. People who patiently toil towards worthwhile goals, building strong character while overcoming adversity and challenge, grow the strong internal foundation to cultivate and handle success. Keep this in mind when engaging with the recommendations I've shared in this chapter.

The Chinese bamboo tree is a perfect parable to our own experience with personal growth and change, whether we are working on ourselves or coaching others. At the start, it may be slow to show any progress. It's frustrating and unrewarding at times. But it is so worth it … especially if we can be patient and persistent.

To bring it all together—your success is driven by your mindset. If you master your mindset and follow some of the simple tips in this chapter with regular and fierce persistence, you will make possible your present and future success. Your outward growth will be astonishing, just as happened with the Chinese bamboo tree.

Finally, I strongly advise you to write down all the "Notes to Self" given in this chapter and place them where you'll see them daily. You could even discuss them with others. Having these reminders enter your thoughts daily will open you to many aha moments that just might bring you closer and closer to success.

Wishing you a fruitful success journey.

About the Author

Christina Kashar is an executive coaching expert, certified in leadership and management capacities development. She is certified by Marshall Goldsmith Executive Coaching Academy (2020), a Master Trainer by iTOL England (2018), an Accredited National Trainer by the Ministry of Administrative Development (2016), and a Trainer by the European Union SEBC (2010).

Christina's mission statement is this: "To be the change maker in business and personal lives of enough people to contribute to the effective development inside and outside Syria."

During the past 12 years, Christina has coached over 190 companies, ministries, universities, INGOs, and business leaders in the Syrian and Lebanese markets. She lectured on "Personal Development Skills" for two years at Damascus University. She has been awarded three international "Creativity in Business—Thinking Out of the Box" awards received in Austria, Tunisia, and Egypt. The Syrian magazine *Aliqtisadi* chose Christina as one of its "Syrian Iron Women" in 2011. Christina was the first Arabian mentioned in "Blue Ocean Strategy," a success stories website, along with other international success leaders like Anthony Robbins.

LinkedIn: https://www.linkedin.com/in/coachchristinakashar

CHAPTER 21

SUSTAINING EXTREME SUCCESS: MINDSET MATTERS FOR PEAK PERFORMANCE

By David Krueger, M.D.
Executive Mentor Coach, CEO, MentorPath®
Houston, Texas

To travel hopefully is a better thing than to arrive.
—Robert Louis Stevenson

Success Anticlimax

The morning after Bruce Jenner's last decathlon, he asked, "What am I going to do now?"

Olympic gold medalist Victoria Pendleton offered a slightly more elaborate comment on the same dynamic: "People think it's hard when you lose. But it's almost easier to come in second because you have something to aim for when you finish. When you win, you suddenly feel lost."

After a long-practiced and anticipated success, people often have to deal with a significant anticlimax experience. The body's sprint system of anticipation is mediated by dopamine, the pleasure chemical, which can sustain the excitement of expectation to anticipate a positive consequence. This can last, as we know from various performers, for years or even decades.

For any physical or intellectual achievement, upon its successful completion we must also address the emotional role and creative closure. I have known a number of authors who describe a letdown after completion of their book. One even described it as postpartum depression. The most successful achievers have evolved their capacities to recover faster from success anticlimax.

What makes super-achievers in sports, arts, or business so relentless in their successes?

> *It's about squeezing every last ounce of juice out*
> *of this life. We'll celebrate some things, but we'll very,*
> *very quickly move on to what's next.*
> —Andrew Garfield

Relentless super-achievers have something far simpler than genes, training, education, and internal drive. The most successful achievers have evolved their capacities to recover faster from success anticlimax. The athletes and executives I have worked with and others whom I have interviewed have learned how to contend with the anticlimax of shifting from stimulating anticipation to sustaining maintenance by returning to a system that reframes anticipation in an effective way.

Matthew Syed, a former Olympian and author of *Bounce*, finds that relentlessness is in part an evolved capacity to deal with anticlimax faster and more effectively, to emotionally disengage from a long-sought goal, and to refocus more quickly on new endeavors. This attitude was succinctly summarized by Manchester United Soccer Club manager Sir Alex Ferguson, who in only a few minutes after holding up a record ninth Premier League soccer trophy said, "I'm already looking forward to next season. Let's get on with it. I'm looking forward to going on to win a European trophy as well as pushing for the league." And the next year they did.

Nick Saban, head football coach at the University of Alabama, consistently tells his players to not think about championships and wins, but about the preparation and the performance of the process itself each day in practice.

The Summit Syndrome

There are a lot of people in the world who will take the challenge to climb the mountain. They don't just climb it but aim to be the first one up, the fastest one up, the first one up a particular route. But when you get to the top of the mountain and achieve that "first one ever" goal, you then become the mountain because everybody's shooting at you. Everyone is aiming to beat your "first one ever" achievement. The great ones can get to the top of the mountain first and say:

> *You know what, I can be even better.*
> —Belichick and Saban, *HBO Sports*

Those supercharged and successful performers who consistently acquire new knowledge and evolve new skills surpass even their own previous benchmarks of excellence. They push their own limits to expand beyond what was expected, at times beyond their own vision. Their identity becomes consolidated around challenge, resilience, and success performance. Their brains have become habituated to the consistent excitement and pleasure of anticipating what is next. Then achieving it, to again ask what is next.

As paradoxical as it may seem, the greatest challenge can come immediately after the completion of a long-anticipated accomplishment, especially at the end of a career of such accomplishments. What it takes to climb the mountain (phase 1) is a different mind-set and neurochemical system from what's required to maintain a position at the top of the mountain (phase 2). And that is also different from what it takes to have a happy and purposeful life after you come off the mountain (phase 3). Different mindsets and different neurochemical systems are involved in each of these three phases.

Someone can become habituated to the unique experience of mind, body, and neurochemistry in any one of these developmental phases. To continue improving performance and to keep dopamine and adrenaline flowing, one must continue to look for ever-ascending possibilities of success or frame continuing success in a different way. Super-achievers who realize significant success after a long engagement and often exclusive focus on achievement (phase 1) then have to make a significant transition in order to not continue searching for the same stimulation.

George Parsons and Richard Pascale offer an interesting perspective to my research and work on success anticlimax for performers. They described the corporate equivalent of this process in *Harvard Business Review*. Their application in a corporate setting outlines how "steps taken at the right time not only can allow extreme overachievers to surmount the summit syndrome but can also deepen their capacity to lead."

Throughout the process of deliberate practice and accumulating successes, the player has generated a heightened appetite for stimulation. Unless this is planned strategically and specifically for what to do next, this can lead to a vulnerability to various stimulating substitutes, including drugs, risky investments, and exciting but bad relationships. Often, the peak of career success when someone is feeling most invulnerable is the very time that they are, in practical terms, most vulnerable. Especially if, at that time, they attempt to recapture or replicate the stimulation in alternate ways.

At this point, internal and external may not match. External metrics of immense success may be in contradistinction to becoming habituated to such stimulation, to wondering about what's next, to being confused about how to sustain the achievement excitement.

This process is prominent in professional athletes after the sudden achievement of a lifelong goal, as in the example of Bruce Jenner, or equally at the end of their career, after injury or retirement. Throughout, self-regulation challenges are in the foreground, ranging from the continued stimulation of "what's next?" to how to sustain the excitement after arriving at the summit of the mountain.

Challenge is diminished or negated if the outcome is certain. This takes away the stimulation of the dopamine-mediated stimulation to attend and continue to pursue an outcome. Think about the major successes you have achieved, probably with sustained immersion and dedication and with the outcome not determined until the very end. Throughout you had sustained engagement of the questions, "What happens next?" and "What do I next need to do?" Think about how differently this may be experienced if you knew that everyone who participated would get the same trophy or the same reward of whatever nature. This is not the way the mind and brain work.

After a significant achievement and the continued stimulation of new challenges and endeavors, reaching the summit of success can potentially have the paradoxical effect of diminishing a passionate edge. The buzz seems to be missing. The continued dopamine stimulation of "what's next?" is no longer there because all the next challenges and opportunities have been achieved.

With no new stimulation and challenge, the edge can morph into boredom and lack of stimulating motivation. Common questions may be "Did I lose my edge?" and "What is left to achieve?" Is this reaching a limit or simply feeling stuck at a plateau? The novelty, challenge, and looking to the next achievement during all the stages leading to the successful attainment are no longer there. Or, at least, they have to be successfully reframed to sustain the evolution of even further skill, challenge, and success. The summit syndrome has to be reframed to a different paradigm of sustaining and enhancing achievement.

Very different from burnout and the depletion of intolerable workloads, this experience simply means that the framework of novelty and the challenge of climbing the mountain needs to be reframed to sustain passion and interest in staying at the top and even exceeding former visions and definitions of successful attainment.

Rather than a plateau, this experience can be a signal to look for access to the next level of achievement and reframe interest and focus to a new level of performance. Knowing that the brain craves novelty, in your reframing of the next challenge and the next level you need to consider what was not previously envisioned.

Transformational Mentor Coaching

The mentor coach as a catalyst empowers others to produce extraordinary outcomes. For each individual player and for the team, this ongoing striving for and achieving of excellence is an ultimate purpose and outcome. Transformational mentor coaches look beyond attaining immediate goals to shaping larger strategies and visions for establishing continuously evolving performance benchmarks.

A successful performance achievement profile is not a single straight line to peak success but a process of continued practice and performance. It includes ups and downs. It especially takes into account how to sustain and enhance success once it is reached, especially when it is beyond what either the player or mentor coach has envisioned.

Often the player does not recognize—or even have reason to reflect on— different stages of the performance trajectory/career or understand the entire process in terms of developmental stages. Their winning formula that works on the ascent of the mountain becomes an outdated game plan and even a handicap once they're at the top. A different system and a different identity are required, and this is its own system of work.

Self-regulation can be a challenge for someone such as a very young athlete who is suddenly paid millions to tens of millions of dollars without having the experience of gradually adjusting to increasing monies, especially when this instantly transports the athlete from life experiences of low income or poverty.

When anyone engages a task or position that moves them beyond a core identity, discomfort and uncertainty lead the way. There is no core bedrock foundation of identity in a new social and economic framework.

More than 80 percent of lottery winners of $3 million or more declare bankruptcy within the first five years. Why? Their money changed, but their mindset did not.

How Can a Sense of Purpose Sustain Success?

Like talent, purpose is not inherent or even discovered, but cultivated. Passion, purpose, and talent need deliberate effort and practice to develop.

A number of research findings reveal an optimistic picture in which individuals with a strong sense of purpose are more willing to take risks, persist, and have a significantly higher degree of successful outcomes, whatever area of performance they choose. Those with a higher sense of purpose are grittier and more persistent in Angela Duckworth's classic study of 16 thousand participants.

It is important—imperative—for a team to have a shared purpose to unite players, so they can achieve individual and collective optimum performance. Many studies of exceptional performance find that the exceptional performer can catalyze teammates to excel. The star performer can be either a distraction or a motivator for excellence. Exceptional immunologists boosted their colleagues' research productivity by 35 percent; the most outstanding 6 percent of physicists led research teams that generated 50 percent of all physics papers published. Wharton School of Business Professor Adam Grant has shown in his research that when people see how their work affects others and have a shared purpose, they work better, harder, longer, more generously, and more productively.

To make purpose come alive, the mentor coach must engage players to understand how their efforts make a difference and how their efforts make a difference for each other and for the greater good of the team. Motivation is enhanced by an appreciation of how each individual's work benefits the well-being of others on the team.

How Can Extreme Success Be Maintained?

The toughest thing about success is that
you got to keep on being a success.
—Irving Berlin

Althea Gibson, winner of 11 major tennis titles and the first African American to be named "Female Athlete of the Year" said very simply, "Most of us who aspire to be tops in our field don't really consider the amount of work required to stay tops." The relentless, grueling, repetitive work of deliberate practice is essential, and it is no less grueling and deliberate to sustain and even expand that success, especially when it reaches remarkable levels.

A specific challenge for those who achieve extreme success is to figure out a way to stay passionate about the pursuit of excellence, rather than simply enjoying the fruits of success. The systematic approach to climbing a mountain cannot be abandoned when reaching the top, yet it must be transformed to continue excellence on top of that mountain.

The challenge is twofold: to continue to sustain the passion of growth and the pursuit of greater excellence, as well as dealing with the specific and unique challenges of success.

Elite performers are not distracted by victories or failures of themselves or others. They concentrate on what they can be effective in determining and let go of everything else. They focus exclusively on the task at hand, the flow of the performance endeavor. This exclusive focus, a type of compartmentalization, fuels resilient practice and sustained peak performance.

Elite performers actually love the pressure and feel immersed in the process and the energy of full engagement.

Elite performers in business, sports, and the arts often are equally passionate about their hobbies. Richard Branson is as passionate about his hot air balloon adventures as he is his primary business. J.J. Watt became consumed in the offseason in helping Harvey flood victims in Houston with a passion equal to his defensive all-pro prowess.

Similarly, the ability to rebound from defeat comes from this intense focus and passion on aspirations and to long-term goals. Small achievements pave the way and provide ongoing incentive in the ever-present and the necessary experience of effectiveness, step by step.

Teams and companies continually push one another to elite performance in ways they would never achieve if they were working alone or with less-accomplished colleagues.

Elite new performers in every domain maintain an insatiable appetite for feedback to use in deliberate practice and performance. They seek advice. They want to improve development and progress. They celebrate their accomplishments. This celebration along the way is more than reward, more than emotional release, but involves continued analysis with enhanced awareness and ever-continuing deliberate practice. A constant dialectic can balance celebration with continued striving and accomplishment. Getting to the next level of performance becomes the purpose of celebration. Celebrations become meaningless with consistent elite performance and victories.

About the Author

David Krueger, M.D. is an executive mentor coach, and CEO of MentorPath®, an executive coaching, training, publishing, and wellness firm. His work integrates psychology and neuroscience with strategic coaching to help professionals achieve and sustain peak performance.

David is the author of 24 trade and professional books on success, wellness, money, and self-development, and 75 scientific papers. His book, *The Secret Language of Money* (McGraw Hill) is a business bestseller translated into 10 languages. David's 2019 book releases include:

- *Engaging in the Ineffable: Toward Mindfulness and Meaning* (Paragon House)
- *Your New Money Story: The Beliefs, Behaviors, and Brain Science to Rewire for Wealth* (Rowman & Littlefield, New York/London)

A mentor/trainer coach and Dean of Faculty for Coach Training Alliance, David has been quoted in *Money, Fortune, Forbes, Town and Country*, the

New York Times, and the *Wall Street Journal*, and was elected to the American Society of Journalists and Authors. Founder and director of his own licensed, specialty-certified *New Life Story*® *Wellness Coaching*, and *New Money Story*® *Mentor Training*, David has trained professionals worldwide and develops internal mentor programs for corporations.

Email: dkrueger@mentorpath.com
Website: www.MentorPath.com

CHAPTER 22

UNSHAKABLE SELF-CONFIDENCE: THE KEY TO SUCCESS AND HAPPINESS

By Dr. Stem Sithembile Mahlatini
Motivational Speaker, Coach, Counselor
Orlando, Florida

There are only two ways to live your life. One is as though nothing is a miracle. The other is as though everything is a miracle.
—Albert Einstein

My struggle to get out of my own way has been my greatest teacher to finding my true self, hence true self-confidence. To understand the reason why I now know that self-confidence is the key mindset to a successful and happy life, you have to understand my journey.

When I first arrived in the USA in 1986 from Zimbabwe, I worked in a nursing home as a nursing assistant for six years. Boy did I hurt my back, which, to this day, continues to bother me when I sit or stand for too long.

After two years of working full-time and going to school for computer science in the evenings, I met a family that was bringing their mother, "Ms. Mary," into the nursing home. Ms. Mary was crying, yelling, and screaming, asking why they were not able to care for her at her home, why she had to be in a home and how her children were not appreciative of all that she had done for them.

I then wheeled Ms. Mary to a private room where I proceeded to talk to her and calm her down. I spoke to her adult children, assuring them that we would take care of their mother and she would be alright. I spoke to them until the charge nurse ordered me to go back to my assigned work. It was heart-wrenching for me to leave this group, but I noticed Ms. Mary had stopped crying and the family was talking without yelling when I left. I made it a point to stop in to see her every day to check that Ms. Mary was doing okay. I was just doing my job. Little did I know I was on a path to finding my authentic self.

One day, I stopped by and Ms. Mary asked me what I was doing in school, as she knew I was also going to school. I informed her that I was pursuing a computer science degree. Shaking her head in disagreement, she said, "You are not a computer person, you are a social worker." I did not know what a social worker was, so I asked. She explained that the way I had spoken to her and her family when they came, reassuring them and following through with making sure she was alright was exactly what social workers did. She told me I was so at ease with talking to her and the family, that it was very natural and, therefore, something I did well.

On my part, I did not know I could get paid to talk to people. I did not know that talking to her made that big of an impact on her and her family. That very moment, I saw the revelation and found myself. I was excited. It was the very moment that the bulb came on that I can do what I love, that is—help others live their best life, through counseling, coaching, motivational speaking, radio and television, and, yes, through books.

Ms. Mary told me to speak to the nursing home social worker whom I had admired for a long time. All I'd known was there was a lady who always came in with families showing them around, but what I'd liked the most about her was the way she dressed in suits and heels all the time. I hadn't known the nature of her work, and I was exhilarated that I could be like her and, hey, wear suits like her!

The next day after speaking to the social worker, I was discouraged. She was very negative and told me it was difficult to get into any graduate programs without experience. She especially said in no uncertain terms that it was difficult to get into the Boston University (BU) program that she had graduated from. I remember feeling so worthless, so dejected, and at the same time infuriated.

I resolved to prove this lady wrong. How dare she insinuate that I was not good enough to enter Boston University. How dare she think she was better than me and only she was good enough to be a BU graduate. I recall very vividly that I abruptly returned to Ms. Mary to tell her, "Guess where I'm going to graduate from? Boston University." I knew that it was possible to get into Boston University if other people were able to enter the program. Funny how we all have that inner belief and knowing, that "I can do it" that becomes the fuel to help us light our light to the world.

I have always believed that there is more in me than meets the eye. However, getting to that place where I could completely let my hair down and know that I have done it was somewhat evasive. That's been difficult for me. The one thing I did, and do even now, is to keep my options open to miracles unfolding every day and every moment. I know that somewhere somehow, I will meet or learn something that will enhance my personal and professional being.

So, yes, I was accepted and graduated from Boston University with my master's degree in social work. Next, I went on to do my doctorate in education at Nova South Eastern University. Sometimes confidence is looking back and seeing how confident we have been in our life without realizing that it's been confidence that's gotten us so far.

While some might think that earning a degree is all you need to be happy and successful, unfortunately, that is not true. Once I finished my schooling, I started a private practice in Boston, where I provided counseling services for individuals, families, and couples. I did okay, not as well as I'd envisioned for myself. I could not understand what was holding me back. There was always a reason why I was not getting as many clients or making as much money.

However, I recall providing business and life coaching to women who, in turn, created businesses, seminars, and conferences that are thriving today because of the guidance I provided them. Why then was that same advice I gave others not working for me?

The answer: I was self-sabotaging myself.

How? I was not confident in myself. I did not believe I was good enough. It is amazing how sometimes we struggle to find ways to become better and do more in our life and businesses, and yet the answer is right within us—confidence.

I remember, I had conflicting inner voices. One said, "Yes, you can do this," and one said, "But is it good enough?" I believe we all have inner voices we grapple with every day. While our loving inner voice can help us dig deeper into who we truly are, it is also our critical inner voice that speaks to us and lets us down in so many ways. Louise L. Hay observed, "You have been criticizing yourself for years and it hasn't worked. Try approving of yourself and see what happens."

I have to say, the loving inner voice that was saying, "You can do this," has always been louder and more consistent than the fearful one.

If you are suffering from lack of confidence or low self-esteem, then there is a high probability that your inner critic has been speaking to you a lot. Thus, you need to talk back to it. I encourage you to question your inner critic and ask yourself why you think you are a failure or why you can't.

Every time your inner critic throws you a harsh comment about yourself, question it. Look for an answer, and you will notice that there is nothing to feel bad or negative about. You possess inner confidence that is ready to serve you each time you pause to give yourself a chance, no matter what you are facing.

Becoming Confident, Unstoppable and Fearless

Self-confidence is key.

As I said earlier, my biggest problem has been my own self-sabotaging thoughts, which affect my confidence to be my best. Building confidence is a journey that requires patience. Yes, it requires patience. Practicing patience is something I can honestly say has taken me forever to learn. My resistance to being patient and to allowing myself to be open to life cost me a lot of painful years. I realize how insecure I was, how much low self-worth I felt, and how much I undermined my ability to learn and do anything I put my mind to. Why did this happen?

Looking back, I see I was an insecure child, always feeling like others shunned me because I somehow appeared a threat to them. In primary school, at Kurai and Wadzanai in Kambuzuma, Zimbabwe, I was teased, bullied, and shunned by girls whom I thought of as, or maybe wanted to call, my friends. I tried to fit in so much, and as a result I found myself minimizing my abilities in order to fit in and prove that I was not a threat. It is only now that I know for sure, as Oprah Winfrey would put it, that "Others saw the light and greatness in me before I did, and they wanted no part of my greatness."

Until now, I hadn't known that my light had been shining way before I knew what I wanted to do in college, let alone in life. In life, you will meet people who will tease you, mock you for being smart, for no reason, for being beautiful, for being cheerful, quiet, smart, or cute—you name it. Know that they are unknowingly helping you to blossom, shaping you into exactly who you were meant to be. In my language we say, "Vanokupa shungu"—the isolation and mockery drive you to do better and be better. It is helping you to be more confident in your abilities because there is something about you that is intimidating to someone, without you saying a word. Step out, do your best, and become your best anyway.

You have to understand that you are on this earth for a reason, that there is a purpose for you, and that no matter what, you can and will be somebody if you learn to love yourself and prepare yourself for greatness. It is important to apply your energy to learning more about what you love, what you want to become, and what kind of person would be ideal for you to be. You are your number one cheerleader before the world.

The one reason why most people are not pursuing their dreams is lack of self-esteem and self-confidence. The reason why those who have all the degrees but hold back from doing more is also a lack of self-confidence and self-esteem. I have noticed many people question their self-confidence and ability to thrive during many of life's phases: teenage years, twenties, thirties, forties, fifties, sixties, and even nineties. It does not matter which phase you are in; it is possible to find new confidence in yourself, deeper strength, and new ways of doing what you love and getting paid for it.

I have had to take responsibility for what I have done with this beautiful gift I have, the gift called life. Every day that I wake up breathing, talking, walking, eating, and hearing, I owe it to myself to give it my all and become unstoppable, free, and fearless. That means being fearless, believing in myself, in all that I love doing, believing that I am making a difference even if it is with one person. I go easy on myself and listen more to my loving and kind inner voice. I love myself, I cheer me on, and I encourage myself more.

My biggest lesson has been to never allow someone else's behavior or thoughts of me make my day, or life, unbearable. Whenever there is an unimaginable hurdle in front of us, we just have to remember that confidence and being fearless is what is going to pull us through.

Adjusting to the New Normal with Unshakable Confidence

There are a few lessons I would like to share with you from my experience of becoming more confident, free, and fearless. Confidence is contagious. Courage is contagious. The company you keep and the thoughts you think will be your number one tools to building a confident mindset for success and happiness. Here are my best tips to boosting an unshakable self-confidence:

- Believing in yourself is the first and most important tip. You are unique and different for a reason, believe in you.
- You may have to take a detour on the way to your dream, but if you remain true to yourself, the time will come when you emerge and become something bigger.
- It is important for you to work through any trauma, self-limiting beliefs, or self-sabotaging beliefs with a professional so that you can be completely open to your true self.
- Though the journey may be painful and challenging at times, remain fearless. It's okay to feel the fear sometimes, but don't let that fear outweigh your courage. Allow courage more than your fear to roar and rule most of the time.
- If it means having to do small odd jobs on the way to your dream life, by all means do it because it is all worth it and it all adds towards sharpening your skills and success in the end.
- Be like that deaf frog from the inspiring motivational story who broke barriers because it couldn't hear the shouts from the crowd that what it was doing could not be done. In the end, the frog did the impossible and climbed the highest mountain and won! Sometimes we have to be deaf to the labels of impossibility that society puts on us. Tell yourself, "Yes, I can," even if you are the only one that believes in you.
- If you ask somebody for help and they don't help you, move on to the next person. Don't hold it against them or be resentful towards them because whoever is destined to help you, will help you. Sometimes, the lack of help from others is actually the help you need to push yourself.
- What the mind can conceive and believe, it can achieve. Practice the habit of writing down your dreams and believing that you certainly can make them happen. I believe in vision boards, they come to life.

- Never underestimate simple conversations you have with people. Therein lies your miracle. Mahatma Gandhi said it best, "Your beliefs become your thoughts, your thoughts become your words, your words become your actions, your actions become your habits, your habits become your values and your values become your destiny."

- Always find a person you can dream with—someone who can believe in you and be your cheerleader. It can be a friend, colleague, relative, peer, or mentor. Writing this chapter was made possible with my new friend and colleague Erik Seversen who found me on LinkedIn. Stay open, miracles unfold every day.

- Be happy, smile, and laugh for no reason at all.

- Never settle for anything you know is beneath your worth. Know your worth. Never let go of your self-respect no matter what! If you feel you deserve more, ask for it, or walk away and knock elsewhere. The right door will open. It always opens.

- Do not give up just because you hear the word no or because it takes longer to get to your desired dream. Embrace it because no, N-O, simply means—next opportunity. Every dream unfolds in the appointed time. Stay confident, believe, and keep working at your dream.

Believe you can and you're halfway there.
—Theodore Roosevelt

I am reminded of a quote by Marianne Williamson that now makes sense in my life:

Our deepest fear is not that we are inadequate. Our deepest fear is that we are powerful beyond measure. It is our light, not our darkness that most frightens us. We ask ourselves, who am I to be brilliant, gorgeous, talented, fabulous? Actually, who are you not to be? You are a child of God. Your playing small does not serve the world. There is nothing enlightened about shrinking so that other people won't feel insecure around you. We are all meant to shine, as children do. We were born to make manifest the glory of God that is within us. It's not just in some of us; it's in everyone. And as we let our own light shine, we unconsciously give other people permission to do the same. As we are liberated from our own fear, our presence automatically liberates others.

I meditated on this quote many a day to get my confidence and courage to go on. This quote has become a lifeline. I hope that you too can be encouraged by my story to go after all your dreams and become successful and happy in everything you do.

About the Author

Originally from Zimbabwe, Dr. Stem Sithembile Mahlatini is a confidence coach, president and owner of Global Counseling and Coaching Services, Inc., and founder of The Empowerment Academy, an online platform with life success programs, workshops, seminars, and books. Her mission is to inspire, empower, and educate others to live stress-free, successful lives through her speaking engagements, books, seminars, workshops, counseling, and coaching services. In addition, she hosts The Dr. Stem Show Radio, Television, and Podcast, which is an educational, empowerment, and encouragement show. You can find her shows on YouTube and all podcast platforms.

Drawing on her background as a licensed psychotherapist, Dr. Stem offers people practical advice on how to tap into their limitless power to change their lives, overcome roadblocks, and aspire to be better than the circumstances that surround them. For businesses, she provides cutting-edge training and coaching programs to help business leaders and employees break through personal and environmental barriers to maximize their success in all areas of their lives. Her lifelong goal is to continue to help others build unshakable confidence to be winners at home, work, and business. Her motto is "Each day is an opportunity to become more confident, successful, and happy."

www.drstemacademy.com
www.drstemmie.com
www.drstemspeaks.com

CHAPTER 23

YOGA AND NEUROSCIENCE TO ACHIEVE SUCCESS

By Claire Morton
Yoga Teacher, NLP Coach
Liverpool, United Kingdom

Realise deeply that the present moment is all you ever have.
—Eckhart Tolle

Your state of mind determines how you experience your life. It is your state of mind that allows you success or regret; satisfaction or longing; presence or distraction. In order to optimally develop your state of mind, thus your life, you must get past the screen of your analytical mind and into the operating centre of your subconscious mind. For it is in the subconscious that your habits, behaviors, beliefs—positive and negative—lie. The question then is—how do you access the subconscious?

In this chapter, we're going to look at how yoga allows you to harness and ignite the positives that lie in your subconscious mind, so you can activate a success mindset. Yoga entails much more than engaging a series of physical postures and stretches. Yoga is much deeper than a fitness class for the physical body; it's a way of life.

First I'll give a brief overview of the many facets of yoga to show how it is more than a physical stretching practice. For the purposes of igniting a successful mindset, we'll then concentrate on these two aspects of yoga: meditation (known as Dhyana) and breath control (known as Pranayama).

What Is Yoga?

There are many myths around yoga that I've heard over the years, some have some merit, but some are quite humorous. Here are some of the comments I have heard from my students, friends, and family:

- ☞ *I don't have the time to practice.*
- ☞ *I'm not flexible or bendy.*
- ☞ *I can't clear my mind.*
- ☞ *I'm not religious.*

As already stated, yoga is much more than physical fitness and stretching. It is much more than yoga pants and mats. It is a way of life. To put it simply, the meaning of yoga is the union of body and mind, being with "the self" or "at one with the universe". The purpose of practising yoga is to realise that you are not the body. The goal of yoga is transcendental, beyond the body and the mind.

> *Yoga is not to be performed. Yoga is to be loved. Yoga does not care what you have been. Yoga cares about the person you are becoming. Yoga is designed for a vast and profound purpose. And for it to be truly called yoga, its essence must be truly embodied.*
> —Aadil Palkhivala

Yoga, which is over ten thousand years old, is a science that originated in India developed from the Tantric civilisation. The first written scriptures originate from the ancient Tantras and after those, the Vedas. One of the four main paths of yoga is Raja Yoga from Sage Patanjali. It became the first definitive and diverse system of yoga. It is also known as Ashtanga Yoga, which is made up of the eight limbs. The ultimate goal for Ashtanga Yoga is liberation. In a ladder-like formation, it moves from obvious and accessible to elevated and spiritual. In Patanjali Yoga Sutras, chapter two, verse 29, the eight limbs are identified as:

☞ *Yamas* and *Niyamas*

At the base of the eight-limbed yogic path are the Yamas and the Niyamas, a series of rules for right living. These cover the basic skills and values needed to prosper in the world. A great read for these purposeful living tools that I recommend is Deborah Adele's *The Yamas and Niyamas—Exploring Yoga's Ethical Practice.*

☞ *Asanas*

These are the steady, comfortable postures for health and meditation, working with the physical body to strengthen, stretch, and tone. With asana practice, the student learns to train the inner body and mind gracefully. Most yoga classes in the Western world practice this aspect of yoga.

☞ *Pranayama*

Prana is the vital life force energy that flows both through the individual and the universe. Pranayama is the control of this vital life force energy, i.e., breathing techniques. We'll be looking more at Pranayama later in the chapter.

☞ *Pratyahara*

This means the detachment from the senses and thoughts, a natural progression from practising pranayama. The mind turns within, and freedom from attachment is achieved.

☞ *Dharana*

This is one-pointedness concentration. The practise of focusing on one object or on one place to eliminate the mind's fluctuations. This can be something as simple as a candle flame, a spot on a wall, or chanting a mantra.

☞ *Dhyana*

This is the continuous flow of perception, i.e., meditation. It takes the aspiring student towards a more spiritual space: deep meditation.

Here the student has learned how to use breath, how to detach, and how to focus the mind. In this space of deep meditation, the student can seek and realise the truth. Because this practice helps us to access the subconscious mind, we'll look at it more closely in this chapter.

↳ *Samadhi*
This is the final limb of Patanjali's teachings. Samadhi is the state of complete and integrated consciousness, in which the yogi is able to free themselves from all that they are attached to and reach a place where they merge with the divine. The divine can also be known as any of the soul, spirit, god, the mind, the self, consciousness, awareness, the cosmos, etc. For me, personally, it's about connecting to my higher self and to a higher energy, where I feel connected to oneness or the universe.

The Brain, The Body, and Stress

Before Dhyana (meditation) and Pranayama (breathing techniques) let's explore some factors on the brain, body, and stress. By understanding these physiological factors, you can better grasp the empowering effects of regular Dhyana and Pranayama.

Through practising meditation alone, neuroscience has shown that this enables a part of the brain known as the Corpus Callosum, the bridge between the left and right hemispheres, to grow. This growth allows us to access both hemispheres of the brain more easily, thus to be able to find solutions, reach clarity, and make decisions much more efficiently and effectively—all of which is essential to have success.

For example, your boss asks you to produce a report in the next half hour. The typical response may be to panic and lose focus, clarity, and creativity on the situation. A regular meditation practice would allow you to deal with these types of stressors, which are the modern-day equivalent of the sabre-toothed tiger, a stressor of our ancestors. In the environment we live in today, we are typically safe and sheltered from most physical-type dangers. However, we have new types of stressors, every-day stressors such as traffic jams, exhausting work schedules, rocky relationships, and social media. From these daily stressors, the majority of us are constantly living in a primitive stressful state of fight, flight, or freeze.

The more that we live in this stressful state, the more we become prone to illness because of the chemical and hormonal reactions and imbalance in our bodies. This then has an impact on the body's immune system. The definition of stress is when your brain and your body are shaken out of homeostasis (balance). The stress response is something your body naturally does to keep you safe. Stressors come in three types:

- *Physical*—such as trauma, accident, injury, falls
- *Chemical*—such as harmful bacteria, viruses, fluctuating blood sugar levels, and food toxins
- *Emotional*—such as traffics jams, mortgages, landlords, family tragedy, and parenting

Stress can be good as it helps to protect us from danger. However, no living organism can live in the emergency state of fight, flight, or freeze for a prolonged period of time. So, by daily generating enormous amounts of energy for some threat in your outer world, like traffic jams or financial pressures, then there is no energy left in your inner world for growth and repair. When this happens, especially when it is a daily occurrence, then you cannot engage a success mindset.

You can turn on the stress response through thought alone. People can become addicted to their own thoughts, so it's a scientific fact that the hormones of stress push the genetic button that creates disease. This means your thoughts can actually make you sick. If you change your thinking and emotions, and begin to open your heart, it is those elevated emotions that begin to restore and rebuild the immune system. And it is also how you establish a mindset for success.

Research by Dr. Joe Dispenza and his team from the fields of neuroscience, epigenetics, and quantum physics explores the science behind spontaneous remissions in people. It's fascinating work and it's one of the reasons why I do what I do, as my passion is to cultivate people's awareness and knowledge, so they can begin to change their life to live a truly, purposeful, authentic, and abundant life. A life of success. Let's spread this message of kindness, love, and a new mindset to others, let's make it a "kindset". Dhyana (meditation) and Pranayama (breathing techniques) help us establish our mindsets as "kindsets".

Energy, Frequency, and Vibrations

When you learn to surrender, let go, and trust through the acts of yoga's Dhyana (meditation) and Pranayama (breathing techniques), the energy field operates from a higher frequency. In turn, you will start noticing synchronicities, meeting new and different people and new relationships and opportunities coming into your life that were never there before. The amount of new relationships and connection I have made in the last seven years has been truly amazing. This is where it might sound a little outrageous and even unbelievable, but trust me, raise your vibration, learn to let go, and just notice new people and new opportunities coming into your life.

This is where we go into the realm of quantum physics and the notion that we are all energy, vibration, and frequency. Check this out over the coming weeks and notice where your own frequency is operating from. Are you high vibe or low vibe? And how does this affect you and the people, places, and things around you?

Your Mind and Brainwaves

Let's look at brainwave states to explain how meditation and getting beyond the conscious analytical mind and into the subconscious works to change your embedded patterns and programmes.

The conscious analytical mind, which is 5 percent of the mind (the size of a golf ball), is what keeps us organised with logic and reason. Then we have our subconscious mind, which is 95 percent of the mind (the size of a beach ball), where our values, beliefs, and habits are formed.

We are living our lives from our subconscious mind (the beach ball). Events, experiences, family upbringing, society, culture, etc., all form the basis of our beliefs, perceptions, and behaviours that encompass the subconscious mind. We all have positive, negative, simple, mundane and life changing events that have happened to us. All of this information is stored in our subconscious (beach ball). So, it's the bigger ball that's running our lives and we may not be aware of it. For example: If you were told by one of your parents that you were no good at maths, that occasion when that was said to you - may embed a limiting belief within your subconscious and you start to believe you are no good at maths, therefore you may not attempt to even try to understand maths and you tell yourself there's no point because you are no good at it, which then in turn puts you into a vicious cycle of spotting how bad you are at maths, because you give up trying to learn. On the other hand, something positive could be said or shown to you and that instilled an inner confidence within you that empowered you. We all have positive and negative stores in our subconscious, however it depends upon the individual and how conscious they are of these thoughts. When one is conscious of their mind, values and beliefs, they can then begin to make changes to the ones that don't serve them.

Through meditation, you are more suggestible to new information to be able to make changes in your subconscious. Meditation better enables new synaptic connections , reprogramming old, embedded limiting beliefs into new empowering and healthy ones, therefore cultivating a creative mind, leading to a success mindset.

A typical, healthy human being operates from a mid-range beta brainwave state at 16 to 22 cycles per second. This is where coherence and organisation are pretty good. If someone is living in a highly stressed state, they'll be in high beta brainwaves at around 22 to 50 cycles per second. This is like driving a car in first gear and stepping on the brake at the same time. This is not good for the body and leads to a narrow focus, incoherence, and brain imbalance. This is where the stress hormones get signaled to kick in, and it creates conditions such as anxiety and depression.

When we come into a meditation practice, it's about getting beyond beta and alpha brainwaves and into theta, delta, and gamma waves. I don't claim to be a neuroscientist, but I do study the brain, yoga science, and behaviour. I know through meditation practice and my work with neuro-linguistic programming, you can begin to reach amazing, joyful, and magical brainwave states through practice.

Positive changes happen when we get into the operating seat of the subconscious mind, the limbic brain which controls the entire body's nervous system. When you come to realise the scientific, physical, emotional and spiritual benefits of this ancient artform, you will begin to understand how re-wiring your brain through the practice of yoga positively makes changes in the mind, cultivating creativity, new ideas and opportunities engendering a mind for success. Many people who discover this become inspired to practice yoga and meditation on a daily basis.

What Is Meditation?

Anyone can meditate. It is a natural unraveling, and it's the heart of awareness. Meditation is the space to observe what is honestly happening in the present moment. It gives the conscious, analytical mind a chance to break through into the subconscious mind. Therefore, becoming conscious in your subconscious mind. As mentioned, meditation is one of the eight limbs of yoga, also known as Dhyana. In a nutshell, it's sitting down with yourself for several minutes and being able to switch off from your senses and go within. Let me add—it's not about clearing your mind.

If someone has an urge to be perfect at everything, then they're usually the ones that will give up sooner as they'll feel they're not getting the perfect meditation practice. Meditation is not about perfection, meaning it's not about sustaining a perfectly clear mind and perfect total presence for the length of the practice. That's not what it's about. Also, each meditation practice can be different. Some days you'll connect to the divine inner self, consciousness, God, universe—whatever you want to call it. Other days you may not. It's about stripping back and removing the ego. Not to judge. To just "be".

Meditation cultivates inner peace and calm with a consistent practice, which assists you to reach a space of creation. You are no longer living in survival mode. You are now the creator of your own life. You can now see through a lens of choice and opportunity. You are now connected to consciousness, the universe, and your creativity.

Between yesterday's mistakes and tomorrow's hope,
there is a fantastic opportunity called today.
—Anonymous

As mentioned, meditation is the formula to get past the screen between the conscious, analytical mind and the subconscious mind.

So many of us have heard the phrase, "Be present" or "Be here now", but what does that really mean? It simply means living in the present moment, that your mind is in the now, focusing on whatever you're doing at that time. You are conscious and aware of your thoughts, emotions and actions in the now. Not thinking about the past or the future. Yogic philosophy talks about meditation as a tool to help you become present. There's now a scientific stance to demonstrate what it truly means to be present and how it can assist you in going beyond your body, your environment, and time itself. This allows you to reach the delicious place of the present moment.

By explaining how meditation works and with the proof of neuroscience and quantum physics, hopefully, this will instill your belief in the value of the practice. You can change your personality into your personal reality because what you think and feel, whether good, bad, or indifferent, affects your energy, which, in turn, affects the outcomes of your life.

Through the practice of meditation, you can re-wire your mind and even genetics. You can change for the better. You don't have to stay the same if it's not serving you. By analysing your personal reality through consciousness (presence) of your thoughts, emotions and behaviours, you can change your personality for success.

Breathing Techniques and Meditations

Pranayama breathing techniques help you with self-confidence, presence, and focus. Deep breathing increases the supply of oxygen to the brain and stimulates the parasympathetic nervous system, which promotes a state of calmness. There are many different techniques, such as Anuloma Viloma (alternate nostril breathing), Kapalabhati (skull shining breathing), and abdominal breathing. We'll look at abdominal breathing here.

Abdominal breathing is to inhale through the nose. As the air comes in, allow the air to enter the abdomen and inflate your abdomen like a balloon. Exhale. Breathe out through the nose, and as the air comes out, the abdomen deflates. To be most effective, repeat this for five minutes or longer.

When you think about how we breathe as babies, we automatically breathe into the abdomen. However, as we grow through life, with life experiences and stress, most of us tend to form a habit of shallow breathing, which is quick and shallow and goes only as far as the upper chest. This physically puts more of a strain on the body. Hence, we have many people with conditions such as anxiety, stress, and respiratory problems.

Breathing techniques are a great way to prepare yourself before a meditation practice. Even if you are feeling a little overwhelmed, upset, or stressful, revert to a tool that you are always carrying: your breath.

When you own your breath, nobody can steal your peace.
—Anonymous

Simple Meditation Techniques

Before meditating, find a comfortable seated position. Simple meditation asanas (postures) are *Sukhasana* which refers to an easy cross-legged pose on the floor, sitting on a cushion or yoga block. You can lean against a wall for support or you can sit on a chair with both feet flat on the floor. Once you have found your position, make sure your spine is straight and your head is in line with the spine, shoulders, and back. Sit up straight, as if the spine is rising up through the crown of the head and close the eyes or take a downward gaze.

Ajna Chakra Meditation

In this meditation, you focus on your Ajna Chakra, the third eye (space between the eyebrows) as your focus point, with closed eyes. This type of practice helps to steady the wandering mind and thoughts.

Tratak Meditation

Constant, steady gazing, known as Tratak, is a good concentration exercise. It involves alternately gazing at an object, photograph, candle flame, or point without blinking, then closing the eyes and visualising the object in your mind's eye. This practice helps to steady the wandering mind and allows you to focus your attention. Here's how to do the practice:

1. Place the object at eye level, three feet (90 cm) away from you.
2. First regulate your breathing, then start to gaze at the object without blinking.
3. Look steadily without straining.
4. After a minute, close your eyes, and keep your inner gaze steady while you visualise the object.
5. When the image from your mind's eye vanishes, open your eyes and repeat.

Mantra Meditation

This meditation starts with repeating a mantra out loud by saying it, chanting it, or whispering it. Correct pronunciation is a must so that the energy can manifest itself to make a specific thought pattern in the mind. With profound practice, repeating a mantra leads to pure thought, creativity, and clarity. There are many types of chants, including:

- *Aum* or *Om*
- *I am that I am.*
- *Lumen de lumine.* (This fills you with power and light.)
- *Ho'oponopono.* This is an ancient Hawaiian word, meaning: "I love you; I'm sorry; forgive me, please; thank you".

In summary, it is easy to change your reality into your success. Your state of mind decides how your life pans out. You can choose the path that you want your life to take. The only thing that stops you or brings you success is your own state of mind—your mindset. In order for you to change your life, you must get past the screen of your analytical mind and into the operating centre of your subconscious mind.

Once inside the subconscious mind, you are now conscious in your unconscious mind. This is where the magic happens—new programmes, new synaptic connections, new thoughts, new experiences, new results, and new behaviours. Therefore, a new life.

You must reconnect your mind with your heart to be able to live in creation, gratitude, and abundance—as opposed to a state of survival, living in lack and separation.

My hope is that you are now informed and inspired to enjoy this beautiful ancient practice, creating a success mindset, and that you go live your life on purpose. Namaste.

About the Author

Claire Morton is a Master NLP (Neuro-Linguistic Programming) practitioner and yoga teacher. She is one of the UK's most sought-after transformational well-being coaches. A multiple award-winner, Claire is a highly motivated yoga teacher with a passion for learning and development with over 20 years' coaching experience in the corporate world in both public and private sectors. After leaving the corporate world, Claire continues to specialise in emotional intelligence, leadership, mindfulness, yoga, and well-being.

Claire evokes and inspires life-transforming journeys through her compassionate and perceptive nature. She also serves as an MBTI (Myers Briggs

Type Indicator) practitioner, Reiki healer, and radio presenter on Wirral Wave Radio, hosting her own show, *All Being Well.*

Claire's vision is to support individuals who want to change to push them through analysis and reflection of every element of their life, emotionally, physically, spiritually, and mentally with every fear, every comfort zone being stretched, to take them from survivor to creator, or from lost soul to purposeful creator.

Email: Claire@thepurpose-pusher.com
Website: www.thepurpose-pusher.com

CHAPTER 24

BREAK THROUGH TO YOUR UNLIMITED POTENTIAL

By Jeff Israel Nthiwa
Breakthrough Coach, Life Coach Trainer
Nairobi, Kenya

Eliud Kipchoge, the greatest marathoner of all time, was on a mission to prove that no human is limited. He was driven by this goal: "To run a marathon in under two hours and to show to the world that when you focus on your goal, when you work hard, and when you believe in yourself, anything is possible."

Anything is possible when we stand in our true power. In my 15-plus years of deep coaching experience, I have witnessed firsthand the fact that humans are not limited. I have seen people unleash confidence, audacity, hope, greatness, and much more from their human spirit by learning how to break through to their unlimited potential.

The secret to wealth, health, peace, and joy lies in releasing our true human potential. If you are experiencing financial difficulties, it is because you have not yet discovered the unlimited power of the human potential. If you are suffering from ill health and bad relationships, it's because you are yet to know who you are and just how powerful you are.

The Destiny Life Coaching program is all about helping people to step into their power by cutting off everything that ties them to a limited experience of life. I put my clients on the path to take back their power.

Power Game

Humanity is driven by a power game. The power game in itself is not a bad thing. In fact, it is unavoidable. As human beings, we can't help but play this game, whether consciously or unconsciously. Our entire existence is defined by this game. It is not about whether you are playing this game or not; it is how you are playing it that determines whether you live a life of fulfillment or frustration. A majority of people play the power game the wrong way.

As with any game, this game has positions, and each one of us unconsciously takes the position of our subconscious programming. You are programmed to play the game a certain way by your brain's hardwiring. To play the game of life differently, you need to change the way your brain is wired. Let's look at the various positions in this game.

What Position Do You Play in the Game of Life?

There are three positions in the game of life. They are:

1. The Victim
2. The Hustler
3. The Master

The Victim

You are playing the victim position if you live like life happens to you. To quote Tony Robbins, "Life doesn't happen to you, it happens for you." Victims believe that other people and circumstances are to blame for the bad things happening in their world. The victim mentality is trained to always find a way to place blame elsewhere and look for excuses for not taking responsibility for their life. They react to most life challenges by thinking, "It's not my fault."

People who play this position lack confidence in life. They are people pleasers with very lethal inner critics. They live a life of frustration and are often angry with a world that seems to be against them. Victims also become resentful of people who seem happy and successful. They only surround themselves with people who "understand" them and not those who challenge them to grow and take responsibility. Victims enjoy the company of those who lavish them with attention and feel sorry for them. The victim position is a powerless position in the game of life.

The Hustler

The hustler has an aggressive approach to do whatever it takes to get what they want, including overlooking their values and the needs of others. They are driven by the need for certainty and significance. The hustler's philosophy is to "make it by hook or crook." Get rich or die trying. When the hustler fails, they never make excuses. They look at a challenge square in the eye and accept it as an opportunity to grow and do better. They play to win even if the win means losing some relationships.

Although the hustler meets their need for significance by achieving and making the impossible possible, the hustler is often not fulfilled. Bravado, egocentric behavior, and greed control the hustler's heart. The hustler may not know there is a better approach to life than the use of force and "trying" to make things happen. The hustler is surrounded by shallow relationships and doesn't have a deep relationship even with themselves.

Achievement is a science that every hustler masters. Fulfillment is elusive to the hustler. The frustration of having achieved so much and not feeling a sense of fulfillment is frustrating to the hustler. The hustler believes that when they reach a certain level of achievement, they will instantly become fulfilled. Since achievement doesn't bring fulfillment, every time the hustler achieves something, they systematically move the goal post farther and farther ahead till they drop dead and die unfulfilled. As Tony Robbins says, "Success without fulfillment is the ultimate failure."

The Master

The victim is a slave of their environment while the hustler is a slave of their ego. The master is not a slave. The master is a hustler who has found their true power. Finding true power is a realization that everything in the universe is an expression of God, who is divine love. We are a part of God. True power is an awakening and acceptance of this truth.

Good news! It doesn't matter whether you have lived your life as a victim or as a hustler. In the rest of this chapter, I'll share the tried-and-tested steps you can use to become a master.

Assume 100% Responsibility for Your Life

Accept 100 percent responsibility for your life. Believe that you have created the life that you see right now with your own subconscious mental conditioning and focus. Believe that you are the one responsible to turn things around and live a new empowered life. Decide to be a master of your life and begin to dance with your destiny. Change begins the moment you accept your "response-ability" over your life.

You have the ability to respond to whatever life places on your path, so you can make the best out of every situation and season. Use your God-given ability to choose your response to what life places on your path.

Believe in Your True Self

To become a master, you must believe in your higher self. A belief is a feeling of being certain that this is the way it is. There is a "true self" inside of everyone. Living a powerfully fulfilling life begins by knowing who you truly are as a spiritual being.

This does not happen when you are stuck in the hustler's world of fear or the victim's world of complaining, but in the master's world of faith that a greater version of you exists and that it is your responsibility to unleash it. To believe in your true self, you must divorce the false self and then live in alignment with your inner self in every situation. As such, your true inner self becomes your true compass. It will help you make decisions on whether something (relationships, money, business or job) is in alignment with your true self or not.

Change Your Story

Our life is powered by the stories we tell every day about who we are and what we are capable of. Every human being has between 55 thousand and 75 thousand stories that we tell ourselves every day! That is about 3 thousand stories per hour or 53 stories per minute. Only 5 percent of these stories are conscious. Ninety-five percent are unconscious stories playing in our minds like a video on a constant feedback loop.

Between the victim, the hustler, and the master, which one have you accepted as your story and how is it serving you? The life you are living today is a result of the story you are telling yourself or the story you have accepted as your story. Your core assignment in life is to remember who you are and tell that story on a consistent basis.

Tell a story worthy of your highest expression. Tell a story that shifts the way you feel about life and the way you experience life itself. Remembering who you are and living that out is the whole idea of life.

What will it take to change your story and adopt the story of your higher self? Who would you be without your old story? The negative stories we play over and over again in our brain are the real reason we never break through to our destiny, no matter how we practice the Law of Attraction or go for miracle prayers.

The real miracle is in changing our stories. We have to divorce the old stories and get married to new, more empowering stories that will help us unleash our destiny.

Decide to Remain in a Resourceful State

Breaking through to your human potential will require that you shift into a resourceful state. People are not limited by a lack of resources but a limitation of resourcefulness. Each of the three mindsets—victim, hustler, and master—are all states of being. A master is in a permanent state of abundant resourcefulness.

According to Tony Robbins, there are three factors that influence our state: our physiology (body), our focus, and our language.

The master knows how to use their body—for example, through breathing techniques—to be in an abundant state. They focus on what helps them grow, and they use language with and about themselves and others that is positive and empowering.

The master is in a "state of flow" where their body, focus, and language are in alignment with their higher self.

Embrace Uncertainty

The reason people upgrade from victim to hustler is that they want to be certain. They want their lives to feel important and to stand for something. They want to prove that they are worthy and that they deserve to be heard.

However, the hustler's world never offers lasting certainty. Having a strong need for certainty denies the hustler the ability to relax and enjoy life.

The life of a master is a life of embracing uncertainty and living in alignment with the universal laws of nature. The master never judges in terms of good and bad because the master is wise enough to know that good can be found in the land of bad and that the bad thing can work for good. The master believes that all is well and trusts that God knows what he is doing.

To break through to our potential and become a master of our destiny, we have to release our need for certainty. When we let go, we allow ourselves to put all our heart into living in this moment, the here and now. Of course, there are things we can control and must control, like our state and our responses. However, mastery of life involves embracing what we have control over as well as embracing what we don't have control over.

Forgive and Flow

Forgiveness is only possible when humans connect with their highest, most God-like selves. It is only the master who can let go of the ego, certainty, and small stories. Small people don't forgive, or when they do, they forgive to get something out of the process of forgiveness.

Look at your habits, behaviors, and addictions in the past or the present that did or do control your life and the way you think, act, and behave. Tune in to the effects of this on your life and make a decision to forgive and let go.

Forgiveness is so powerful it has been found to affect even our immune system, reduce pain, reduce stress hormones, and lower blood pressure. The practice of unconditional forgiveness creates a positive state that enhances our performance. I am talking about unconditional radical forgiveness, which only comes with the practice of accepting things as they are. It comes with the understanding that we cannot change the past, but we can shape the future with the choices we make in the present moment.

Forgiving takes strength and maturity. It takes a belief that God knows better and that the divine can use any experience for our good as long as we remain in "good" vibration. Infuse your emotions with self-love and no judgment.

God at the Center of Your Life

"Stay in your head and you are dead," says Tony Robbins. The master becomes a master because of their spiritual alignment. Masters keep God at the center of their lives because they know and understand that God knows best. Their true self is connected to their higher self, which is characterized by pure, unconditional love.

The purpose of life is to be restored in the image and likeness of love (God). "Our true home is called love, and this is where we walk and return to moment by moment. That journey home to love is a personal responsibility," explains Tony Robbins.

Therefore, the choices are two: (1) you can walk towards love or (2) walk towards fear. You can make love your home or make fear your home. Unfortunately, a huge number of people in the world choose fear over love, and that is unfortunate.

As we spend more time with our true self, we realize that all that we need is within us and that we are one with God and God is part of us. That is a powerful realization because God is everything we can ever need or imagine. Slow down and be aware of the loving presence of God within your heart. Practice daily rituals that anchor your soul in love. Visualize yourself as an ocean of infinite love. Look at everything from the eyes of love. Listen from a place of love and take note of when you are slipping into non-loving places and come back home.

Hunger for Your Life's Assignment

A master has a hunger for a life mission. A master has mastered their life's mission, and they focus their life, time, and money on that mission. The journey of living your mission begins by creating it.

The master is driven by a high calling. While the hustler is simply trying to make a point, the master doesn't have the need to prove their abilities. The master has a mission; they have a contribution to make to the planet.

A true mission is not a hidden treasure that no one else should know about. It is a treasure that the world must know and benefit from. Talk about your mission and let people around you hold you accountable to your mission statement. Frame it on your wall. Create a daily ritual of saying your mission statement out loud. This will help to record it in your subconscious mind and make it a part of you.

Imagination

Imagination is a tool that gives you the permission to experience what you desire. Imagination allows you to put yourself in that place you wish to be right now, in this moment.

Start imagining yourself in the reality of your ideal self. Use the five senses to see, feel, touch, smell, hear, and taste yourself being and doing whatever you desire. Imagine a life where you are a master or where you have started taking actions towards mastery. Begin with the end and write down the small steps you took to arrive there.

How does it feel to be a master of your destiny? What emotion do you think will help you take action towards mastery?

Imagination helps us to shift into an emotional state of resourceful abundance. This empowers us either to let go of the painful past or attract our dream. Through imagination we can create the life we desire.

Imagine the most powerful being that you are capable of becoming. Imagine that you have the power to steer the ship of your destiny and that you are totally in control of your happy life.

Be Vulnerable and Present

The ultimate goal in life is to be happy. One of the critical break-through activities is when my coaching clients, both male and female, allow themselves to be vulnerable. Vulnerability takes courage, and I find it integral to a happy, joyful, and fulfilling life. The impact of vulnerability is experienced in all areas of life: interpersonal, intrapersonal, and professional.

If you want to master your life, you must let yourself be seen. I don't believe in role models, and the reason I don't believe in role models is that I think role models only play a role, and that's different from being real.

Vulnerability allows us to be real and authentic in all our interactions and experiences. To be vulnerable is to trust that all is well and to let your creativity flow in every area of your life. You allow feedback from others and quickly get involved with hard conversations.

My prayer is that you will allow yourself to be vulnerable in this moment. Adopt the physiology and state of vulnerability, and see the universe open up for better and more fulfilling experiences in all areas of life. The courage to be vulnerable is what helps humanity to crush fear, shame, anxiety, over-caution, perfectionism, and self-hate.

I consider vulnerability a power. As you show up more vulnerable, you will experience freedom from pleasing people and the joy of being present, and you are able to trust that the universe has got your back and that everything is somehow working for your good.

About the Author

Jeff Israel Nthiwa is a catalyst for those who want to break through to a better life. He began helping people break through to a better life in the church. He worked with the Christ Is the Answer Ministries for seven years. He transitioned into full-time professional coaching after earning certification in intervention coaching. Throughout his over a decade of professional coaching and counselling, Jeff has helped hundreds of individuals create breakthroughs in their lives and reconnect what matters.

Website: www.jeffnthiwa.com | www.dlc.co.ke
LinkedIn: https://www.linkedin.com/in/lifecoachkenya/
Twitter: https://twitter.com/CoachingKenya
Facebook: https://www.facebook.com/LifeCoachKenya
Instagram: https://www.instagram.com/breakthroughwithjeff/

CHAPTER 25

DEVELOPING A CULTURAL MINDSET FOR SUCCESS

By Marilyn O'Hearne, MA, MCC
Global Executive, Leadership, Team and Mentor Coach
Kansas City, Missouri

"It is impossible not to work interculturally." Perhaps—just like 90 percent of global leaders in 68 countries and the US head of PricewaterhouseCoopers—you agree with or are curious about this statement. Let's read it again: "It is impossible not to work interculturally." Perhaps you too are ready to discover more about how increasing your cultural intelligence (CQ) can contribute to your personal success and the overall success of your family, community, organization, and/or business.

In our complex world, we are bombarded with frightening examples of how lack of cultural intelligence (CQ) results in misunderstandings that lead to costly conflict; loss of business, talent, and even lives; and how it is tied to shootings, bombings, and the inequitable impact of the 2020 pandemic. It is easy for you to be afraid of crossing the line and your organization ending up negatively in the headlines, and it can be challenging to be aware of what the line is.

You may end up either doubting yourself or blindly forging ahead, over-confidently believing you already are sufficiently culturally intelligent because you have taken a training, traveled, or have had some intercultural experience.

The truth is, like much of life, you never fully "arrive" because the world, your team, organization, clients, family, and community keep changing, and so do you.

I have extensive training and experience in the area of CQ. I've lived in three countries and coached leaders, teams, and coaches in 40 countries, including the United Nations. I wrote a book on the topic. I served on the International Coaching Federation Global Board. And still, to this day, I continue to develop my cultural intelligence.

It is impossible to not work interculturally—this is true even in your own community and organization, when you consider each of our multiple cultural identities including gender, generation, ethnicity, region, sexual orientation, religion, ability/disability, education, appearance, income, etc.

Cultural intelligence is recognizing and understanding the beliefs, values, rank, and behaviors of those cultural identities and groups; and then effectively applying that awareness. Applying that awareness can lead to teams, organizations, communities, families and even nations that welcome, appreciate, respect, and leverage for success any and all cultural differences. In turn, this leads to an unlocking of all potential and a creating of environments where everyone enjoys a sense of belonging and all are living in prosperity and peace. That's my vision.

You can increase your prosperity and peace as well as that of your team, organization, family, community, and nation by you committing to increasing your CQ, with a little guidance and coaching. Organizations with greater diversity and CQ are up to 35 percent more profitable (McKinsey & Company, "Diversity Matters," 2015). Talent retention improves by 19 percent as well as a reduction of the 60 to 80 percent of difficulties related to "strained relationships among employees" (Zeynep Ilgaz, "Conflict Resolution" 2014). The median coaching ROI is 300 percent! (ICFGC Client Study)

New Zealand's leadership demonstrates CQ through its understanding, respecting, and leveraging the strengths of its indigenous population. For example, since 1867, the New Zealand Parliament has reserved seats for indigenous leaders, so that their voices are always represented. Prime Minister Jacinda Ardern incorporated Māori words and images in the poem she wrote and shared to draw her country together with a message of compassion during the challenges brought on by the 2020 pandemic. According to Julie McCarthy in a 2020 NPR interview, "[New Zealand] Prime Minister Jacinda Ardern has applied her trademark empathy to rally her country to attempt what few states have tried: eradicate the novel coronavirus." And compared to many other countries in the world, at the time of this writing, New Zealand has made impressive efforts against COVID-19.

Franklin Delano Roosevelt, US President during the Great Depression, demonstrated empathy for and awareness of the varying needs of those across a range of socio-economic levels. He demonstrated his compassion through his "fireside chat" radio broadcasts, uniting the country and contributing to economic recovery.

Both these leaders exemplified the "cultural mindset," the ability to integrate different cultures and consciously shift into another perspective or cultural frame of reference, without fear of losing their own. As mentioned in this chapter's opening, a cultural mindset is cited as necessary to achieve business success. As noted in *Cultural Intelligence* by Ang, Van Dyne, and Rockstuhl, "Ninety percent of leading executives from 68 countries identify intercultural skills as among the most important capabilities required to remain competitive." All in all, there's convincing evidence across a variety of areas that a cultural mindset contributes to a success mindset.

Shifts to Increase CQ for Success: David's Story

To help you increase your cultural intelligence and develop a cultural mindset for success, let's turn to an example from my leadership coaching. In this example, we're calling the business leader "David." David was a leader of a Western European business that was starting to work with business partners in South America.

"David, can you give me an example of one of your goals for improving negotiations and partnerships?" I asked in our first coaching session together.

David answered, "I want to know how to convince them of the truth! [i.e., that they are wrong, and we are right]" David said loudly and firmly.

At this response, alarms sounded in my head. "Is this leader coachable?" I caught myself silently wondering.

"Would you rather be right or in a relationship?" I then asked him. By the way, this is one of my favorite coaching questions that I ask in hopes of playfully shifting a client's mindset.

Fortunately, David was able to laugh when I asked him the question. This showed he recognized that improved, sustainable partnerships and insistence on being right do not go together.

How would David be able to shift his approach for better results?

He came from a Western European business setting and culture. He was working in South America. For David to achieve better results, I invited him to shift his mindset. With this in mind, I asked about the cultural differences. Specifically, I asked, "How direct is your communication? And how direct is that of your South American partners?"

Asking him this question was pivotal for David to make the needed shift in his mindset to achieve his business goal for success. Through this question, he moved from the place of seeing his beliefs and culturally direct communication as "right" and his South American partners' beliefs and indirect mode of communication as "wrong," to accepting their cultural differences and even adapting to them.

The classic question in intercultural work (remember, all work is intercultural) is—who adjusts how much? David had, without being aware of it, expected the host culture, i.e., the South Americans, to adjust to his cultural style of communicating. He realized that in order to win in his goals of negotiating and improving relationships, he would need to shift both his mindset, i.e., "My culture is right, others are wrong," as well as his expectations and, strategically, his cultural communication style. David had to trust he could make these strategic shifts without losing his own culture.

By making these adjustments, David could then see beneath the surface of the other party's behaviors, business practices, and customs, which at first he found irritating and frustrating, to identify the underlying beliefs and values. In turn, this would allow him to work with his South American partners toward a shared vision.

At the conclusion of our coaching engagement, David shared his development through our coaching, pointing out the following lessons he learned to instill a cultural mindset:

- Speak less, listen more, and try to understand.
- View with the eyes of someone else (empathy).
- Ask what and how questions (as modeled by his coach, me).
- Consider it a game of chess (be more strategic and realize it can be fun!).

David demonstrated increased cultural intelligence through awareness, curiosity, humility, and empathy, which removed the goal barrier of trying to prove he was right. I see those as key ingredients for cultural intelligence—

awareness, curiosity, humility, and empathy, as drawn from multiple sources such as J. Bennett's "Cultivating Intercultural Competence" and Greater Good Magazine's Science-Based Insights for a Meaningful Life from UC Berkeley.

Of course, we cannot stereotype or generalize that all South Americans are indirect communicators; all Western Europeans are direct communicators; or all _____ [cultural identity] are _____ [any adjective]. Because we have multiple cultural identities, each dimension of culture, such as communication, will vary by generation, gender, education level, time spent in or working with other cultures, etc.

Continual Development of Our CQ

To help you understand this is not all about international cultural differences or business settings, I share my own cultural "oops" moment, where my children caught me in a judgment of a cultural group within my own nation and community. Remember, we never fully arrive. We can continually develop and increase our own cultural intelligence.

My adult daughters and I were enjoying ourselves in conversation. Shifting to national news, I commented in an adamant voice, "Can you believe these fear-based commercials and how 'those people' are actually falling for it? And imagine how they are going to vote in the election!"

"Mom, we have never heard you talk this way about a group of people before," my daughters both told me.

I was caught in the act of judging. Even though I am a coach and strive to approach everyone with an unconditionally positive regard and with compassion, I am human. As such, I make judgments. While judgments can be helpful for looking at what can be further developed and for making good decisions, they can also get in the way and even signal biases we all have. As shown by Rita Carter in *The Human Brain Book*, Judgment shuts down the brain in .07 seconds!

The fact that judgments stop thinking is being taught in medical school. Just imagine how dangerous it could be for a doctor to immediately judge a skin rash as measles without ruling out life-threatening toxic shock or an allergic reaction. Unchecked judgments and bias can be equally dangerous to our relationships, decision-making, and quadruple bottom line (people, planet, profit, and purpose) organizational results.

How did I flip my judgment on its head? Thanks to my daughters holding me accountable, I did what I teach others to do. I encourage you to try the following and share your results.

1. *Awareness*—pause, take a few deep breaths to move into awareness.
2. *Curiosity*—consider the person or group of people you are referring to and what you think you know about them: socio-economics, educational level, regional location, occupation, appearance, religion, age, gender, sexual orientation, etc. Get curious!
3. *Humility*—ask yourself, "Are my assumptions 100 percent true?" Humility check!
4. Ask yourself, "How could my assumptions get in the way of my thinking (or our communication or relationship)?"
5. Ask yourself, "What assumptions or biases do I want to update?"

In my situation, it would have been easy to keep "those people" in a remote box based on some media coverage. Choosing not to cut off half the US population, I was aware that some of my very friends and university classmates were among the group I'd harshly judged. From there, I could implement ACHE: awareness, curiosity, humility, and empathy.

I became *aware* of my assumptions. I could get *curious* about why "those people" could be "buying into" fear-based commercials. What might they be afraid of? How might they see this candidate as their "savior"? What were my and my political party's fears? How might we work together for a win/win with *humility*, knowing neither group was 100 percent right nor had all the answers? Choosing to see "those people" or "others" as more like me and becoming more aware of our shared hopes and fears triggers more *empathy* rather than condemnation.

In our fast culture we may be tempted to skip the first step, the pause with deep breathing. The pause with deep breathing is important because it actually shifts our brain's blood flow from reactionary and back to the front of the brain, the neocortex, where it can be used for effective decision-making. *Presence Based Coaching* author Doug Silsbee advises the practice of deep breathing with centering ten times a day, claiming, "It will change your life!" With frequent practice you can more quickly and easily access this centered, present state for better decision-making and relationships.

We make hundreds of judgments a day, so what's the big deal? Judging becomes a problem when we make harmful or unfair judgments based on little evidence (or quick judgments based on unconscious bias). Doing this can result in shaming others. Also, it shuts our brain off to other possibilities, resulting in unproductive conflict, limited opportunities, and strained relationships.

Clues we are moving into harmful judgment that may include bias include the following:

1. Talking negatively about "those people."
2. "Should-ing" or advice giving (implying someone or some group should change) without empathy.
3. Sighs or groans in response to behavior or appearance; or ignoring or avoiding.
4. Condemning something or someone as "bad," "stupid," "unworthy," "deplorable," etc.

Note: the last two can include you doing it to yourself. Check and flip if necessary your judgments about yourself and others, shifting your mindset to become more compassionate and empathetic for greater success and impact.

To Increase Your CQ with ACHE

How can you further develop your cultural mindset and CQ with ACHE?

1. *Awareness*

You can become more aware of others' cultural identities and your judgments and biases towards those cultural identities by going through the previously given five steps that I used to flip my judgment on its head. Be ready to engage the five steps when you meet someone new. Also, you could consider who triggers an emotional reaction or judgment, even as you listen to the news or read, and then engage the five steps.

To grow your CQ, you can place yourself in different cultural situations by attending a different place of worship; tuning in to a different news source; making a goal of meeting or talking with three new or different people at a meeting rather the same people you would normally interact with; or inviting someone outside your cultural identities to a gathering; and for any of these, be sure to go through the five steps.

You can also pay attention to how others describe your own cultural identities. Doing this should help you to increase your awareness of how your cultural identities are being perceived. As Hal B. Gregerson, director of MIT Leadership Center, advised, "Get out and seek unexpected surprises, seek dramatically different people. Find out what you don't know before it's too late."

2. *Curiosity*

Ask questions to gain an understanding of others' mindsets. For example, "What are you experiencing?" or "Tell me more." Ask yourself questions to reveal your assumptions, judgments, and biases (we all have unconscious bias, and that does not let us off the hook for identifying and managing them). And listen.

3. *Humility*

Humility is a lack of arrogance.

- Move from believing your culture is "right" and "the only way," that others are "wrong," or that "we are all alike" (because that denies people's uniqueness that can be leveraged for greater success).
- Move to accepting that other cultures have their own wisdom.
- Choose to integrate and leverage other cultural perspectives without losing your own. Leveraging differences exemplifies an advanced developmental stage of intercultural sensitivity per Milton J. Bennet.

As Cher Wang, HTC CEO, said, "It takes humility to realize we don't know everything, to know we must keep learning and observing."

4. *Empathy*

Empathy is the ability to sense other people's emotions and imagine what someone else might be thinking or feeling. To practice empathy, you can:

- Listen to understand rather than judge.
- Pay attention to nonverbal cues, including facial expressions, including your own.

☞ Along with integrating and leveraging differences, keep in mind what you and the others have in common.

One example of "stretching with curiosity" that I wrote about in my 2017 book *Breaking Free from Bias* is a program where community members who were at odds with police interviewed the other party and then did presentations based on their results. Part of the presentations included speaking from the other party's position, doing songs, doing role plays, etc. This resulted in greater respect, empathy, trust, and reduced community conflict. Community members involved in this, when interviewed, started by explaining their mistrust of the police and ended by sharing their greater understanding of the police officers' position. And vice versa. I even heard some lightness and playfulness after they interviewed each other.

The Value of Diverse Perspectives

Who speaks up in your team or community meetings, or family gatherings? Is it mostly the elders or youth, males or females, someone of a certain ethnicity or educational level? Hearing from diverse perspectives not only contributes to innovation and success (resulting in up to 35 percent more profit, as referenced in the "Diversity Matters" McKinsey report), but also when people feel heard as respected contributors, they are more likely to stay in the family, organization, or community.

In some direct cultures, if someone is not "jumping in" and speaking up in meetings, they could be labeled "not a contributor" and be passed up for special assignments and promotions, or possibly even let go. In indirect, more hierarchical, elder-oriented cultures, to speak up before the elders and organizational seniors have spoken is considered rude and offensive, with the same potential results. Talent loss is expensive.

How could this be handled with a cultural mindset, ACHE, win/win/win approach?

To increase *awareness*, the boss, let's call him John, has a caring conversation with Ana, to share that others in the organization are concerned about her not speaking up enough in meetings and how they are viewing her as a non-contributor. John is able to explain that in their Western, direct-communicating setting, meeting participants are expected to speak up. "Please tell me about how speaking up in meetings might be viewed in the culture that you grew up in," he says, expressing his *curiosity*.

"Interrupting elders and those with greater authority is considered rude, offensive, and risky," Ana replies.

John and Ana explore alternatives, based on mutual respect, trust, and humility. Neither take an "I am right, you are wrong" approach. Instead, they appreciate each other's position and take an *empathetic* "we" approach. They ask, "How can we work together for a win/win/win?"

The result is a win/win/win situation for the organization, Ana, and John. They even expand the options for dealing with Ana's speaking up in meetings. The leadership could ask her questions during meetings, ask her to submit her comments in advance of meetings, and/or break into pairs during the meeting to encourage more participation. This approach would benefit not only Latinas, Native Americans, and those of Asian descent who are taught to wait until the elders have spoken or when they are called upon, but also women from rural or other communities who grow up seeing women mostly in the background.

In this case, Ana chooses to speak up. She wins because as she contributes more in meetings, her value to the organization becomes more recognized, increasing her impact and influence. She is now in a position to advance within the organization. Her boss John wins because his department gains more recognition, as Ana does and as her ideas are leveraged. The organization wins because it benefits from Ana's ideas and the resulting productivity in John's department. The organizational culture and employee experience are also enhanced as additional workers of diverse cultural identities see Ana's ideas being recognized, valued, and put into action, preparing her for promotion. This, in turn, enhances talent retention and recruitment.

You can apply this in any setting: a board meeting, community organization get-together, your family meals together. Observe who is speaking and who is not speaking to become aware and get curious about why, all the while demonstrating humility and empathy.

Developing a cultural mindset for success is truly a life-long journey, so how will you continue to develop yours? How will you apply awareness, curiosity, humility, and empathy to increase your cultural intelligence and further develop your cultural mindset for success?

About the Author

Marilyn O'Hearne, MA, International Coach Federation Master Certified Coach, is globally experienced—since 1998 and in 40 countries—and is known for her big-picture approach, producing sustainable results.

Leaders, teams, coaches, and organizations, including the United Nations, move from the overwhelming uncertainty of our rapidly changing, culturally complex world, to confidence with renewed focus and vision via Marilyn's break-through coaching and programs. Marilyn is a recognized thought leader in bias, CQ (cultural intelligence), and EQ (emotional intelligence) as demonstrated in her book *Breaking Free from Bias,* many articles, and popular speaking and interviews.

Marilyn's compassionate listening and truth telling inspire trust. Everyone deserves the opportunity to achieve their full potential, to prosper, and to live in peace, Marilyn's vision. Unlocking people's potential results in reduced conflict (25–40 percent) while also boosting prosperity (35 percent), a quadruple bottom line result (people, profit, planet, and purpose). A leader herself, Marilyn served as a director in Brazil and on a global board.

Email: marilyn@marilynoh.com
Website: www.marilynoh.com

CHAPTER 26

CONNECT TO CREATE SUCCESS

By Alyssa Poggioli
Emotional Intelligence, Life and Health Coach
Chicago, Illinois

To become successful, the one action you need to take is to give yourself permission to feel.

When you allow yourself to feel, you will become more connected. The state of connectedness is where we are able to access success. And when I reference "connectedness," I do not mean gathering with a group of friends for a happy hour, taking a mental health day to binge-watch television, or booking a vacation to enable escape patterning.

By "connected," I mean connecting to your mental or emotional roadblocks as well as societal conditioning that prevents you from being your authentic self. In other words, making the effort to come to terms with the mindset or dis-servicing beliefs you might have that prevent you from being able to articulate how you feel, who you are, and what you want in leadership, personal relationships, and self-actualization.

This chapter will highlight five phases where connection and creation of success can occur at any moment in time. Connection creates the sense, and your mindset creates the state. These are the five phases we'll be examining:

- 𓂃 Phase 1: Be Curious
- 𓂃 Phase 2: Confront Disconnect
- 𓂃 Phase 3: Reidentify Yourself

☞ Phase 4: Get Clear and Live into Your Values

☞ Phase 5: Commit to Habits That Align with Your Values

Phase 1: Be Curious

What if I were to tell you that you are very likely living your life under a preconceived idea that someone else has conditioned you to believe about how you are intended to live?

Let's take 50 percent of today's population of 8 billion people and apply the above to it. That would mean there are 4 billion people in the world living a life they think they should be living based on the preconceived ideas of others. Four billion people living confused and disconnected and going through the motions that society has cultivated for them.

In my professional opinion, this is a crisis and must end.

If you are reading this book, there is a high probability that your life is lacking something, or maybe you are just passionate about self-growth and development. Either way, both scenarios symbolize the mindset that things can always be better. In the coaching world, we call these "reframes" and "paradigm shifts."

The reality for most is we have been conditioned to think we need to be a certain way, to have a specific identity. The belief system that by a certain age, we should have a specific degree, profession, or relationship status. The pressure of being in a specific profession means we are meant to live a certain way or behave in a specific way. And the problem is, this conditioning neither supports nor allows our mindset to become creative. It prevents us from being able to increase our awareness, especially towards emotional intelligence.

Why is emotional intelligence important?

Your lack of emotional intelligence prevents you from being able to connect and experience yourself, others, and the world from a lens of truth, security, and connectedness, what I call a TSC lens. Without TSC in the internal and external way of how you are living and showing up, the likelihood of you experiencing a true sense of success will not be possible.

Author and founder of the Heartmath Institute, Doc Lew Childre says it best, "Realize that now, in this moment of time, you are creating. You are creating your next moment based on what you are feeling and thinking. That is what's real."

A helpful tool to reference to enhance your emotional intelligence can be Dr. Marc Brackett's cognitive resource called the RULER:

- ☞ R = *recognize*. Pause throughout the day and check in with your mind and body. Ask yourself, "At this exact moment, what is my emotional state?"
- ☞ U = *understand*. Be an "emotion scientist." Why are you feeling this way? What is causing it? Ask yourself, "What could have triggered this feeling?"
- ☞ L = *label*. Put your feelings into words. Be specific. Broaden your emotional vocabulary. Ask yourself, "Am I sad? Melancholy? Unfulfilled?"
- ☞ E = *express*. Converting emotions into words improves your health. Talk about your problems or write them down. Ask yourself, "Who do I know with whom I feel safe being vulnerable?"
- ☞ R = *regulate*. Experts recommend three strategies for regulating emotions. 1. Perform positive self-talk in the third person (i.e., he, she, or they). 2. Reframe your feelings in a positive way. 3. When you feel a negative emotion, ask yourself, "What would my best self do?"

This brings us to a particularly important theme of this book—what is success and how do you achieve it?

Most of us know that success means different things to different people, yet for some reason success seems like a challenging thing to acquire. For instance: to person A, success is determined by the state of mind a person is in. To person B, success is having a tangible status, such as family, professional title, house, or car. To person C, success is being able to do what you want when you want.

All answers are relevant but not reality. What felt like success at 15 years old will be different at 51. What last month's success was will be different from what tomorrow's success will be. This is reality. This is how life works.

However, if you are disconnected and living on autopilot from a preconceived notion of what you think you should be doing, you will miss the opportunity to feel your current day's success.

Success is created internally. The sooner you take personal responsibility in creating it, the sooner you will experience it. The energetic state of success is always present, interchangeable, and ever-evolving.

This sounds like a simple concept, but, as a society, we have lost our fundamental ability and our disciplined way of life to slow down, stay present, become creative, and play through curiosity.

The preconceived conditioning prevents you from knowing or making the choice to get a clear read on:

- 👉 Your state of mind
- 👉 Your desires
- 👉 Your true wants vs. needs
- 👉 Your habits

Therefore, we are going to dive into these a little deeper. You cannot experience or feel a state of success if you are unable to articulate and know what the context of success means for you. This is often the biggest mistake we make in our search for the creation of success. We focus entirely on creating a mindset we think we should have to become successful versus feeling the present-day success we already have (again, a conditioned tactic).

If we are unaware of the current state we are mentally, emotionally, financially, physically, and spiritually in—becoming successful will not happen. Our demand for security and values are two primary pillars that create success. Without having a sense of understanding solely of these two pillars of our lifestyle, there will be roadblocks that create a disconnect. Knowing, articulating, and applying these areas is how we can become proactive in experiencing a state of success. And having the mindset of understanding that our security and values will change as time evolves will allow us to stay in a state of mind where success is always present.

Phase 2: Confront Disconnect

Our awareness and ability to articulate how we feel and acknowledge what it is we are thinking is a practice. There are many external factors that get in the way of us being able to fully commit to staying connected. Whether it is our workload, family obligations, or lifestyle hobbies that allow us a sense of community, having a default of disconnectedness and distraction is easier than we would probably like to admit.

This is why confronting disconnect is so important in the first place. Half the world is living off a disconnected software system and completely unaware of it. To move away from this, we have to have the courage to connect and address the elephant in the room before believing it can be eliminated. Confronting disconnect can look something like this:

Dear Disconnect,

I am ashamed to admit how much I have relied on you lately and want to take a moment to acknowledge you for all the hard work you have done. No one deserves to be taken advantage of like this. So, I would like to set some boundaries on how we should move forward.

When I think back to when it all started, it is somewhat of a blur. As a child, I was unable to understand what was happening. Fast-forward to adolescence—as a young adult, I used you as a safety mechanism to protect me. And throughout my corporate, professional, and entrepreneurial phase, you served well as a destructive distraction.

All this time, I have been using and abusing you to either keep me safe or beat me up further. Your ability to build a mask and manipulate the mind is impeccable; to that point, I am surprised I have any friends and family left after my poor behavior. Not to mention your silent strength of doing everything possible to avoid conflict. This included sweeping pain under the rug, placating unwanted reality with food, substances, and other such external factors, or turning me into a hurtful villain that uses cowardly communication to resolve conflict.

I cannot imagine how exhausted you must be. When I think about the time, energy, and physical effort it takes to multi-task, managing emotions, manipulating reality, and pushing people away, I am in awe. Never catching a poor break to feel something, except disconnect. Alone, automated, depressed, heavy, lethargic, numb, predictable, and stagnant. That is your reality.

You leave me asking: what am I doing with my life? What is the purpose of it all? Where did the erotic, playful partner I fell in love with off and disappear to? How come everything seems like a battle to overcome? Why can I not seem to get through to my children? Who am I? What makes me, me? From where am I emulating my values, dreams, and truth?

All these questions are a necessary exercise in human evolution. However, sometimes you are too good at your job and you prevent others from doing it because of the uncertainty that resides in being connected.

The truth I have realized is with you present, I cannot feel alive. You box me into a preconceived space where your method of protection forces me to try and survive without the necessary tools I was born with. If I want to experience any sense of connected living, euphoric bliss, and illuminated success, I cannot have you in my life.

For a long time, I avoided changing my perception and mindset to create something different because of the "work" it was going to take. No one likes to address their inner critic or self-evaluate their destructive patterning. The work and mindset shifts were enough to stop me in my tracks before I could even get started. But here I am—alone, disconnected, and wildly unfulfilled, believing my reality can be different but knowing this mindset and way of life will not work.

World-renowned lecturer, consultant, educator, and author Karen Kaiser Clark once said, "Life is change, growth is optional, choose wisely." So here I am, making the choice to eliminate you from my ecology. You are no longer to be part of my operating system because it turns out I have a lot to give this world. Every individual does. But I cannot give if I do not feel, so it is time to effectively become and apply being eternally connected—with myself, with others, for the world.

Good Riddance,
The Successful, Creative Mindset

Many more people than you think live with disconnect, and many don't even know it. To evaluate your level of disconnect, answer the following questions:

- ☞ Am I willing to admit that I am disconnected right now?
- ☞ When was the last time I felt joy?
- ☞ Where do I feel disconnected? Finances, health, work, relationships?
- ☞ What would "connected" feel like?
- ☞ What action can I take within the next 24 hours to create a connection?

If you felt something regarding those questions, take action now!

Phase 3: Reidentify Yourself

Reidentifying yourself can be as easy or as difficult as your mindset makes it out to be. You will either go into this with curiosity or confrontational discomfort and stigma around what it even means. And whichever reaction you have will shed light on your willingness to create a mindset and energetic experience of success. The three-step process of reidentifying yourself includes (1) reidentify, (2) rebuild, and (3) reapply.

First, reidentify. Get clear on how much of your life you are human-doing versus being. Values are an actionable self-evaluation of this phase. A different way to put this is, do you experience life from a space of obligation or opportunity? If we are not careful, life can become an obligatory, run-down, scarce space in the blink of an eye. But when we stay present and connected to a mindset that practices honoring our truth, values, and desires, we can operate from a space of opportunity, resilience, and abundance.

Second, rebuild. Create the shift from doing to being. Boundaries are the actionable self-evaluation in this phase. There are tons of ways to hold ourselves accountable in this process. To name a few: meditation, keeping a gratitude journal, hiring a coach, having an accountability partner, having consciousness timers/trackers, and joining a mastermind group to have safe, vulnerable conversations.

Creating success with the reidentification process is no easy walk in the park. It is very important that you know and realize it is a continual practice where some days you will feel like you are owning it, and others you might feel confused and question the point of all the mindset reframing business. However, success is always present with a mindset reframe.

Third, reapply. Discover what your current-day values are. What do you want? What do you need to feel secure? Where do you get in your own way? What methods do you use? How do you allow others to get in your way? Reapplying is, in essence, retraining or rebuilding, which makes it one of the most crucial components in being able to create a new identity or way of life.

Give yourself permission to feel and become aware of what those feelings are. Your awareness enables understanding. Understanding allows you to articulate. Articulation provides a connection. Connection creates a mindset of fulfillment and reassurance, which then becomes a sense of success.

Phase 4: Get Clear and Live into Your Values

In terms of creating success through being connected, you need to be clear on your values. Values are a person's principles or standards of behaviors; their judgment of what is important in life. When you are not cognizant of and committed to your values (your why), it is easy to fall down the trap of prove, perfect, perform, or please. This will let others get in your head and hijack your efforts.

What does it mean to live into your values? You do more than profess your values. You practice them. You walk your talk. You are clear on what you believe and hold important. Take care that intentions, words, thoughts, and behaviors align with those beliefs.

When you are neither clear about nor connected to your values, you can forget WHY you went into the arena in the first place, you can forget the reason you are there, you can forget your values, or more frequently, you may not know what they are or how to name them.

Pick two core values that you feel are most important. Why only two? Because if you have more than three priorities, you have no priorities. The more values you deem "important" to yourself, the more it becomes a piece of paper of gauzy feel-good words. Additionally, your two core values are where your secondary values get fueled and tested. Your core values should be so crystalized in your mind, so precise and clear, that they do not feel like a choice. They are simply a definition of who you are in your life—personally and professionally. They guide you to make the choice to pick what is right versus what is easy or fun.

Your core values are the lifeline of who you are and the integrity of why you show up. Make them count. For Brené Brown's core values exercise, visit https://daretolead.brenebrown.com/workbook-art-pics-glossary/.

Phase 5: Commit to Habits That Align with Your Values

Your current habits are perfectly designed to deliver your current result. End of story.

When it comes to creating a space of success, your habits will make or break you. However, your habits are living proof of where your mindset is from a level of consciousness as well as whether it is operating under a fear-based or grounded-based mentality. Both are choices you make on a day-to-day, action-by-action basis.

Every action is a consequence of a thought. Your thought is a consequence of what you consume. And in the modern age, what you consume is largely a consequence of how you select, how you connect, and where you refine your boundaries and relationships. Choose better inputs. Get better outputs.

You can tell a lot about a person's core values and mentality based on their level of commitment as well as the types of habits they commit to. Your habits are where it is often safe to pass or make excuses, which are harmful because your commitment towards them is not only how you show up but why.

So, sit down and look at your habits. What is being reflected back to you? It can be a comforting truth or an unbearable excuse.

It is your job as a purpose-driven, success-connected thinker to always be willing to learn from and evaluate what your way of being is saying back to you—mentally, emotionally, financially, physically, and spiritually.

To learn more about your habits, read the book *Atomic Habits* by James Clear or visit https://jamesclear.com/habit-tracker.

Summary

Being connected is the backbone of your ability to feel success. If you eliminate the energy you put towards human-doing and become more intentional in who you are being, it will allow you to feel grounded in having purpose and belonging. That is why permission to feel is so important. You are human, you belong and have a purpose. Do not let societal standards fog your vision of what you can have and disconnect you from experiencing the everyday success you could be celebrating.

Action Steps

Nothing changes without action, so here are a few simple things you can do to move toward a successful mind:

- ☞ Become connected mentally, emotionally, financially, physically, and spiritually.
- ☞ Remain curious, dive into what your habits and lifestyle are reflecting about your beliefs.
- ☞ Confront disconnect and articulate your core values often—what is working in your life, what is not working, and connect to the why.
- ☞ Be unapologetically you, feelings and all.

About the Author

Alyssa Poggioli is a connection and leadership coach with an emphasis on emotional intelligence, as well as a writer and vlogger. Alyssa is certified in holistic health, life, and transformation coaching. A professionally certified coach with more than a decade of experience, she has helped others create massive change in their health, habits, and mindset. Alyssa has traveled extensively around Latin America and Southeast Asia, learning about the culture and relations of human connection. She is currently living in Chicagoland but is ready for her next great adventure.

Learn more and stay connected with Alyssa at www.alyssapoggioli.com, where you can also sign up for her blog, vlog, and monthly newsletter.

Email: alyssa@alyssapoggioli.com
Website: www.alyssapoggioli.com

CHAPTER 27
PSILOCYBIN MUSHROOMS AS SPIRITUAL ALLIES

By Chi Psilocybin
Psychedelic Guide, Coach, and Retreat Facilitator
Chirripo, Costa Rica

Only when the last tree has been cut down,
the last fish caught, and the last stream poisoned,
will we realize we cannot eat money.
—Cree Indian Prophecy

For millennia, humans have consumed psychedelic mushrooms to receive visions, heal diseases, and commune with the gods. Psilocybin, the primary psychoactive ingredient in these mushrooms, connects us with our innate intelligence and rewires our hearts and minds to be positive, open, and joyful. Having evolved and survived for more than a billion years, these magic mushrooms can help humanity transform into a more intelligent, loving, and harmonious species.

Our connection with Mother Earth is key to our survival. In cities, vehicle noise and fumes pollute our senses. Bird songs and the scent of flowers are foreign to many. We shuffle in and out of lifeless concrete buildings, instead of living amongst trees and rivers. We interact with screens more than with people around us. Many of us eat alone, mindlessly, without thanking all the hands involved in bringing food to our mouths. We feel like cogs in a machine—disconnected from ourselves, each other, and the environment.

But we are conscious beings—cells in a breathing organism. We are social creatures who *need* community and a sense of belonging. We want to surround ourselves with people who love us unconditionally. We despair in the absence of human affection. Humanity is experiencing a mental health crisis. In January 2020, the World Health Organization estimated globally more than 264 million people suffer from depression. Suicide rates worldwide have skyrocketed 60 percent over the past 45 years. The opioid crisis and other drug epidemics have ravaged families and communities. However, even though mental health problems seem to be increasing, and most people in need aren't getting the help they are looking for, a powerful solution is available almost everywhere: psilocybin mushrooms.

Magic mushrooms flourish on every continent except Antarctica. They are easy to grow indoors. Research from Johns Hopkins, Imperial College London, NYU, Beckley Foundation, and other universities supports long-established anecdotal evidence that psilocybin can improve our emotional states and reconnect us with nature and each other. These findings may come as surprising news for many. For me and others who have experienced the life-changing benefits of mushrooms, the excitement about a "new treatment for depression" feels like a return to ancient wisdom. Certainly, in my life, the mushroom has been one of my greatest teachers.

Before mushrooms found me, I struggled with chronic depression, low self-esteem, and destructive habits. I never felt good enough. Although loneliness tormented me, I pushed people away to protect my heart. I found myself in bottomless pits of shame, guilt, anger, and frustration. To escape these emotions, I pursued adrenaline rushes and intense pleasures. A series of overlapping addiction cycles propelled my life. I binged on sweets and cannabis. I played cards, sometimes sitting in smoke-filled poker rooms for 20 hours or more. I spent hours on the Internet watching pornography and playing games until my eyes could barely stay open. Of course, these habits deepened my angst. I caused grief for many, especially those who loved me most. Consumed by psychological pain, I considered taking my own life.

By my late-twenties, I felt hopeless. My strategies to avoid and escape difficult feelings were failing, but I didn't know what else to do. I felt unfulfilled even after immersing myself for many months in intensive meditation at Buddhist monasteries and retreat centers. Although several people over the years shared stories about their psychedelic awakenings and urged me to experiment, I dismissed these substances as "dangerous drugs," reserved for addicts and crazy hippies. As my desperation grew, though, I was willing to try anything.

My first few psychedelic adventures transformed my opinions about these stigmatized substances. Spiritual dogma and rigid thinking began to fade away. Masks dissolved. As I faced painful parts of myself from which I had previously run and hid, my heart released rivers of pent-up emotions. I laughed. I cried. I felt playful, bright, and authentic. My energetic center started to shift from head to heart, from intellect to intuition.

How could such effective medicines be illegal? Needing to understand, I dug into the history of psychedelics. I discovered that authorities banned magic mushrooms and other eye-opening substances not for health reasons, but for political ones. Psilocybin mushrooms, referred to as "flesh of the gods," were a cornerstone in Mesoamerican culture for thousands of years until Spanish conquistadors violently suppressed their use in the early 16th century. According to Paul Stamets in *Psilocybin Mushrooms of the World*, Catholic missionaries, wanting their subjects to commune with Christ instead of mushrooms, branded those using the latter as "devil worshippers." Psilocybin ceremonies went underground.

In the late 1950s and '60s, mushrooms experienced a brief resurgence in the wake of a *Life* magazine article titled "Seeking the Magic Mushroom." Gordon Wasson, a former JPMorgan executive, wrote about his adventures participating in ceremonies conducted by Maria Sabina, a Mazatec shaman who lived in Oaxaca, Mexico. Inspired by Wasson who wrote, "We chewed and swallowed these acrid mushrooms, saw visions, and emerged from the experience awestruck," many Westerners followed his footsteps in search of their own epiphanies. From these humble origins, psilocybin and other psychedelics energized the global counterculture and anti-war movements during the '60s.

By 1970, fearing collapse of the social order, the US government under Richard Nixon placed psychedelics on Schedule I of the Controlled Substances Act. In the eyes of the law, mushrooms and heroin were the same—both drugs "have a high potential for abuse and the potential to create severe psychological and/or physical dependence." Although researchers had published more than a thousand studies touting the therapeutic potential of hallucinogens during the prior two decades, Nixon declared a "war on drugs," threatening to imprison those caught with illegal substances. Federal authorities sought to stigmatize psychedelics and halt related research, but some dedicated academics, psychiatrists, and therapists continued to work clandestinely with the medicines.

Decades later, we are living in the midst of a psychedelic renaissance. The US Food and Drug Administration has granted psilocybin "breakthrough therapy" status twice: first in 2018 for treatment-resistant depression and again in 2019 for major depressive disorder. Researchers are once more studying the effects of this substance on a host of illnesses including depression, end-of-life anxiety, obsessive-compulsive disorder, anorexia, addictions, and cluster headaches. Calls to decriminalize, if not outright legalize, psychedelics grow louder each day as more people experience the benefits firsthand. For many, the inhumanity of criminalizing citizens who experiment with mind-expanding substances has overshadowed any perceived utility. When fresh evidence challenges our worldviews, we must be willing to change our minds. Our magic mushroom journeys help us see through a different lens.

Our psilocybin experiences urge us to think for ourselves and to question everything we *think* we know. They reveal how society distracts us from deeper truths. Perhaps for the first time, we admit we lack answers to fundamental questions. Who am I? What are my values? What do I really want? What brings me joy? What is my contribution to the world? Why are cigarettes and alcohol widely available while magic mushrooms are illegal? When we examine our beliefs, we face the unsettling possibility that our life has been built on falsehoods. Disillusionment leads many to embark on a spiritual search.

With mushrooms as our guides, we dive into our own hearts and rediscover childlike attitudes of openness, curiosity, and wonder. A newborn enters this world a clean slate without preconceived notions. They welcome new information and perspectives. Our journeys train us to be a child who sees through new eyes. With a flexible, soft, and supple mind, we lower expectations and start to appreciate our blessings. We empty ourselves and return to being receptive vessels.

As the mind opens, we become sensitive to vibrations emanating from our surroundings. We notice how environments color our mood. When I enter a crowded city, I feel disconnected and anxious. Many are lost in thought while they stare at phones and rush to their destinations. Hugs and eye contact are rare occurrences. The suffering of homeless people disturbs me. In contrast, I remain at ease when I walk through a forest or bathe in a clean river. In natural, open spaces, life seems complete, nurturing, and rejuvenating. I feel less compelled to numb myself. Earth reminds us to slow down and return to a simple existence in harmony with the rhythms of life and death. Because no matter how fast we run, we cannot escape the law of impermanence. Mushrooms are a reminder of this, both within and outside of cities.

Communing with psilocybin allows us to practice dying before we die. We drop attachments to old ways of thinking, acting, and relating. In some of our journeys, we experience transformative states of ego dissolution. The edges of our bodies melt into our surroundings. Thoughts disappear. In the absence of a concrete sense of self, joy radiates. We are one with the Universe, Heart of God, Infinite Light, Eternal Love, and Christ Consciousness. Bodies return to dust, but life continues beyond our death. The medicine gives us the ability to feel and release fear.

During our journeys, we are like snakes shedding worn-out skin, or caterpillars in metamorphosis preparing to emerge as butterflies. Every time we commune with the mushroom, our faith in the process of transformation grows. We forgive rather than punish our demons. By relinquishing control, we feel light and free. Tensions dissolve. Our faces glow. We feel reborn. And even when happiness appears, we continue the practice of non-grasping.

As we mature, we become aware of our self-centeredness. We humble ourselves before life does to avoid the dangerous trap of perceived invincibility. We abandon the need to prove ourselves or be better than others. We take ourselves less seriously and laugh at our folly. We are quicker to say, "I was wrong," "I'm sorry," and "Please forgive me." When others harm us, we pardon them and thank them for allowing us to practice patience. We listen fully instead of thinking about how we are going to respond. When we let go of small-mindedness, our hearts become more magnanimous, nurturing, and joyous. We cultivate respect for all beings.

Mushrooms remind us life is a vast interconnected web. All around us, countless beings move and breathe, grow and evolve, and compete and cooperate with each other. Trees, insects, birds, rivers, and oceans are as much part of life as we are. Our journeys allow us to feel connected to all beings. When we see ourselves in others, we treat everyone the way we want to be treated. We may even sacrifice our own pleasure for the sake of others. By forgetting about ourselves, we gain freedom. Our guiding principle becomes to abide as a source of happiness for others.

As our experiences reveal universal laws of cause and effect, we sense ripples of even the most subtle thoughts and actions. Past intentions have led to current conditions, and the present mind creates the future. Positive outcomes result from practicing kindness, compassion, forgiveness, generosity, and joy. Dire consequences follow when we scatter seeds of greed, anger, hatred, fear, and arrogance. When we recognize the repercussions of past deeds, we become careful about the energies we transmit. Our life is the result of every seed planted since the creation of the Universe.

As we explore our hearts and minds, we feel more connected to our ancestors. We are not separate from all those who came before us. Our life is a tapestry of their blood and bones, hopes and dreams, shame and grief. We are a leaf growing at the tip of the infinite tree of life, the culmination of generations of evolutionary struggle.

Our mushroom journeys allow us to relive and release ancestral traumas. The Native Americans say every action affects seven generations in each direction. When we heal and mature, we transform our entire ancestral lineage whose spirit flows through us. Our descendants are able to live without our energy blockages. And our epigenetic healing impacts not only our own bloodline but the whole of humanity. One person's transformation benefits everyone. As ancient wounds continue to surface, we accept the infinite and privileged nature of inner work.

You may ask, "Why would I want to relive painful intergenerational wounds?" In my experience, the healing process can be unpleasant, but its benefits outweigh any discomforts. Psilocybin has helped me mend relationships with my parents, particularly Dad, who is Chinese. Since my childhood, we have struggled to maintain a healthy relationship. Our education and upbringings were completely different (I was born and raised in the US, and Dad in Taiwan), and I felt we had a shallow connection at best. Dad's angry and violent outbursts, though infrequent, carved deep wounds into my heart, which I buried with an insatiable drive to be "good" and liked. To compensate for my pain, I focused on becoming a capitalistic machine—a star student and relentless entrepreneur. I strove to be a successful, confident, controlled, and purebred American—everything Dad was not. For many years, I was ashamed to be his son.

Then, in the summer of 2018, I tripsat for Dad's first two psilocybin journeys when he visited me in Amsterdam. Both of us were ready to give space to and release painful emotions. During his second experience, Dad's hurt inner child emerged. A dam broke—decades of unsaid words and repressed confusion, fear, and heartbreak poured out without a filter. He missed Mom who had been his rock for more than 30 years before their divorce in 2015.

As I watched Dad sob for hours, I allowed myself to feel sadness, compassion, and love for a human being beyond the label "Dad." Instead of a villain, I saw a Divine Child of God. He knelt, bowed his head to the ground, thanked me, and begged for forgiveness. I felt like his father and his son, and we were one. Every judgment dissolved and transmuted into a bright, soft, loving energy. It was a miracle.

Our relationship now is still mostly painful, but these events gave birth to an entire lineage of feelings I had previously suppressed. I stopped hating the Chinese half of myself. I became even prouder of my paternal grandfather, an Air Force Colonel who escaped to Taiwan when Communists won the Chinese Civil War. He was passed up for generalship because he protected the 2 thousand men under his command when his superiors wanted to maneuver them into dangerous situations. His heart was full of love. In the months after I tripsat for Dad, waves of primal warrior energy surged through me. During one journey, I was a military commander as I walked briskly up and down an open field. I saw fires and armies marching and entering battle. Mushrooms revealed these ancient visions stored in my psyche.

My ancestors move through me, especially when I take mushrooms. When I study and contemplate the sometimes brutal Sino-Japanese history, I choose to explore complex emotions rather than run or hide. Curiosity and compassion, not fear and bitterness, guide me as I examine the relationship between the two nations, along with the role America has played in shaping modern Asian history and my perspectives. The cultural rivalry that underlies my parents' relationship provides me with a microcosm. Although I used to think Mom was always right, I now accept she is a fallible human—a wounded child. As I recognize and grieve the destructive consequences of anger, pride, and violence, I am able to practice compassion for all beings. When we heal relationships with family, we restore relationships with everyone else.

Since tripsitting for Dad, I have had the honor to support hundreds of journeyers from all walks of life. The mushrooms have taught me lessons that books alone cannot. When we open to our own pain, we allow ourselves to feel the suffering of others. Healing is a cyclical process without an end. When we get too excited, we are bound to fall. Sometimes, the pain overpowers us. We contract and return to old habits. And it's okay. Deep-seated wounds take time to heal. Let's be patient and kind with ourselves. We all need community—family, friends, teachers, therapists, and others with whom we can share our deepest thoughts. Indeed, the Buddha explains that spiritual friendship is "the entire spiritual life." This wisdom also applies to the mushroom journey.

While some people like to journey alone, others find it more comforting to have someone watching over them. When we experience overwhelming emotions during our journeys, the presence of a mature tripsitter can be a soothing balm. A tripsitter reassures us that we are safe and loved. This person may assume various roles: friend, babysitter, therapist, nurse, cook, and angel. A skillful tripsitter does not do or say much. Lacking ambition, they make no effort to lead. They sit, listen, and send love. They help us go to the bathroom, get tissues, and drink water. In challenging moments, they may hold our hand or give us a hug. Blessed are those who have a trustworthy tripsitter and those who tripsit for others.

I am convinced that psychedelic medicines are humanity's most reliable partners in our urgent struggle to replace toxic systems with regenerative ones. They are teachers—mirrors that allow us to take an honest look at ourselves. They give us opportunities to relinquish old habits, restore relationships, and meet death with joy. As our minds expand, we think less about what we can get, and more about how we can serve others. As Shantideva writes in *A Guide to the Bodhisattva's Way of Life*, "All the suffering in the world comes from wishing our self to be happy. All the happiness in the world comes from wishing others to be happy."

Mushroom journeys fill our hearts with gratitude. They show us that though we are insignificant specks of dust, we are also perfect manifestations of the infinite and eternal. Every moment since the beginning of time has led to our present existence. Nisargadatta Maharaj, the late Indian nondual master, said, "Wisdom tells me I am nothing. Love tells me I'm everything. Between the two my life flows." Every mushroom journey reaffirms this paradox.

May the mushroom find all those who seek peace and wisdom!

About the Author

Chi is a psilocybin guide, advocate, and retreat facilitator whose life is dedicated to sharing the mushroom message of love and light. He is the founder of Truffles Therapy, a psilocybin retreat organization that has guided hundreds of people on their psychedelic journeys. He is also the founder of Global Alliance of Psilocybin Practitioners, which provides community, training, and mentorship for guides, and connects those seeking the medicine with those providing safe access. Finally, he advises individuals and companies involved in the emerging psychedelic industry.

Chi has had the privilege of spending more than 16 months in silent retreat, including a month in dark retreat. He credits his success to his parents, his spiritual teachers, and psychedelic medicines. He bows down to all the Buddhas and bodhisattvas throughout space and time.

Learn more about the work at www.trufflestherapy.com, www.tripsitters. org, and www.psilocybinfoundation.org.

Email: chi@trufflestherapy.com

CHAPTER 28

THE WELLNESS MINDSET IN BUSINESS: SUCCESSFUL COMPANY CULTURE CHANGE

By Michelle Greene Rhodes, MHS, CMCN, RN
Managed Care and Wellness Consultant
Tampa, Florida

There is a major crisis in businesses worldwide. This crisis is the lack of a total health and wellness culture within companies. More and more businesses are realizing how valuable employee health is to an organization's overall productivity and profit, but there are still many companies that ignore wellness as a factor in company success.

As a wellness consultant, it is my job to help with this problem.

Before beginning any business-wellness project, I must envision the epitome of wellness within the business in which I am requested to assess. I must see what wellness programming can improve to get a positive result. Can any of these become a reality: a culture where leaders attend yoga class with workers, where leaders participate in a monthly meditation class, or where leaders share their hobby of bike riding or walking? When leaders value wellness to the extent that the entire organization will benefit holistically, then it's a likely yes. When onboarding an organization, the team and I determine together the greatest and best use of wellness services within the organization.

Even still, I have worked with business leaders that only want to invest in the level of "checking the box"; to say they've addressed wellness without actually embracing and valuing it in their business and their own mindset for success. What would be the result of wellness initiatives for businesses in these not even half-hearted circumstances? Probably, the result would not be good. Welcome to the importance of how the mindset of leadership can influence the outcomes for many, many employees and, in turn, the business's bottom line.

This is important because company wellness shouldn't be to get employees to a neutral place of no problems and no benefits. Rather, to create win-win situations. Therefore, the goal for total wellness should be beyond average.

There is a paradigm within healthcare called the "illness-wellness continuum" created in 1975 by Dr. John Travis. This continuum demonstrates the correlation between beliefs, lifestyle behaviors, and health outcomes. On the far left of the continuum is premature death with disability, symptoms, and signs moving toward the center, which is the neutral point (no discernible illness or wellness). The treatment is usually to get people from premature death to the neutral point. On the far right of the continuum is high-level wellness with awareness, education, and growth as points along the continuum from the neutral point to high-level awareness. Whereas the "treatment paradigm" starts on the left of the continuum and ends at the neutral point, the "wellness paradigm" starts also on the far left of the continuum, but it keeps going all the way past the neutral point to high-level wellness. This place of high-level wellness is where business leaders' with success mindsets aim to get their companies' wellness cultures to.

With this "illness-wellness continuum" in mind, I argue that the healthy outcomes of an organization's employees as well as the financial health of an organization itself must be in balance, and the recognition of the importance of both should be in place. If a leader is strictly focused on providing the minimum amount of wellness programming for the sake of the balance sheet, or to check a box, then the claims expenditure for health plan costs may very well overtake that. You see, we must tackle wellness at the very beginning of this continuum and implement the services that will serve the employees where they are, along it. This is done to slow down their progression on this continuum.

The effects of a robust wellness program have been shown to be widespread, from increased productivity, improved engagement, and cost savings in other beneficial areas. To achieve these positive effects, it is imperative that leaders grasp this concept, instill it in their success mindset, adopt it into the culture of the organization, and lead with it. This can only be achieved if the business leaders have adopted the mindset of creating a "culture of wellness."

There are multiple ways that a culture of wellness can be established from the top down. When it comes to creating a culture of employee wellness within an organization, a top-down establishment of it remains the best practice. You see, if the goal is to help an organization transform from the inside out, the leaders must stand out as early participants and champions of what is to come.

Why is employee wellness important, and why must we embrace this at work? If you are a business owner or leader and desire outcomes such as high-functioning teams with high productivity, then wellness programming is designed especially for the culture of your organization. These programs pay for themselves, but how do we get there? It all begins with the mindset of the leader who sets the tone for the culture of wellness in the organization.

It's Bigger Than Claims Data

Ideally, when cultivating a "culture of wellness," if the leader does not incorporate it into their personal lives, does not show enthusiasm about the movement, or does not have values that match what is being adopted, then the movement might be lost before it has begun. Employees are more likely to take the time to propel this movement forward—and actually adopt demonstrated behaviors—if the workplace culture is designed to receive it. If top management are willing to commit the budget, support systems, and even their time to the wellness initiatives, employees will sense that wellness is a top priority for the organization, and that is where the mindset shift begins for the employees.

This is why the mindset of the leader is so important, and what I call the "culture of one becoming the culture of many" happens. Business leaders must be willing to trade the focus of claims data and the cost of healthcare in exchange for this type of vantage point. The leader is in a unique position to align the organization's strategy, processes, and culture to wellness initiatives. Health and wellness have to become an integral part of the strategy. Processes and policies must be in place to demonstrate the full support of top management with claims data only being a secondary outcome of their efforts. This becomes highly beneficial because when it comes to claims data, we see that the further one goes down the left side of the "illness-wellness continuum," the higher the price to be paid out.

Champions Help Begin a Movement

So how do we now integrate this "top-down wellness" way of thinking into an entire organization? As a part of the implementation strategy, we do cut the leader some slack. Of course, they could not be held responsible for transforming cost savings and peak performing teams of an organization in this manner single-handedly. This type of work requires delegation. A training system should be developed to showcase not only the top leaders adopting wellness principles, but their senior management team as well. Delegation is the next step that our firm prepares for, and we begin to strategize a train-the-trainer approach with senior leaders, which will then bring in "champions" for our movement. For this movement to become successful, it has been found that business executives must dedicate time and effort into this integration.

Here's how to strategize with the "champions":

- Organizational strategy—the who, what, when and how, starting at the top
- Meaningful meetings—what to communicate and how frequently?
- Budget—money, time, and accountability
- Teamwork—who will be responsible for what?
- Implementation—taking action individually and collectively

As the "champions" are at the crux of this movement, let us discuss their critical role at this juncture. Who knew that it would take an entire team to contribute to organizational behavior change? Would you have guessed that the work environment could help save lives? You see, change is a bitter pill to swallow, and it is more widely accepted if it's distributed amongst the organization by those who are ready, willing, and able to champion the cause. They are known to have an influential effect amongst those that they work with, in an effort to create buzz. You see, human behavior often works such that if we see an organic trend, we tend to trust its roots. Nowhere can just one person sharing a message from a mountain top create major change, nor can change occur quickly without everyone being part of the new change. It's the gradual one-by-one results that we tend to value the most. Our natural and inquisitive nature kicks in, and listening and adapting to the environment tends to kick in. This, however, can be the case for negative and positive behaviors. Business leaders, if you are listening, let us use this strategy to implement positive and methodical behavior change.

Create Momentum, Then a Movement

If leadership goes in with the mindset of creating lasting change, then it must be committed for the long run. Wavering support will signal to employees an untruth, and momentum gained might dissipate. As already mentioned, in order to provide employees with support that they need to create an impetus towards wellness programming, senior leaders within businesses should consider creating a team of champions that will create ways to connect with the organization.

Let me mention that messaging is very important to be on one accord to help formulate the culture as well. Please ensure that team members carry the same message and are on one accord. Next, contemplate a company kick-off announcement and pre-launch activities. During this time, if a beta group can try out various initiatives, their testimonials can help towards creating heightened awareness down the road. This strategy is just the beginning of creating programming that yields maximum ROI when the entire culture is challenged towards growth in its wellness. Contests or interactive activities are a great way to begin to launch fully.

Begin with intentional meetings that are designed to create programs that support physical, emotional, mental, intellectual, and occupational well-being.

We All Win

It is more important than ever that companies promote wellness. Believe it or not, employees are looking for some inspiration to stay happy and healthy during these tough times. At the time of this writing, we are in the midst of the COVID-19 worldwide pandemic. We are uncertain of what is yet to come for organizations, as many have closed and moved to virtual platforms. Even now, the importance of staying well is a key message for fighting this pandemic. As you can imagine, those who are unhealthy or have pre-existing health conditions may not fare too well during this time. There is no better time than now to implement initiatives that will transform the culture by ridding the organization of old or nonexistent ways of engaging wellness. It is never too early to begin engaging wellness in the workplace.

The key to successful transformations is not about getting your employees excited about a one-time walk, a 30-day challenge, or an annual health fair. This is a method of "checking another box" and not truly investing into the culture of your organization. A true wellness program starts with the mindset of the winners in the C-suite. The reason they are winners is because they decided to implement a wellness culture that begins with themselves! Next, they establish a senior leadership team who shares the vision and mindset of this intended plan of direction. Let us not neglect the fact that this is not a plan to be passed on or instructed without causing change in all hands that touch it. Through the champions who carry out the intended message on one accord, your business's organizational culture can then be created, inspired, and empowered. Fueled by momentum, if leaders are married to the cause, an organization should see a significant return on investment in as little as 18 to 24 months on average. That is a major win-win success.

With a shared mindset aimed at total wellness within a company, the company can become more healthy (and profitable), leadership can become more healthy (and effective), and employees can become more healthy, filled with a wellness mindset, improved lifestyle, and avoidance of unnecessary morbidity, which would reduce company productivity overall.

About the Author

Michelle G. Rhodes is a wellness consultant with a background in managed care and registered nursing. She has been recognized by the Florida Nursing Association as an ICON Winner for Nurse Entrepreneurship. After serving as a registered nurse for 20-plus years, Michelle decided to marry her background in managed care/population health with her innate ability to create educational programs and cost-saving solutions that are uniquely designed for each client. After multiple successes in cost saving and exceeding targets, she now utilizes her gift to help organizations meet and exceed performance measures and goals.

Michelle has worked with clients such as the UnitedHealth Group, the City of Tampa, and Gaudenzia, Inc. to create wellness initiatives for awareness campaigns and total culture transformations.

Email: support@greenerhodesconsulting.com
Website: www.GreeneRhodesConsulting.com

CHAPTER 29

RECIPE FOR GREATNESS

By Annie Salvador
High Performance Coach, NLP Master Coach
Chicago, Illinois

I begin this chapter by inviting you, for a moment, to lend me your imagination and consider your desires of success. Perhaps you have a specific challenging goal that has grasped your attention, and the idea of accomplishing this goal excites you. Imagine yourself, if you will, five or 10 years ahead, living your best life, doing your best work, and relishing in the joys of the journey. You are thriving, and you, along with everyone around you, knows it. You have a sense of pride in your accomplishments. You did it. Everywhere you turn, you are receiving positive feedback, and it feels good. You are blessed and are appreciating it all. As this mental movie plays out, feel the emotions of your success. Take a moment to consider your amazing accomplishments and how you present yourself to the world. What is it that you gave every day that made accomplishing all this possible? What skills did you bring to the table? How have you been turning up?

Perhaps you might also now consider someone you hold in high esteem; someone you admire who has or is doing the things you want to do. What qualifies them to be esteemed? Is it something they do? Is it something they don't do? Is it specific accomplishments? Is it their reputation?

Now pause for a moment and ask yourself: are you today, in the here and now, a match to that future version of yourself? Are you a match to your admired individual?

Part of my role as a high performance and personal development coach is bridging the gap from where you are and who you must be, to live that experience of accomplishing your goals. I help individuals raise their standard of greatness. I help people do everything better, to follow through and reap the rewards of their efforts.

One of the questions I am often asked by new clients is "What makes some mediocre and others great?" or "What makes the greats, great?"

I always get excited when I hear this question because interestingly, the greats I know, those thriving in their domain, have at some point in time asked themselves this same question in a compare-to-self manner. This is relevant because it is not the case for everyone. For many who ask themselves the same question, it is merely a fleeting thought that leaves as fast as it arrived. The curiosity, the desire is not there.

I believe greatness is a recipe that you cook up over time. It isn't one specific ingredient, but it is having the right collection of habits, behaviors, attitudes, and understanding that allows you to be great. In life, rarely does a person have all they want handed to them on a plate. Those fortunate enough to be blessed with natural talents dedicate a lot of time and energy into honing their skills. Even then, having skills is merely one aspect of greatness, it's what you do with those skills, what you add to those skills, and how you make those skills work for you that makes you a cut above the rest. In this chapter, I will share some of the ingredients to success that have become apparent over the years of my work.

Greatness Is a Choice

Greatness is primarily a choice that cannot be forced upon you. You must choose it for yourself, so you ought to choose wisely. Mediocre can be a satisfying life and will require less of you. Nowhere is it written that greatness is easy. Yes, with an understanding and the application of the laws of the universe, you can make the journey less bumpy. It will require much effort and sacrifice. Particularly in the early days, you are very aware that by choosing to be your greatest, there are a lot of other things you are choosing not to do, for example, a lot of fun, distracting stuff that could be very pleasing ways to pass the time. No matter how tempted you are, you will have to choose greatness and choose it repeatedly, refusing distracting desires for the sake of the greatness you wish to experience in the future. You must give before you receive. There is rarely instant gratification.

Greatness Is Fueled by a Worthy Goal

Because the road to greatness will be thwarted with challenges and demands a lot from you, you need a worthy mission. It must be bold enough to make it worth your while; you must really, really want it and know specifically what it will give you and what it will do for you. When you weigh what you are willing to give to what you will receive, it must be worth it to you. When you have the right motive, you have the motivation. The rewards and incentives need to be so juicy; you are happy to wait for them. If you are doing it right, you will also be enjoying the journey.

Greatness Is Being Bold Enough to Self-Evaluate from a Growth Mindset

To become the greatest version of yourself requires you to be brutally honest when considering your skills, character, and attributes. Even within self-evaluation, you must be kind to yourself and do so from a growth mindset. According to Carolyn Dweck, Ph.D. at Stanford, "In a growth mindset, people believe that their most basic abilities can be developed through dedication and hard work—brains and talent are just the starting point."

No one can be good at all things. Our objective ought to aim for bringing the best performance we can, and where we are weak, work to improve that area. Many of our weak spots are simply venturing into new territory; other weak spots though, tend to be interlinked with those elements we avoid and procrastinate on. We avoid for many reasons: because it feels uncomfortable, because we know we are not equipped to confidently make the right moves, or because we are making something else more important in the moment. Perhaps, sometimes, we are right for our inaction. We know we are not prepared. We are indeed weak, because we haven't learned to a reasonable level what we need to be confident within a certain skill.

Once we have thrown some energy in that direction, when we have tried and failed and then tried again, when we have served our time in practice, we approach in an entirely different manner. Our expectations are different because we are turning up different, not as weak but as a person who believes they have the ability and who is the right person for the job.

Sometimes it's not as easy as enhancing a skill; sometimes it is the individual's character that needs to evolve. No one likes to be under character assassination. You must be willing to scrutinize yourself though if you want to reveal the best of yourself. Much of our communication and learned response habits do not serve us well when it comes to persuasion, leading, and getting results. You can have all the talents in the world, but for the most part, if you are not likable, if you can't communicate well, then you may struggle to coerce people into working alongside or for you. If you are too arrogant or if you can't confidently direct people, if you can't relinquish control, then you may just end up doing all the work yourself and become exhausted.

Greatness Is Discipline in Action

Self-mastery and discipline are keys to success. There is no room for excuses or laziness; they are for the mediocre. There will always be multiple justifiable excuses readily available to your mind. The secret to success is to know this and plan accordingly. Anticipate their sneakiness and set yourself up to win. Truth is when planning anything, your mind already knows all the excuses you could use to not follow through. It comes down to choosing. Choose to do it or don't. Don't use excuses when you know, if you really want it, you will make it happen. The only person you are cheating is yourself.

The problem with excuses is they easily become bad habits that breed other bad habits. Such as blaming. People who make excuses all the time often blame everyone else for that which does not go according to plan rather than taking responsibility for their actions or lack thereof. This is not the habit of someone living their greatest self who instead takes full responsibility for their errors and accomplishments.

One of the unfortunate consequences of being a habitual procrastinator is that you live with a baseline of anger, frustration, and sometimes even jealousy. Ultimately this is because you live within constant disappointment of the worst kind, disappointment in yourself with anything you don't get done, being used against you.

Greatness Is a Willingness to Make Mistakes

It is going to happen; it is inevitable. There is simply no room for progression if there is no room to make mistakes. Of course, in finance you only want to risk what you are willing to lose without regret; other than that, holding the space for error and being bold can be the exact ingredient for creating new, workable opportunities. When a screw-up does occur, it is important to own your errors, especially if you have a team. Not taking responsibility for your misgivings usually means someone else is taking the fallout. It is most likely that the relationship will be tarnished for the long term. Good business thrives on great relationships. When you take ownership, it speaks volumes about your honorability. Truth is, in all mistakes, there are great lessons. It's the culmination of all these lessons and adjusting actions accordingly that makes for truly living your greatness and thriving both in life and business.

Greatness Is Being Strategic

The greats are strategic. They look before they leap and are always appropriately cautious. They aren't just winging it and are not looking to leave anything to chance. They hold the space for chance and luck, but they will be taking matters into their own hands. They know what they want, whether it's achievable and worth the investment, and they identify the obstacles to getting there. What they can control and influence they do. They do not cut corners! They would never want to be known for that. More importantly, they are not kidding themselves; they are not being what I call "avoiders." Avoiders are those individuals who refuse to look at something they fear may reveal something they don't want to see. For the greats, if something could be a problem, if there could be a block, they face it head-on. They are not 'wishful thinking' that it will resolve itself. They are not praying and taking no action to support the manifestation of what they ask for.

Of course, they may make a mistake; they are far from planning for it though.

Greatness Is Emotional Mastery

Some people are academically and financially successful yet lack the one vital component to truly being great, which is emotional mastery. The ability to allow your initial reaction to pass you by without it dominating your behavior and, thus, allowing yourself the opportunity to choose how to respond—that is a powerful capability. When you are emotionally invested in a goal, and if your goal is worthy, it can be easy to react too strongly under strenuous or disappointing circumstances.

You must know your own stress-response. Without doubt there will be trials and tribulations on the path to achieving your goals; within any kind of business environment the tide could change in an instant. How you respond when the going gets tough can make or break you. The four stress responses are fight, flight, freeze, and fawn. Many people fall victim to a habitual stress-response that is deceitfully wrapped up in elaborate excuses of justification. If you are not aware of your own response, if you do not have a plan on how to manage such situations, you are not in control of the situation but a victim to it. Many poor decisions are made from rash, emotionally charged responses rather than thought-through, rational responses. A simple pause by taking a breath and allowing the wave of emotion and the reactive thoughts to pass is sufficient to prevent a reactive and detrimental response. At least by not responding, you haven't escalated anything. I wouldn't recommend trying to master this in the heat of the moment; instead, throughout your day, get into the habit of taking a breath and slowing down all responses.

Greatness Is the Success Mindset

Surpassing all these in importance is a baseline belief that all things are possible with the right attitude and implementing the right strategy. This is a key point. Because there is rarely instant gratification, you will often play the waiting game, and as they say, the idle mind is the devil's workshop. Being fragile and at unrest within the period between work and rewards manifestation is the simplest way to make all prior work irrelevant. Sure professionalism, doing due diligence, and keeping your eye on the ball is essential for success. It serves you well, though, to allocate a specific time for such contemplation. In all other times, second-guessing, planning how you will recover from failure, and anticipating disappointment can sabotage your best-laid plans.

The greats are not doing this. They have prepared to win. They rest easy knowing they have done their best to secure their success. If a challenge arises, they can rely on themselves to deal with it. In times of inaction in one area they are usually making most of the time and focused on another important area. Hopefully, they are throwing some fun in there.

Greatness Is Self-Love

Unfortunately, this is an area I see lacking in many leaders. They are so busy, they always come second to every task that needs action. It is the very reason why so many eventually end up in poor health, whether mental or physical. Even the smartest and most active minds benefit from downtime. It benefits you to be clear when you are on the work clock. When you are not officially on the work clock, reward yourself by being present where you are, enjoying the calm. There is a time to knuckle down to business and a time to enjoy your friends and family. Often the latter gets forgotten, and career spills over into living or the activities of living become just as hectic as working.

The only way to avoid looking back and thinking you missed out on all the great stuff, the free time of life, is to make it important and schedule it in. This I mean literally. When you break it down, there are 168 hours in a week, sleep uses 49 hours, work at least 40 hours, about seven hours of hygiene care, which leaves us, before feeding ourselves and taking care of errands, a mere 72 hours. Throw kids and a lover into the mix, and the one thing that soon becomes apparent on the path to success is that time is the most precious thing. You can't buy it, and you can't get it back. Use your time wisely. Sometimes doing nothing for nothing's sake is the perfect remedy.

Greatness Is Being Humble

Greatness is playing the long game. It is a series of hurdles you must overcome and an ever-evolving animal. We are all on our own path, evolving at the appropriate rate as designed by ourselves. There is no right or wrong in having a desire to be great or not. It's a preference. There is a tendency for greatness to become tarnished with arrogance. Be aware and remain humble. The way to consistently grow in your greatness is to seek to constantly raise others up. The ultimate greatness is living your dreams that you worked so hard for and deserve while being humble, kind, and hopefully paying it forward.

If you want to live out your greatness in this lifetime, get hungry and take action! The only thing that can get in your way is you. We are blessed to live in our current time and space, and to choose how we flourish, so choose greatness. Your potential is endless.

About the Author

Annie Salvador, a British Chicagoan is a high performance and personal development Coach who, for almost two decades, has been developing individuals and raising the bar on success utilizing a diverse toolbox with modalities in coaching, strategic intervention, energy psychology, NLP, hypnosis, and mindfulness. Annie has licensing from some of the leaders in the industry, namely Robbins-Madanes-Peysha, Richard Bandler, Paul Mckenna, Michael Breen, and Jon LaValle. When taking a break from conquering the world of high performance, Annie is exploring all things metaphysical, mystical, and energetic, and surrounding herself in nature, all while enjoying the rewards of motherhood.

Email: info@anniesalvador.com
LinkedIn: https://www.linkedin.com/in/anniesalvador/

CHAPTER 30
BEING *THAT* GOOD!

By David Saville
Creator of Pure Coaching
Ilford, United Kingdom

My game was my biggest endorsement.
What I did on the basketball court, my dedication to the game,
led to all this other stuff ... My game did ALL the talking!
—Michael Jordan

Michael Jordan has made over a billion dollars through endorsements from brands like Nike and Coca-Cola, but he didn't seek them out. He dedicated himself to excelling at basketball and drew those opportunities towards him like the gravitational pull of the sun.

Those brands wanted to be in his orbit, and everyone else wanted to "be like Mike". He was admired by millions and influenced filmmakers like Spike Lee. This kid who loved to play basketball changed the way the world worked. He is a unique phenomenon, and yet his approach contains lessons for us all about how we can develop our own gravitational pull.

The mindset we are going to be focusing on in this chapter is "being *that* good!"

The phrase, "being *that* good", has a feeling of power and freedom to it. It represents a way of being, living, and working that will have you experience life in a way that is rare and beautiful. It's not an easy path, but, if you stay with me, you'll see why this is a very strong choice to make and how it is relevant for you whatever your current circumstances or history.

It doesn't matter how good or bad you think you are right now. You can make a choice to develop this success mindset within the life you are leading, and it can become a clear path to a brighter future.

When most people think of success, they are using money as the measurement. It is important, but there are problems with having money as the main focus: it clouds judgement, makes us selfish, brings out neediness, and blinds us to other important factors.

Before I became a professional life coach, I worked for the same company for 17 years. I started in the warehouse picking stock and ended up doing most jobs that no one else wanted to do. One of them was processing faulty goods and sending them back to suppliers, a job rejected by most of the staff. They said they wouldn't do it because they weren't getting paid enough.

I saw it as a way of adding variety to my days and an opportunity to learn something new. It was horrible at times, going through goods that had been used and sent back, but it allowed me many opportunities to grow my skills, like negotiating with suppliers and other tasks that challenged me.

Before having this position, I had severe anxiety, being scared to speak to people, so being forced to do that as part of my job helped me learn to communicate better. At first, I became okay talking on the phone, and over time I became good at it.

I didn't know when I accepted this part of the job that it would lead to anything, but a few years later I was promoted into the office and became assistant to the owner. In this new position, I needed to draw upon the skills I had developed, and I learned a whole lot more.

That "dirty job" that no one else wanted got me a large pay raise and opened up more opportunities while the others who refused to do it worked in the same roles for years and were miserable. Their need to get paid first prevented them from getting paid a lot more later, and they missed out in many other ways too.

Absolute Responsibility

Taking responsibility is important. Don't look for short-term payoffs, seek to take on more responsibility than is reasonable for anyone to expect. The skills you develop and the person you become make you far more valuable. Your worth increases exponentially. Rather than avoiding responsibility, ask yourself, "What other responsibilities could I take on?"

You Are NEVER Good Enough

"You are NEVER good enough" has a bad reputation, yet it is key to becoming so good that opportunities come to you. "Good enough" means we don't need to try any more. "Good enough" is the bare minimum.

Right up until he retired in 1999, Michael Jordan continued to adapt and improve his game and also took responsibility for upping the game of his team. In that last year, he led them to a sixth championship win in eight years (he led all six victories!), he was MVP in an All-Star Game—which meant he was the best of the best—and *that* is when he said goodbye to professional basketball. That's how good *he* was.

His last year was a big factor in his continuing to receive endorsements long after his career ended and why I am now using his example to help you. Like Jordan: don't seek to be good enough, seek to become *that* good.

Evidence Gathering

Tracking the measurable results of your work will add a lot of weight to the gravity of your service, which will pull far more opportunities into your orbit. This is far more important than getting testimonials, which are useful, but nothing compared to this.

I am going to focus on coaches in my examples, but this is relevant for any service-based business.

When I ask coaches to talk about the results their clients have experienced, they usually run out of things to say pretty quickly. They might have done great work, but they haven't found out how far the changes they facilitated with their clients have reached, and they can reach *really* far.

Five years ago, I began working with the director of an animal charity in South Africa, the Vervet Monkey Foundation. Her name is Josie Du Toit. She wanted to do a good job on camera for a documentary they were filming, but for our first call, she didn't even want to be on video with me because it scared her so much. Needless to say, we had some work to do.

We actually sorted that out during the first session and continued working together in a much broader and deeper sense. The charity wasn't doing well financially, each month was a struggle. Through the work we did on transforming her, Josie opened up to a very different way of thinking and behaving, and the entire foundation changed as a result.

They gained more volunteers all year round, received a lot more funds and donations, started an internship programme, became internationally accredited, took on more permanent staff, improved facilities, installed leadership training, and became a leader in the sanctuary world.

Long after our work ended, Josie continued to grow herself and the foundation, and they have just been featured on a mainstream TV show in the UK called *Work on the Wild Side*. It has been viewed by millions of people.

The depth of transformation within Josie can be measured by the overwhelming evidence of the changes around her, in her personal and professional life. As we stay in contact, I get to find out how the ripples of my work continue to flow, which adds weight to my sense of what could happen to anyone I choose to work with. In turn, this helps me to better understand the lasting value my service provides (which is important when it comes to setting fees). Gathering evidence of the lasting impact of your service is an essential part of creating your own gravitational pull.

Here's how to gather your own evidence:

1. Reach out to all your previous clients and learn what your own ripples have been.
2. For your current clients: ask bigger and wider questions to track their life progress more closely.

Remember: *your* gravity is in *their* detail.

Don't Just Be the Best, Be the Only One

A good friend of mine, Orissa Kelly, is an acrobat. She, like many others in her position, used to gets calls at 5 pm to do a gig that same night. She never knew when or where her next job would be or what they would want her to do.

After her older brother saw a viral video of a girl shooting a toy bow and arrow with her feet, he bet Orissa that she couldn't do it. They have always been competitive, so she took it on. It wasn't enough for her to do it the same way though. She drove to an archery shop, bought a real bow and arrow, and went to a local cricket field to try it out.

One cold wet day in April, she set up a target, walked 15 metres away, picked up the bow with her toes, and got into a handstand. She arched her back, her legs above her head and horizontal to the ground, pointing the arrow at the target. From this very awkward position Orissa pulled the string back with the toes of her other foot and let go—*choo*! She hit it on the first try! There is a wonderful video of her screaming and jumping around, having shocked even herself.

Orissa could have left it there, but she wasn't able to hit the bull's eye every time and that wasn't good enough for her, so she practised for hours, returning every day, her toes often so cold she couldn't feel them. What began as a dare, became a mission. After a few weeks, as she was getting better, she wondered how she could turn it into an act.

A couple of years later, Orissa became known as the world's first professional foot archer. She was invited to go on *Britain's Got Talent*—where she did a hilarious bit for the extra show. She influenced a school in America that then started teaching foot archery because of her. She has been invited all over the world to perform her unique act. Google her and you'll see why.

Orissa created her gravitational pull, which is extremely rare in her overpopulated industry. Many have copied her since she went public with it, but they will never compete with her because she is the one who created it from nothing and continually evolves it into something more. She is not just the best; she is the *only one* who does what she does.

You can be that too, in *your* way. This isn't something you can force, but it is a natural result of embodying the mindset of "being *that* good!" Even though Orissa did something that is exceptional, she wasn't connected to what it could *really* mean for her. This realisation helped her take ownership of her uniqueness and is a key aspect that enables her success.

You may not think you have anything that is exceptional like that, but if you dedicate yourself to living through the mindset principle I have laid out here for you, you'll surprise yourself with what you are capable of.

Everything Matters

Every interaction is an opportunity to do something better. However experienced you are, there is *always* more you can do. There are many touch points between you and your clients, and each one is filled with the potential for higher quality: your website and social media profiles, emails, text messages, videos, written posts, webinars, podcasts, radio and TV appearances, coaching sessions, talks, workshops, retreats, and immersive adventures. All of these. Each individual part of your business can be upgraded significantly, and there is a layering effect that happens. It is like a snowball. The more you improve, the more you are able to improve.

You don't know how much better you could get until you take action in improving things. And, you can start small.

Let's explore this through written posts on social media. Most coaches use social media badly. They want clients and focus on writing posts that get attention. They have bought into the lie that you need to be marketing 80 percent of the time, so they chase algorithms, post multiple times a day, and have a full content calendar. This lowers quality and prevents them from developing the unique, powerful, voice that would make the whole process feel meaningful. Plus, if you don't have a very good assistant, it means wasting a lot of time!

If you take 1,000 coaches' posts and put them next to each other, you are going to see a lot of the same phrases being repeated and many of the same quotes shared. If I mixed them up and asked you who they belonged to, it's unlikely you could tell me.

It can feel like there is a lot of competition and that it is hard to stand out, but that isn't my experience or that of my clients. Instead of chasing and competing, when coaches use their posts as tools to become better at articulating, to more clearly explain the principles they coach on and to develop their storytelling ability, then something important happens—their voice becomes unique and powerful. When that unique voice aligns with the high-quality service they are providing, every post becomes a beacon that draws more of the right people in. If you start doing this, the results of this approach won't take long to be revealed to you.

One of my clients, Arti Joshi, coaches people to date fearlessly, so they can connect deeply with anyone they want without holding back or hiding who they really are. She was tagged in a post recently, where someone was asking for dating advice. She took her time and gave an in-depth, considered response inside a comment; she was focused on being of real service.

As a result of that single comment, she had three people connect with her who were interested in becoming clients. Think about that for a moment—a single comment created three opportunities so far!

Other coaches would likely have given a rushed easy answer or asked the person to DM them, thinking that if they speak to the person privately, the person is more likely to become a client. There is truth to that, but it is also short-sighted. What Arti did served the person who posted the question and anyone else who saw the comment. It is a much better way!

It takes longer to give that kind of deep attention, but your words reverberate through social media and reach more of the kind of people you would love to have as clients. It also trains you to speak naturally with the kind of clarity and authority that answers the question, "Where can I find more clients?" with "Anywhere I happen to be". It is a beautiful way to work.

Give More of Yourself to Even the Smallest of Interactions

By focusing on excellence, you get to grow while also getting noticed. In addition to our careers, it is equally important to bring this mindset to other areas. "What, in your life, needs most attention?" This is one of my favourite questions to ask. It's easy to get caught up focusing on success in our work and ignore the incredible resources that every area of our life contains.

Many of the people I have coached were seeking greater success in their work and to make more money. With each person, it wasn't as simple as developing a strategy and doing the work. There were some significant personal challenges that were holding them back.

We are complex beings and we carry our emotions from one part of our life into another. If there is something we are avoiding personally, it requires energy to suppress it and that pressure builds up. We can't escape ourselves, so it is important to give attention where it's needed most.

Use the mindset of "being *that* good!" with your loving relationship, family, friends, fitness, and other parts of your life. When no one is there to see what you are doing, especially bring it there. This isn't about seeking perfection but about being better than you are now and discovering how great you can be.

It is also important to "critique not criticise". We are messy human beings who make loads of mistakes and have a lot to learn. This is true for me, true for you, it's even true for Oprah! If you take on this approach and truly want to "be *that* good", evolve beyond criticism and begin critiquing. It has a very different energy and enables you to be direct with yourself and feel good.

Three-to-One

Three-to-one is a simple strategy for critiquing effectively. After you have done something, ask yourself: "What three things did I do well?" and "What is the single most important upgrade I can make?" I recommend the ratio of three-to-one because it will train you to notice the good more than the bad. By knowing what you have done well, it becomes easier to be direct about what needs improving and to rapidly make the needed changes.

In time, you can go straight for the jugular without it choking you. This will enable you to get better really fast. It's important to answer by being specific.

Let's use Arti's comment as an example. For one of the positive reflections, she might have said, "I gave a complete answer to the question within the comment", and for the upgrade, "I could have shared the same content with fewer words". Next she could get clear on which words she could have removed to make her comment stronger. By doing this, she would become better at articulating clearly and would improve every interaction from then on. It can be *that* simple! The ability to communicate our expertise clearly and powerfully is a vital part of increasing our gravitational pull.

Strengthen All Your Weaknesses and All Your Strengths

This is at the heart of the success mindset we have been exploring together. In all aspects of our lives, we can get better and not just a little bit better. We have an almost never-ending ability to keep improving. If you try out my recommendations for just a few weeks, you will notice a vast improvement in the areas you bring attention to. It has a compound effect, meaning your success grows exponentially. Do it for an entire year and your life will be so vastly different, you will be shocked at what you have achieved!

So, if you want to be truly successful, treat everything in your life as your training ground and, just like Michael Jordan, dedicate yourself to "being *that* good!"

About the Author

David Saville is the creator of PURE Coaching. This is a method that enables the coaches he trains to create profound and lasting transformations, using a very light touch. He also supports coaches in developing services that are a unique expression of themselves. As a result, no two clients' businesses look the same.

Growing up, David experienced severe anxiety, panic attacks, and body dysmorphia; he hid from life. In 2012, the death of his dad, Jack, who had Parkinson's disease, hit him very hard. He felt he had let his father down and had lost the chance to make things better. David resolved to never fail like that again. He sought out teachers, mentors, trainers, and coaches to help him transform. He dedicated himself to living a better life. Through being coached so meaningfully, he decided that was the direction he wanted his career to go.

David has coached hundreds of individuals around the world, from many different backgrounds, delivered numerous transformational talks, workshops and immersive adventures, and has been working with coaches since early 2016. He lives outside London with his mum, Heather, and two dogs, Bessy and Pepper. He has a Ninja Warrior course in his garden in hopes of competing one day because he loves a good challenge.

Email: david@davidsaville.co.uk
Website: www.davidsaville.co.uk
Linked In: www.linkedin.com/in/davidsaville78

CHAPTER 31

LIVING IN THE GRAY: A POWER STRUGGLE WITHIN

By Kari Schwear
Gray Area Drinking, Discovery Coach
Richmond, Virginia

Change your thoughts and you change your world.
—Norman Vincent Peale

Inner mind chatter, racing thoughts, and triggers.

We all have them. And we always will. For our entire life. The question is—what do you do with them? Do you give in to the trigger? What action, or inaction, might you take? It can feel like a power struggle in your mind.

The power struggle comes from two or more "incongruent" thoughts. Our mind knows these thoughts do not align and gets stuck trying to reconcile them. The power struggle emerges when we are in a state of transition. Examples include relationships, jobs, health, and parenting. Let's take a look at each of these:

Relationships—you break up. One thought is the positive memories of that person, a feeling of pleasure. A second thought is how much you miss them right now, the feeling of pain. Thinking of this person brings up both thoughts, and they are incongruent in your mind.

Jobs—you strongly dislike your job and you're unfulfilled. One thought is to leave and find something else, and this produces excitement. A second thought is to suck it up and accept it since you're making good money. This thought creates fear of losing what you have currently. These thoughts are incongruent.

Health—you want to be healthy. One thought is how much you enjoy ice cream. A second thought is that ice cream causes you to gain weight.

Parenting—you want to support your child. One thought is your desire to step in and help during a difficult situation. Another thought is to step back and let your child figure it out on their own, so they can grow.

Now that you've seen a few examples, I want you to think of an example of an incongruent thought that is happening for you right now. It could be big or small, but unless you grab an example from your life, this chapter won't make sense. It won't resonate with you. You need to play along. Write one of your own thought power struggles in the margin of this page.

I learned about this power struggle as I made a shift out of the gray area of drinking. I had used alcohol as a coping mechanism. As I changed that habit, I ran right into incongruent thoughts that alternated between the pleasure I felt from drinking and the desire to remove this coping mechanism that no longer served me.

Alcohol worked until it no longer worked. After ten years of having wine nightly, I found my consumption grew from one glass to three glasses. I needed more to feel better, which turned my coping mechanism into a new problem.

I was a typical gray area drinker—more than a social drinker, but not quite an alcoholic. I was living a double life. The outside world saw me as a successful achiever, but inside I felt like an imposter. I never experienced a rock bottom, so I thought I was fine. Like other gray area drinkers, I grew tired of lying to myself that I could learn to be a "normal" drinker (whatever that means). I tried to moderate but inadvertently gave in to drinking more than I intended.

Looking back, I can see these incongruent thoughts so clearly.

I finally reached my "enough" in August 2016, the 15th, to be exact. I quit drinking, but my mind was still in the power struggle. One thought was how much I enjoyed alcohol. A second thought was my desire to be free from alcohol as a coping mechanism. These two thoughts never learned to cooperate inside my head. Add in the occasional urges and triggers, and the tug of war began.

Oh, yes, the triggers.

Everywhere I went, there it was—wine. It was displayed on TV ads, suggested with meals at restaurants, offered at friends' houses, and expected at networking events.

After two years of being alcohol-free, I thought I had the triggers and the desire for wine behind me. I was wrong. Out of nowhere, while walking swiftly towards the seafood department at Wegmans grocery store, my mind fell into the power struggle. Before me was a perfectly arranged display of my former favorite drink of choice. My mouth literally watered at the thought of sipping a good Chardonnay. Even though I'd been to Wegmans numerous times, this was the first time I'd been triggered. Who knows why the trigger happened? Maybe a rough day, too much on my plate, or something work-related?

Let's look at the power struggle between incongruent thoughts you chose for your example. What is one trigger that takes you into that power struggle? Write the trigger in the margin of the page.

Like you, these triggers come to me out of nowhere and catch me off-guard without warning. For example, those struggling with a breakup, it might be a song that you hear on the radio.

When the trigger sets the power struggle into motion, we search for a way to reconcile the incongruent thoughts. Since the thoughts don't reconcile, the power struggle continues. Happily, there is a way out of this, as you will understand shortly.

The Shift

I was standing there in the store, triggered by the wine display, calling me to do something I didn't want to do. As my mind began to imagine the buttery taste of the Chardonnay, the only thing I could do at that moment was yell out loud, "Stop!" In doing this, the power struggle in my mind was suddenly interrupted.

I quickly looked around me. Whew, nobody was staring at me or wondering why this crazy woman would yell out the word "stop" in the middle of the store.

I immediately acknowledged the thought as a trigger. I didn't really want the wine. I only thought I did and realized it was a former neuropathway carved in my brain that had gotten activated. It was my familiar go-to pattern.

At the moment of the trigger, I was back into my old routine. I'd pick something up for dinner and grab a bottle of wine to complement the meal. Okay, let's be honest, it was more like buying the wine I was craving and then selecting dinner to complement the wine.

After yelling "stop" and acknowledging the thoughts, I took a few deep breaths. I knew I had to calm myself.

I know now that the wine display moved my mind into a sympathetic stress response due to the immediate longing. While this is a normal function of our autonomic nervous system in times of stress, it wasn't serving me well at that moment.

The stress came from the romantic pull of the wine. I had associated a powerfully soothing feeling with the wine, and at that moment, I wanted it *so* badly. The longing was so intense that by walking away from the display without placing a bottle in my cart, I felt like I was leaving behind a loved one. And if I didn't buy the wine, for me, it was like the loss of a loved one. And yet, I couldn't buy the wine. I wasn't going back to the coping mechanism. I could feel the stress taking over.

Breathing is one of the best techniques to relieve stress. For me, at that moment in Wegmans, I was able to move into a parasympathetic response, which brings a feeling of calm, simply by conscious breathing.

I knew I had to give myself grace and permission for this moment. After all, it wasn't my deliberate intention to think that I wanted the wine. It was subconscious programming that took years to create.

I shifted into gratitude for the choice I'd made to stop drinking two years before and for trusting I was okay at that moment. I hadn't forgotten the delicious taste of wine, nor the sluggishness I felt when I consumed it. Good and bad memories were present, but I walked away from the wine display. I went home to enjoy my salmon dinner with my new go-to beverage—club soda with a splash of cranberry juice.

I didn't know it at the time, but I was creating new thinking in my brain, new neuropathways.

Recalling my experience in the grocery store the next morning, I wrote down the flow and sequence I'd taken to deal with the conflicting thoughts.

> Let's look at your conflicting thoughts. You identified a trigger that takes you into a power struggle. Write two or more of these conflicting thoughts in the margin of the page. These conflicting thoughts are what is engaging your brain in a power struggle.

Habitual patterns of self-sabotage cloud our lives, as it did for me. We may think we're fine amidst our habits, but unless we can see the truth, we can get lost in the fog.

I call that "living in the gray."

The Flow

Let's walk through the sequence together with your habitual pattern or trigger in mind and put it to the test. Until you have identified a personal experience to apply this to, you won't internalize the potential for this flow in a way that will make a difference in your life.

You have two states of being and can be in only one at any given time:

1. *Protective*—afraid, anxious, angry, annoyed, worried, complaining, suffering, stuck, confused, disgusted, sad
2. *Expansive*—happy, joyful, loving, kind, grateful, energetic, clear-minded, productive, creative

Both states serve us, but too often we end up protecting ourselves unnecessarily. There is always a path into the expansive state, but we must find a way to diffuse the power struggle.

Depending on your example, despair and pain may be too much to step into an expansive state. But remember, we are building new neuropathways. The more often we can step into an expansive state and experience a sense of calm and fulfillment, the easier and more natural it will become.

Let's take your example through the sequence. As you walk through it, I expect you to get stuck somewhere. Don't judge yourself. Simply be aware that is where you are at with the power struggle today. As you continue to work through it at your own pace, you will find you are able to get further. Once you get through the entire flow, you will have successfully defused the power struggle in your mind.

1. Stop—Interrupting the Power Struggle

Our brain creates habitual patterns from things that we do without having the conscious awareness that it's happening. We live on autopilot for many of our actions. For example, consider driving an automobile. You don't consciously think about your foot pressing the pedals or turning on the blinker. You just do it.

We have approximately 70 thousand thoughts per day. We can't stop a thought from coming into our mind, but we do have a choice on what to do with it once we're aware of it.

Your brain has formed loop patterns that wire and fire together. They become embedded as familiar patterns of behaviors and beliefs. When you have a circumstance, such as a trigger or a stressful situation, your brain will want to protect you. You'll instinctively feel discomfort in your body. This is an autonomic response in the nervous system, also known as a fight-flight-freeze response. This response is necessary but serves you only when you need to take massive action or when you feel threatened by a predator.

The moment you experience a protective mindset with the mind chatter, racing thoughts, or trigger, immediately say aloud, "Stop." This will cause an interruption and an immediate response to waken your prefrontal cortex to process rational thinking. This action will allow you to gain insight into the next step, acknowledging the thought.

2. Acknowledge—Being Present with the Incongruent Thoughts

Once you've temporarily interrupted the power struggle by saying "stop," it's time to acknowledge what is happening in your mind. There will be emotions present. There will also be a set of rational thoughts trying to justify your situation. The more you can be present with these emotions and thoughts, the more you will be ready to move forward in the sequence to diffuse the power struggle.

> Do you feel anxious, lonely, angry, frustrated, envious, or something else? Write it in the margin of the page. Notice what emotion is stirring for you. See it as your current truth. What you're accomplishing is shining a light on your feelings. No judging, just noticing.

3. Breathe—Calming Your Nervous System

By the time you "stop" the thought and acknowledge it for what it truly is, you will naturally take a big breath to release some of the stress. Stay with it by adding deep, controlled breaths. This step is crucial. You will be calming your central nervous system while moving into a desired parasympathetic response. When this happens, your mind and body will act as one.

Here are three breathing techniques to try:

1. *Deep and deliberate breaths.* At your pace, breathe in slowly through your nose and exhale through your nose. You can also choose to exhale through your mouth as if you are blowing through a straw. Stay with the breath for a count of three or more rounds or until you feel a sense of calm.
2. *Box breathing.* Start with a four-second inhale. Hold for four seconds. Exhale for four, hold for four. Repeat three rounds.
3. *The Weil Method—4, 7, 8.* Dr. Weil's method is similar to the box breathing but with a different breath count. Empty all air from your lungs to begin. Inhale air for four seconds through your nose and hold for seven seconds. On the exhale, blow out through your mouth for eight seconds. Repeat for a total of four rounds.

   Notice how you feel. By calming your nervous system and moving into a parasympathetic state, you'll be ready for the next step: embrace.

4. Embrace—Being Kind to Yourself

The process of stopping a thought, acknowledging it, and performing deep breaths is incredible work. You're rewiring the thought patterns in your brain.

It's time to give yourself grace.

Notice and embrace the emotions and thoughts. Some may be expansive, but most are likely to match the protective state described above. Be kind to yourself, knowing that you didn't cause this thinking to happen. It is coming from a set of circumstances that are present in your life right now. Circumstances can and will change. Sometimes we must be patient for circumstances to change. However, you do have a choice of what to do with your emotions and thoughts now that you have awareness.

Have gratitude for this moment and the work that you're doing. This is next-level thinking that can drastically improve your life. If you're ready to move on, let's continue with redirecting.

5. Redirect—Finding a Restored Sense of Peace

The first time you try to redirect from the old to something new, you will likely fail. You may not know what the new thing is. You may not have the courage to step into it. You could retreat backward. You may not be ready. That's okay. Redirecting is a process. It takes time. It takes exploration.

This flow helps you move out of the gray. To do that, you are letting go of the incongruent thoughts and replacing them with new thinking that is congruent. Typically, this flow kicks in when we are going through a grieving process from having lost something. For me, I lost alcohol as a coping mechanism and as something that I enjoyed doing in the moment.

As I replaced drinking alcohol with other coping mechanisms for stress, I was able to redirect my thinking away from the incongruent thoughts triggered by the wine at Wegmans.

Doing this will create a restored sense of peace in your life, as it did for me. The path forward is to reach an expansive state of mind. That's the success mindset.

Putting It All Together

Neuroscientists talk about the process in which we can create new thinking, also called neurosculpting. This happens when we shift our brains from a primal state to an intellectual state with deliberate awareness.

Many psychologists agree there are six core emotions that are identified universally. From the core emotions, we can experience a range of corresponding emotions: anger, disgust, fear, happiness, sadness, and surprise.

Emotion triggers an action. This five-step flow helps you to break that trigger when you're in anger, sadness, disgust, or fear. This awareness helps you continue your journey to move out of the gray and into an expansive state.

The flow sequence that you just walked through is an example of deliberate thinking, regardless of what emotion you identified. You stopped and acknowledged the thoughts. You breathed to calm your mind and body. You embraced the moment knowing you have a choice to make. And finally, you redirected your thoughts.

My coaching clients often use this process as a verb. They say, "using the SABERS," or they're "SABER-ing their thoughts," or simply, "SABER-ed."

Each step of the flow spells out the word SABER. Feel free to call it whatever you'd like, but it may be helpful to remember it as SABER. When a trigger hits you, immediately: stop, acknowledge, breathe, embrace, and redirect.

Whatever your power struggles are today, remember, there is a way into an expansive state and a better place. I recommend you don't do this alone. Invite a friend into the process. Not only will their support lift you up, but their perspective will help you look at it differently. Once you successfully move through the power struggle, you will be grateful for having walked the path together.

About the Author

Kari Schwear has spent most of her professional life helping people find the story they want to tell about the choices they make in their lives. For the past two decades, she has helped companies grow by finding new ways to serve clients. Kari believes the best way for a company to expand is to help its clients expand. She founded GrayTonic and Question the Drink (QTD) in 2018 for professionals, like herself, who are using alcohol as a coping mechanism for stress. Kari is always on the go, which stems from her favorite place to be—on a racetrack driving Porsches.

Email: Kari@graytonic.com
Website: https://www.graytonic.com/

CHAPTER 32
LIFTING, INTENTIONALLY

By Richard D. Seaman
Beacon Leadership Development
Salt Lake City, Utah

"N-2-2-2-M-D, Salt Lake Center … N-2-2-2-M-D, Salt Lake Center, do you read me?"

Very early in the morning on a winter day in 1995, a business jet departed Salt Lake City Airport number 2. The aircraft was chartered by the Coca-Cola Bottling Company to fly local Coca-Cola and Albertson's grocery store executives to a location grand opening event in Idaho Falls, Idaho. On board were four passengers, a pilot, and a co-pilot. The load was very light for the Mitsubishi Diamond jet with no cargo and two empty seats. The flight was planned for around one hour in the air, and the return trip was to happen after a celebratory lunch with city and construction officials. All in all, about an eight-hour day and back to Salt Lake in time to spend time with family on a Saturday afternoon.

Take off and climb out were routine and quiet. The airspace was quiet, and the air traffic controllers handling the flight saw nothing out of the ordinary. About halfway to Idaho Falls, the aircraft was quietly cruising at 22 thousand feet and 380 knots. It was a mostly clear morning with a few cirrus clouds. As the sun came up over the Wasatch Mountains to the east of their path, the view must have been spectacular.

It was around 6:30 in the morning, and the young air traffic controller working the southeast Idaho sector had just begun his shift. I was the supervisor in the area for the dayshift and had arrived about 6:00 am. At that time of day on a Saturday, there were very few airplanes in the sky, so our job was routine, and we engaged in some light conversation while controllers watched their radar scopes.

The Diamond jet had radioed in normally to the young controller as it entered our airspace, and no other conversation occurred. Routine, routine, routine. Everything in its place. All systems normal.

Suddenly, the young controller sat straight up in his chair and called for me to come over for a look. He pushed the "talk" button on his microphone and said, "November 2-2-2 Mike Delta, Salt Lake Center." He paused and pointed to a data block that had gone into coast track. There was no radar return from the aircraft. The computer was trying to guess where the aircraft should have been by coasting the track and data along its projected route, but radar was not seeing the aircraft.

The controller was on my team and had only been in the FAA for about five years. He told me that he watched the aircraft overfly the Malad, ID navigation aid (MLD), and then just disappear. He had called out to the aircraft multiple times, but there was no response. I ask him to call again.

"November 2-2-2 Mike Delta, this is Salt Lake Center, how do you hear?"

Silence.

Silence on the frequency. Silence in the control room. The rest of the controllers in the control room had stopped everything to lean over and listen in.

"Diamond 2-2-2 Mike Delta, Salt Lake."

Air traffic controllers share a very strong bond, especially when it comes to aircraft accidents and incidents. No one wants to be the controller when something goes horribly wrong, and no controller wishes that on their controller brother or sister. But, when it does happen, the empathy and sympathy are almost tangible. In fact, if an accident occurs on the East Coast, controllers across the nation take notice and, to a degree, share the pain and anxiety with the controller involved.

A great testament of this admirable yet burdensome controller quality is the tragedy of 9/11. Every controller in the nation harbors deep emotional sentiment for the occurrences of that morning, even though the center of air traffic involvement was in Boston and New York. All of us share tremendous empathy for what the air traffic controllers saw on radar and heard on two-way radio frequencies. The air traffic control events that transpired that day are part of one of the darkest days in US history. Most controllers can still feel the pain and, of course, wonder if they could have done anything better or differently.

The Supervisor's Role

Have you ever noticed that sometimes silence is worse than chaos?

It hit me. "I have to jump into action!" I was not a spectator. I was not a fellow controller mustering empathy. I was in charge.

Once over the mindset of still being a controller, I remember thinking, "What are my priorities? This is the moment why I was promoted to supervisor. What do I do first? Focus, Richard. I have a missing aircraft that needs to be reported. I have a young controller very upset and worried about the outcome of this anomaly and whether or not he has done anything wrong. I have a room full of other curious controllers, distracted from their own duties." I feared that as soon as I reported the incident to my manager-on-duty, my phone would ring off the hook with endless questions and curiosity.

I had to do the right thing. In the right order. With courage and calm from somewhere. The monitoring controllers in the room would follow my lead. I had to lead by example, word, and demeanor at that crucial moment. It was my own personal expectation as well as the expectation of my manager, the Federal Aviation Administration, and the public. Oh yeah, there was a checklist somewhere. A checklist of who to notify and what to record. "Later," I thought.

I eventually calculated that my most important and immediate task was to ensure that my other controllers continued to provide optimum safety to their aircrafts. I had to restore order and their focus.

I had been a controller, just a few years prior, in a similar emergency situation. Fortunately, it wasn't my incident, but I had a front-row seat. As I watched the supervisor in charge that day, I remember thinking that he wasn't doing the right things at the start. That he was way too concerned with the telephone that kept ringing. He seemed to be frazzled, and I'd thought, "I could handle that better."

And thus, the seed was planted. I was already starting to think about becoming a supervisor. The financial temptation had already been there, but now I was starting to see and believe that I had something to offer. Maybe something better.

I turned to the other controllers, who were all staring at the southeast Idaho radar and controller, and I said in a calm but serious voice, "Face your scopes. Let's not have another incident." Then I called the breakroom to get another controller back to relieve my young, shaken-up controller. I went over to him, looking over his shoulder to ensure that everything else on his scope was okay. I quietly asked him if he was okay. He seemed well enough, but his voice was definitely shaking, as he anxiously asked me, "What do you think happened to them?"

"I'm not sure," I said, "Did you see anything unusual?"

"No, not at all," he said. "I talked to the pilot when he checked on, and he was tracking just fine, but then after Malad (NAV-AID) nothing. No radar returns at all. Where the hell did they go?"

I noticed a catch in his voice and decided that I needed to remain physically close to him until the replacement controller made their way back. I went over and picked up the cordless phone and called the manager-in-charge and asked him to come down to the area.

"What's up, Richard?" he asked, rounding the corner into my area. I turned away, so my nervous controller couldn't hear, and told my manager about the missing aircraft. I told him I felt like the involved controller needed my attention until I could get him relieved, and then I would report the incident properly. He volunteered to help and started the reporting process for me. The replacement controller returned and as far as the area appeared, nothing had happened, and everything seemed to be back to normal.

Things came together. Later that day, the manager-in-charge told me I had done a great job, and he appreciated the way the controllers had been facing their scopes and not been distracted when he'd come around the corner. The perfect compliment.

As my young controller heard the results of the initial investigation, he was relieved to learn he had not been culpable for what had occurred. However, he was still upset and anxious. Like most controllers, he wondered if he could have done something differently. He was back to work in a few days. I watched him closely at first, but he recovered quickly.

He was very helpful during the investigation, especially as the immediate search began, and he was able to point out exactly where he had last seen the aircraft on radar. I made sure to recognize his attitude and execution of his duties with a formal written letter of appreciation. After all, he had done his job very well, and I was his supervisor and needed to recognize his admirable conduct. I wanted to encourage him to continue his work and validate his performance in front of his peers.

The N222MD: Facts and Assumptions

As for the missing aircraft, it was found a couple of hours later by a county sheriff, pretty much right under its last known radar position. There wasn't much left. It had nosed into the ground at full throttle, apparently in a full spin. The 21-foot-long cabin had been reduced to just over three feet in length. The nose was buried approximately 12 feet into the very dense, frozen clay soil. There had been a small fire but no large explosion. The crash site was in a remote, snow-covered flat draw, sparsely littered with sagebrush.

After much investigation and calculation, it was determined that the aircraft's autopilot was engaged for both speed and altitude at the time of the stall. The autopilot features were still in the "on" positions on the ground.

It will remain a mystery what exactly transpired in the cockpit. It was a beautiful morning. Maybe everyone on the aircraft was distracted. Maybe they were all engaged in a conversation. Maybe everyone on the aircraft had fallen asleep. The flight was very routine. Everything in its place. All systems normal.

Facts

- Recorded radar data indicated a very gradual nose-up angle of attack and slight loss of airspeed.
- The aircraft's anti-ice protection systems were not engaged.
- The aircraft stalled and entered a nose-down spin and did not recover before impact with terrain.
- There were no survivors.
- There was no indication of gas or anything in the cockpit environment that would have caused the crew to be unconscious.
- The sun was just rising and at the four o'clock position to the pilot [behind and to the east of the aircraft] and not a factor.
- The air temperature at the altitude and location of the last known radar position was zero to 10 degrees below zero, Celsius, or freezing.
- There was no precipitation near Salt Lake City. The skies were reported as clear. There were high [cirrus] clouds and moisture in southeast Idaho that morning.

These facts add up to the probable assumption that the aircraft's wings were taking on ice buildup. Ice would have caused the aircraft's autopilot to increase thrust to compensate for a very gradual loss of airspeed and lift. The autopilot also would have compensated by gradually increasing the aircraft's angle of attack (the elevation difference between the nose and the tail in order to maintain level flight). As the angle of attack increased, the aircraft would lose speed and the autopilot would have increased throttle more and more, fighting to maintain altitude and speed until, consequently, the thrust of the Mitsubishi Diamond jet would have maxed out its capabilities and stalled.

In simpler terms, the aircraft lost its ability to create lift due to the presumed presence of ice on the wings' surfaces. It fought against itself, increasing thrust and altitude in order to maintain the speed and altitude that the pilot had selected in the autopilot. As the aircraft pushed its nose higher into the air in order to maintain its autopilot set altitude and speed, eventually the aircraft would have completely stalled and rolled to one side as the nose fell toward the ground. It is very difficult to recover from a stall in a high-performance jet, and the aircraft impacted the ground, still at full throttle, at an estimated 580 miles per hour.

Whatever happened in the cabin just prior to and during the stall would be speculation.

As for me, while I was very happy with my performance, I also began looking back at the episode with introspection and a critical eye. What could I have done better? I realize I could not have changed the accident, but could I have helped my troubled controller more? Up until those moments, I did not know who I needed to be and wanted to be for my team. I was a relatively new supervisor. I had not planned or designed my methods for dealing with emergencies.

How much better could I have addressed that whole scenario if I had thought of how I would have reacted ahead of time? Why did it take that incident for me to decide what kind of supervisor I wanted to be?

Floating in the Current

Similar to the aircraft accident, there were other defining and/or discovery moments in my life. Unprepared, sometimes awkward, at times I have been reactive rather than proactive. I did things, even accepted new jobs, because it fit in the river current in which I found myself. There was no personal design. I was merely in the flow of someone else's plan or design. Here's another example.

The day I hung up my football cleats for the last time wasn't significant, but months and then years later, it became more and more monumental. I missed it all: the work, rewards, friendships, common goal, and even the loud coaches.

Through all those successful seasons and years, I had the mindset of essentially swimming/floating with the river current. At the time, my vision seemed clear—WIN! Whatever that took.

Team win? Yes. However, the wins didn't feel like mine unless I was the recognized star. I needed contribution, acceptance, and reward. Ironically, a direct result of not having a personal vision. A vision complete with a plan, personal growth, work, patience and flexibility, calculated milestones, and accomplishment and celebration.

I now know that what I was missing was a guiding mindset of my own plan and belief. I was part of the team, but I had not thought about where I was headed personally and what "trophy" I would hold at the finish line. I had a vision of how I would celebrate, but I hadn't thought about what I would do when the spotlight extinguished and the river's current around me became still.

My success on a football team or in the air traffic world was determined by someone else's "river current," not mine. My mindset as an employee and manager lacked vision, intention, structure, a concept of what success looked like, and how to recognize and celebrate milestones. My mindset was to "survive and please." My progress was tied to the organization, not personal progress and life balance.

What's Your Vision?

Establishing a dynamic personal vision creates intentionality, design, structure, confidence, and motivation. Dynamic, because your life and priorities change and grow. Dynamic, because a personal vision should include elements from all elements of your multifaceted life.

When football ended for me, what replaced it wasn't football or a different sport. Floating along with the current resulted in me becoming rather one-dimensional. Pleasing or fitting in, based on someone else's ambitions.

Who was I becoming? What did I want to do? What did I want to possess?

When thinking about your vision, consider your personal mission, purpose, passions, faith, love, family, and notions of success, including timeframes.

How is your life or management/leadership journey? Are you staying balanced with all that's important to you? Steven R. Covey said, "Most of us spend too much time on what is urgent and not enough time on what is important." Have you given up on achieving greatness? Making a difference, whether in or outside of your organization? Are you floating along in someone else's river current? Are you busy meeting someone else's urgent needs? Do you have a success mindset geared for your success or for someone else's?

Together, as we take this written journey through the successes, trials, missteps, and humor toward our individual personal visions, I encourage you to develop your personal vision or guiding success mindset. I hope to influence you, in a positive way, to discover who you are becoming, what you will be doing, and what you will achieve. I also hope you will then follow John Quincy Adams' definition of leadership by influencing others to "dream more, learn more, do more, and become more." It all starts by simply defining your personal vision and living it every day.

About the Author

Richard Seaman retired from the Federal Aviation Administration (FAA) in 2011. He now operates Beacon Leadership Development. Among others, his team has assessed, coached, trained, and evaluated Florida Health Care Association, BMW, Apple, L3-Harris, Rio Tinto, One Oncology, and several federal, state, and local governments. Beacon's target industries are medicine, manufacturing, government, and college athletics. Richard is also an adjunct professor at Davis Technical College and Weber State University. He has personal passion for working with young people.

Email: vfr.otp@gmail.com
Website: http://getbeaconlead.com

CHAPTER 33

THE HALLMARKS OF A GREAT SPEAKER

By Vince Stevenson
Founder, The College of Public Speaking London
London, United Kingdom

For many years, I worked at the operational face of IT. I moved from Manchester to London in 1987, just in time for the recession of the late '80s to bite. I had a vast mortgage at 15 percent interest, and I was made redundant twice within three months. It was always boom or bust in the IT industry. Mostly I worked in change management, project management, and programme management. But the most reluctant person to change was me.

Eventually, I moved into freelance IT training for Sun Microsystems and Oracle, which was fun. Working with well-educated, highly motivated, and talented students was novel, but it was another ten years before I found what I truly loved.

I married and started a family, but the work fluctuated enormously. The money wasn't happening. It was a real bummer because I'd always held well-paid jobs, and now when I needed the money, the well was dry. One day at my local library, I stumbled across a speakers' club leaflet (UK's equivalent of Toastmasters). I attended the meeting that night, and I was dazzled by an unknown array of talent. There were so many ways I needed to improve—it was mesmerising. I wanted a slice of it, and that was when my love affair with public speaking began.

To try and create a second income, I started applying to manage European Social Fund contracts to run sessions for NEETs, young people who are "not in education, employment, or training". Essentially, I applied to run sessions for young unemployed people to teach them how to communicate.

At this stage, I had some fantastic breakthroughs working with young people who had fallen through the UK's education system. They lived on a notorious council estate, and the centre manager laughed at my project. He told me many of the students were illiterate, petty offenders, drug addicts, trainee alcoholics, gamblers, and abusers—they had no structure or role models in their lives, and it was a waste of time to help them. He told me the three-day course was too long. If they showed up two out of three days, take it as a moral victory. That said, after running many NEETs sessions, the feedback from the "notoriously bad" young people was terrific. I had two dropouts from a hundred students over two years.

Today, my work pays well, and it is great fun, but I'll always remember my NEETs students. On the last day of a project, two sisters bought me a bottle of wine. I was touched because these young women had no money to waste on me. But what came with it were two of the shortest and most-heartfelt speeches I'd ever heard. There are broken families, and there are severely fractured families, and Clare and Jill came from the latter.

Jill told me, "You're the first man I've ever met who didn't try to take advantage of me."

Clare said, "You're the first person that didn't make me feel like I was a problem. You've raised my spirits and given me hope for the future."

Working with this profile of student was an excellent education and training ground. By building trust, I created closer bonds and found a clearer understanding of their motivations. Your clients need to know that you're their advocate and that you're in their corner. Unlike the IT people I'd worked with before, these students had no resources to fall back on and no support. They asked me awkward questions that I struggled to answer. I became interested in psychology and philosophy as I searched for the answers. My IT work became less exciting and less fulfilling and after a 20-year career, I never once regretted saying goodbye.

From that day onwards, my mindset changed. I wanted to act as a change catalyst for people who had no or limited resources. Alongside my College of Public Speaking London work, I have volunteered for NGOs in Bangladesh, universities in the Middle East, and a large variety of charity and voluntary organisations in the UK.

> *Fear is a reaction. Anxiety is a choice.*
> —Winston Churchill

The altercation at 8.03 pm brought proceedings to a halt. Nobody was prepared for the marital flare-up that evening. Had the janitor not taken his Easter holiday, there was a danger that we'd lose our special venue.

The speakers' session began at 8 pm exactly. The jovial and expectant audience assembled in the art centre's drawing room. Still-life works of fruit bowls, urns, and coffee pots adorned the spot-lighted walls. Outside the French windows, the trains of wisteria signalled another glorious late spring evening.

As the founder of the club, I made the opening remarks. I spoke of the club's ethos—to allow people from all backgrounds the opportunity to improve themselves for professional, personal, or social reasons. My opening remarks came easily:

> *At the heart of endeavour is courage—the word "courage" derives from the French word "coeur" meaning heart. A life without courage is an empty life. To achieve our goals, we must extend ourselves, and we must learn and grow.*
>
> *For many, public speaking is an inhibitor. It stifles your personality. It prevents you from sharing your message and being your best self. Only by sharing our knowledge and experience can we help others grow. If you want to help yourself, help others. Speaking is a leadership role. You're managing people's time, and people's time is their most valuable asset. As a leader, set high standards for yourself and for others to follow. Share a message of hope and optimism that creates an environment for individuals to transcend themselves.*
>
> *As a young man, I was a terrified speaker. But I was determined not to wallow in the shadow of mediocrity. The only way I could move was forwards. And the exciting thing about stepping toe to toe with anxiety is watching just how*

quickly it backs off. Anxiety is an illusion that can strangle your soul if you allow it.

The only time that public speaking matters is when you're doing it for real. Please see the club as a training space where it's okay to make mistakes, and it's okay to explore the tools of expression. Public speaking is a skill; we'll talk plenty about theory, but this is where the theory and the practice hit the road.

Thank you for coming this evening, and it's terrific to see so many new faces. We have a diversity of talent in this club, and everybody's contribution makes it a unique and special occasion. So, relax and make yourself comfortable, and please enjoy the ride and come back next time.

Before the gentle ripple of applause began, the door flung open. Raised voices broke the audience's concentration, and they craned their necks towards the door to find out what on earth was happening. Then an enormous man half stumbled in, only to be dragged out again a moment later. The door closed with a bang.

They say there's a first time for everything. It was unusual and incredibly distracting, especially in the art centre's tranquil setting.

I put my head around the door, and there stood the enormous man with his head in his hands. With him stood a tiny woman, the person who had pushed him in and dragged him out.

"Can I help you?" I offered.

"Are you in the speakers' session?" asked the tiny woman.

"I am," I assured her.

"Can you take this lump and make something of him?"

I looked at the man who was sweating profusely. He was about six-foot-six and built like an armoured car. His knuckles were large and fleshy.

"Have you made a speech before?" I asked.

"No, and I don't want to", he snapped back.

"What are you doing here then?"

"My wife made me come".

"She wants you to speak, but you don't want to?"

"He's got an important exhibition in three months. He's a genius, and he needs to sell his work", she interrupted.

I told his wife the session finished at 10 pm, and I guided him into the drawing room where he settled in the back row. His name was Ray. Ray, the silversmith.

With so many guests in attendance, I asked if they'd like to say a few words about their life, work, family, but Ray settled for giving his name and artistic interest. His voice contained a rich vibrancy. Big man, big lungs, and a massive anxiety of public speaking to match.

At the end of the session, we exchanged contact details, and I thanked him for coming. He was trying to explain something, but he was struggling to breathe. The next meeting was in fourteen days, and I was optimistic he'd attend.

The following week, the phone rang. It was Ray. He apologised for the disturbance, and he remarked that he enjoyed the meeting. I thanked him for the call and asked him if he would elaborate on his work as an artisan silver-smith. At which point, the floodgates opened. In that next five minutes, he went through a brain dump of his extensive experience, and though a little disjointed, it contained an excess of invaluable material.

"Ray, that was excellent! Could you deliver that at the next meeting in the form of a speech?" I suggested.

There was a long silence followed by a muffled conversation with his wife.

"Yes", he eventually replied.

The following week, Ray arrived early, though dripping in sweat. Having devoted hours to his speech, he couldn't make it work. Was it okay to listen and learn from the rest of the group? He enjoyed the atmosphere and the sup-portive feedback offered to each speaker. Everybody felt welcomed, accepted, and acknowledged, way beyond the activities in the room.

That comment was insightful, as was his dissection of other members' contributions from last time. Ray had an excellent memory for names and details. He demonstrated a high level of critical analysis, and he understood what effective communication looked like, even though he was a rookie.

At the break, Ray approached. His large frame dwarfed me.

"Vince, I'd like to make a speech entitled, 'The Modern Artisan'".

I checked the schedule.

"Sure, Ray, but aim for about five minutes, could you?"

"I'll be lucky if I can hold it together for one minute". He grimaced and took his seat.

Fifteen minutes later, to tumultuous applause, Ray and "The Modern Artisan" were introduced. But no sign of Ray.

As the applause faded, Ray's legs had frozen in the chair. Unable to move, his body leant forward over his legs, and sweat ran down his face. With an enormous smile, he outstretched his arms playfully, and it took three men to haul him to his feet.

Ray moved awkwardly with his back to the audience. He had begun talking, though nothing was discernible. At first, I thought he was joking. I stepped on to the stage and whispered, "Ray, turn around and talk to them".

"I can't", he said. "I feel sick".

"Then go and be sick". I led him by the arm to the door.

"No! I want to speak", he insisted.

"Ray, the audience is comprised of nice, ordinary, everyday human beings. Look them in the eye and say a few words about yourself and your work. It's your first speech—don't overthink it. Just do it! It's a journey, so focus on one step at a time".

"What if they don't like it?" he asked.

"It's a speakers' class. They're here to listen and learn. The audience wants you to be yourself. So, talk about your life, your family, and your work. Open the door to your world and invite them in. These themes are universal. It's how we connect. We share our knowledge for the good of the group and the community. We're all part of something special because we contribute to each other's education".

That was one of my most concise speeches for many years. It did the job because Ray was now on stage, facing the audience.

Ray spoke for seven minutes. He touched upon his upbringing in Scotland. Meeting his wife at university, he started a family as a poverty-stricken student and some tough decisions ensued after settling down in London and becoming an artisan silversmith.

There was a theme, and that was "the first time for everything". It wasn't well-structured, but the potential was there. He became more relaxed as the speech progressed, sharing personal stories about hardships and opportunities, false dawns and disappointments. It succeeded because he related to the audience. We all empathised with his difficulties and shared the joy of his success.

Sure, there were areas for improvement like eye contact and some awkward moments of body language. But with a little guidance and focused practice, Ray had the hallmarks of a great speaker.

The next three months saw Ray move from a novice and anxious, to speaker first-class. He was often at the meeting venue before I arrived to help set up the room. We'd talk about the club and his growing business ventures. A few months later, I stepped down as club chairman, and Ray's election to my role was a precious moment for us all. Ray had absorbed the club's courageous ethos at a cellular level and became its latest torch-bearer. Through his words, he became an exceptionally supportive and talented leader of the club and its membership. He subsequently became area and district representative.

One of his favourite sayings was, "It's not where you start, it's where you finish. And I'm not finished yet".

Taking courage, diving in, and immersing himself in public speaking stifled his anxiety. Like a fire blanket smothering a flame, take away the oxygen, and the fire ends immediately. The battle was always with himself.

Public speaking clubs offer a phenomenal community service. They create safe spaces for people to explore their anxiety and develop expression. Participants have to learn something new about themselves. It happens when they discover that they have a well of courage in their tank. The method, as described by psychologists, is called systematic desensitisation. Tiny step by step, you expose the speaker to a supportive audience. You make short speeches and receive constructive and supportive feedback. It's a slow burner, but it's worked for millions of participants across the world. For me, it's provided hundreds of hours of leadership, management, and public speaking opportunity, as well as creating a body of research, knowledge, and experience, which enables me to work confidently with people from across the world. The greatest gift that you can offer somebody is to create positive change in their lives. It's a mindset of service.

About the Author

Vince Stevenson is a speaker, trainer, author, and CEO of the College of Public Speaking London, one of the UK's leading public speaking, management, and leadership development organisations. Vince is the author of *The Fear Doctor* and *Anxiety Quick Wins*, both available on Amazon. Vince is currently working on his memoirs of a five-month road trip to South America in 1995. *The Truck 1995* will be available for Christmas 2020.

Email: vince@collegeofpublicspeaking.co.uk
Website: https://www.collegeofpublicspeaking.co.uk/about-us/vince-stevenson

CHAPTER 34

HAPPINESS AND SUCCESS

By Erik Seversen
Author, Speaker, Coach
Los Angeles, California

*Always bear in mind that your own resolution to succeed
is more important than any one thing.*
—Abraham Lincoln

If you're like me, seeking answers to fundamental questions is one of the greatest rewards in life. For me, seeking the answer *is* the rewarding part. It is the little wins that make me smile with the occasional mind-blowing revelation as well.

When I was living in Paris as a young man, I decided to take a French class at the Alliance française. Before this, I could communicate fairly well through self-taught French that I picked up while traveling through North and West Africa, but my ability to communicate with correct grammar and syntax was lacking.

One day, about six weeks into the class, the instructor asked me if I was enjoying myself. My response was, "You know when you're reading an esoteric poem, and you know there is some powerful message just out of reach, and while reading and re-reading the poem, the image of what it might be becomes more and more clear until that beautiful moment, when it all comes together. It makes sense and it is beautiful. Enlightening. You feel that overwhelming sense of honor at being included among those who understand and appreciate the poem?"

"Yes, I understand that perfectly," my instructor said to me in French with a smile and glowing eyes showing that she was recalling such a moment.

"Well," I continued, "Yes, I'm really enjoying the class because every day is just like that aha moment with a poem."

Really, we were still learning how to conjugate verbs and how to ask simple questions, but for me, my mind was expanding in momentous ways each day of class. What was relatively easy for the other students who possessed a basic education in French was mind-blowing to me, and the daily increase in my knowledge of French felt wonderful. You see, I didn't have to be fluent in French to consider myself successful.

While I enjoyed the goal of speaking better French, and I looked forward to more engaging communication, I appreciated that my success in learning French lay in both the process and the goal. In this way, I never became frustrated at learning too slowly or wishing for something better. Rather, I was happy with the process. I enjoyed exactly where I was in my French education, I enjoyed each level of improvement, and I enjoyed the future idea of speaking more fluently.

This story about my learning French can be applied to almost any growth situation. It can be applied to learning another subject, creating a company, seeking the answer to a question about life, and striving to reach any goal. The main idea is simply that we don't have to get to some point, or accomplish some act, to be happy and successful. All we have to do is choose to be successful right now and choose to be happy right now. No matter how good or how bad your situation is right now, you can choose to see either success or failure; you can choose to be either happy or sad. And, this applies to any situation.

The day my father died in March 2019, I could have screamed in anger over his untimely death. I could have blamed doctors, God, or the universe for his death. I missed him terribly, and my natural inclination was to cry out in pain. That was one option. Instead, I chose something different. No matter the external forces acting on me that day, I was still in control of my own mindset. Really, I had a choice.

The day I learned of my father's death, I was sitting at a desk working in an office. I received a phone call from my sister. When I heard the news, my eyes teared up and a massive lump appeared in my throat. As I hung up the phone, I closed my eyes and decided how I was going to handle this painful moment. I gathered my things, walked out of my office and told a colleague that my dad had died and that I was going home. I drove to my house, parked, and asked myself what my father would want me to do. He was always such a hard worker, both at his job and at home. I knew exactly what I should do. I walked straight back to the shed in my backyard, put on some gloves, and mowed the lawn. During that time, I celebrated my father with happiness rather than mourning him with sorrow.

Now, as you come to the end of this book, *The Successful Mind*, I hope you've gained something from the many authors who sought to show you some way of thinking that might make your life better. From realizing that you are born for success and that there is greatness in you; to learning about direct actions that might create a mindset shift whether from yoga, meditation, a psychedelic experience, or firewalking; to becoming more productive through intercultural communication or controlling addiction to alcohol; or to discovering something in yourself through a new challenge such as public speaking—whatever it is, I pray that you found something just for you within the pages of this book.

If there was anything that you connected with, please don't let it just pass by. I encourage you to return to anything in the book that jumped out at you. Skim or reread any sections that you think apply to you and TAKE ACTION. Decide and write down the set of small steps you want to take to increase happiness and success in your life.

I leave you with an exhortation to answer one question right now. Ask yourself, "Do I feel happy and successful right now?" No one can answer that question but you.

If you answered yes, celebrate this moment and continue striving to live in the moment (or flow) of happiness and success.

If you answered no, only you can change this. I encourage you to take a deep breath and take control over your mindset immediately. Realize you have the power to simply be happy and successful.

Regardless of your place in life right now, I want you to remember that there are 33 authors who care about you and who want you to experience the happiness and success you deserve. There exists a Successful Mind in you. All you have to do is decide to use it.

About the Author

Erik Seversen is on a mission to inspire people. He holds a master's degree in anthropology and is a certified practitioner of Neuro-Linguistic Programming.

Erik draws from his years of teaching at the university level and years of real-life experience to motivate people to take action creating extreme success in business and in life.

Erik is a writer, speaker, adventurer, entrepreneur, and educator who has traveled to over 80 countries around the world and all 50 states in the USA. His travels and intersections with people were a deep study of love, struggle, and ways of thinking that Erik relies on to tackle problems in school, business, and life. His most current ambitions are sharing the lessons he's learned with others and climbing mountains.

Erik lives in Los Angeles with his wife and two boys.

Email: Erik@ErikSeversen.com
Website: www.ErikSeversen.com

DID YOU ENJOY THIS BOOK?

If you enjoyed reading this book, you can help by suggesting it to someone else you think might like it, and **please leave a positive review** wherever you purchased it. This does a lot in helping others find the book. We thank you in advance for taking a few moments to do this.

THANK YOU

Printed in Great Britain
by Amazon

23571281R00172